lcl

HANNAH MORE

and Her Circle

To

Mary Lurena Webster

Hannah More (1786)

From an engraving by Heath of a painting by John Opie for Mrs. Boscawen.

HANNAH MORE

and Her Circle

by

MARY ALDEN HOPKINS

LONGMANS, GREEN AND CO.

New York · Toronto

1947

LONGMANS, GREEN AND CO., INC.
55 FIFTH AVENUE, NEW YORK 3

LONGMANS, GREEN AND CO.
215 VICTORIA STREET, TORONTO 1

HANNAH MORE AND HER CIRCLE

PUBLISHED SIMULTANEOUSLY IN THE DOMINION OF CANADA
BY LONGMANS, GREEN AND CO., TORONTO

First Edition

Printed in the United States of America
Montauk Book Mfg., Inc., N. Y.

Acknowledgments

My introduction to Hannah More occurred when my father brought home from a Sunday School library which he was overhauling and bringing up to date for the Hammond Street Church in Bangor, Maine, a shabby, fine-printed volume from which he read to me, a child of ten, the once famous tract *The Shepherd of Salisbury Plain.* The quaint language amused me, the pious viewpoint did not bore, and the story of the eighteenth-century English laborer, his family, his cottage, and his daily activities, remained vivid in my memory. When, years later, at Columbia University, I found posted as a thesis suggestion the relation of Hannah More to the French Revolution, I eagerly renewed and increased my knowledge of her personality and her writings. Again a long period elapsed before in her own city of Bristol I entered the building which once housed the famous More sisters' girls' boarding school and visited the beautiful home Hannah built in Wrington from the fortune earned by her writings. I have always loved the woman and regretted that she is usually thought of only as an old lady who wrote religious tracts and hymns, when in reality she was in turn a dramatist, a light verse writer, a best seller in non-fiction, as well as a tract writer; and at all stages she was a delightful, lively individual.

As soon as I began my search for additional data, I found

a wealth of unpublished More letters scattered in libraries and museums and in private ownership in both England and the United States. A store of these is a part of the Garrick Correspondence in The Folger Shakespeare Library in Washington and includes a series of letters written by Hannah More to Mrs. Garrick. An almost equally interesting series, in The Henry E. Huntington Library and Art Gallery, San Marino, California, was written by Hannah More to Mrs. Elizabeth Montagu. The R. B. Adams Collection, in the Rush Rhees Library, University of Rochester, contains letters written by Hannah's sisters as well as her own. Correspondence of less personal interest, on business matters and social engagements, is to be found in the libraries of The Historical Society of Pennsylvania; The Massachusetts Historical Society; The Treasure Room of Harvard College Library; The Yale University Library; The J. Pierpont Morgan Library; The New York Public Library; The John Rylands Library, Manchester, England; The Bodleian Library, Oxford; and The British Museum. All these institutions have been so kind as to allow me to have photostats made of the manuscripts. Private collectors have been most generous in giving me access to their More letters and among those living in England I am especially indebted to Mr. Cuthbert Becher Pigot, great-grandson of William Roberts, Hannah's first biographer; Mrs. Theophila Copland-Griffiths, descendant of Hannah's lifelong friend Mrs. Gwatkin; and Mrs. Lintorn Orman, a member of the Lintorn and Simmons families who were bound to the More family by ties of friendship. In this country Frederick W. Halles of Yale University, and Henry March White of Middlebury, Connecticut, have most kindly provided me with copies of More letters which they own; and I have been able myself to collect a few of Hannah's missives.

More than to all others I am indebted to Miss M. F. H. Ellis of Little Dean, Gloucestershire, who, unable to follow her own line of research because of war conditions, gathered information for me in Bath and Bristol during those terrible months of the blitz. Miss Winifred H. Dunham, Curator of Paintings and Engravings in the Bristol Museum and Art Gallery (much damaged), assisted me in obtaining copies of the More portrait by Frances Reynolds and of a charming miniature of Hannah as a very old lady. Miss E. A. Russ of Bath, and Miss M. R. Gleed and Miss Mundy of Bristol went through dusty newspaper files in spite of the hurried, crowded discomfort of war times and unearthed delightful bits of old news for me. This book could not have been completed at a time when war made library research so difficult had it not been for the help given me by English friends.

I appreciate information received from Mr. Charles L. Simmons, descendant of Hannah's executor, and from Mr. E. M. Forster, descendant of Hannah's friends the Thorntons. Bits of information have come to me from unexpected sources. The Misses E. and S. A. Bell of Bristol wrote the anecdote of the Fishponds school and an English clergyman, name unknown to me, asked that I be told one of his family legends, namely, that an ancestor, asking the name of a co-dinner-guest, was informed simply, "That is Hannah—you do not need to be told her last name." Mr. G. H. Spinney, Department of Printed Books, British Museum, familiar with Hannah through his work on tracts, sent me his excellent monograph *Cheap Repository Tracts; Hazard and*

Marshall Edition, containing information on Hannah's writings along that line.

Among those who have helped me in this country, I am especially grateful to Dr. Wilmarth Sheldon Lewis, Fellow of Yale University, who first revealed to me the fascination of unpublished, faded, illegible letters and the delight of searching for forgotten correspondences. I wish also to thank Dr. Giles E. Dawson of The Folger Shakespeare Library; Mrs. Marion King of the New York Society Library; and Dr. George Winchester Stone of Washington University, for interest and assistance.

CONTENTS

There are eight pages of illustrations following page 16.

Chronology of Hannah More's Life

1745	Hannah More born in Stapleton, Bristol, England
1757	Mary More opens famous girls' boarding school in Bristol
1760	George III crowned
1767–73	(approximate) Length of Hannah's engagement to Mr. Turner
1773	*Search after Happiness* published
	Hannah meets John Langhorne
1773–4	(Winter) Hannah's first trip to London. Went every year thereafter for thirty-five years
1774	*The Inflexible Captive* presented in Bath
1775	*Sir Eldred* and *Bleeding Rock* published
1776	Sees Garrick's farewell performances (Mar. 7 to early June)
1777	*Ode to Dragon* published
	Norfolk visit (April to June)
	Essays for Young Ladies published
1777–8	*Percy* presented at Covent Garden (Dec. and Jan.)
1779	Garrick dies—January 20th
	Fatal Falsehood produced at Covent Garden
1782	*Sensibility* and *Sacred Dramas* published
1783	Jacob More dies
1785	Hannah builds Cowslip Green
1786	*Florio* and *Bas Bleu* published

1788	*Thoughts on the Manners of the Great* published
1789	*Bonner's Ghost* written
	Sisters give up school in Bristol; build in Bath
	Hannah opens first Sunday School in Cheddar
1790	*An Estimate of the Religion of the Fashionable World* published
	Open school in Shipham and Rowberrow
	The Slave Trade published
1791	Opens schools in Congresbury, Yatton and Axbridge
1792	Opens Nailsea school
	Publishes *Remarks on the Speech of M. Dupont*
	Begins *Cheap Repository Tracts*
1795	Opens Blagdon school
1798	Opens Wedmore School
1799	*Strictures on Female Education* published
	Trouble in Wedmore about school
1800–4	"Blagdon persecution" of Hannah More
1802	Finishes Barley Wood. Sisters give up Bath house in 1804
1803–5	Hannah has her "great illness"
1805	*Hints for Forming the Character of a Young Princess* published
1809	*Coelebs* published
1811	*Practical Piety* published
1812	*Christian Morals* published
1813	Mary More dies
1815	*An Essay on the Character of St. Paul* published
1816	Elizabeth More dies
1817	Begins a new series of tracts
	Sarah More dies

1819	*Moral Sketches* published
	Martha More dies
1820–27	Hannah becomes an invalid
1820	George IV crowned
1825	*The Spirit of Prayer* published
1827	Hannah moves to Windsor Terrace, Stapleton
1830	William IV crowned
1833	Hannah More dies

CHAPTER I

The More and Grace Families

HANNAH MORE is today a forgotten writer and an unknown personality. Even when she died something more than a hundred years ago, she was scorned by the rising generation which was reading Shelley, Byron, Paine, Godwin, and Wollstonecraft. In her last years she was paid deference largely by very religious people, conscientious bishops, pious reformers, and earnest individuals like the anti-slave advocate William Wilberforce, the missionary-minded Henry Thornton, Zachary Macaulay, and other members of the Clapham group of evangelical churchmen. She was too far back from the younger folk for them to understand her and at the same time too near for them to appreciate her; to them she was an old fogy left over from Dr. Johnson's time and the *Bas Bleu* ladies. She was like a piece of old-fashioned furniture, not yet treasured as an antique.

Today we are far enough removed to see her as an extraordinary eighteenth-century character who, in spite of conforming in every action, thought, and feeling to the conventions of her period, was a vivid, arresting personality whose humanitarian activities in her day directly advanced the cultural, ethical, and spiritual standards of the English people, and indirectly the standards of all people. The span of her life stretched from 1745 to 1833. She lived in the reigns of George the Second, George the Third, George the Fourth, and William the Fourth, missing Victoria's accession by only five years. She was born in an agricultural age and died in the machine age. During this time spinning and weaving went out of cottages into factories, small farms gave way to agriculture on a large scale, the American colonies gained their independence, the French Revolution took place, and social welfare work began. Hannah More saw a great deal in the course of her eighty-eight years and historic changes are reflected in her writings and in her manifold activities. Although from today's viewpoint her opinions seem reactionary and her efforts toward social betterment seem conservative, yet in her day she was savagely attacked as a dangerous radical.

During her long, energetic life, she wrote poetry, taught school, was betrothed and jilted, wrote tragedies, enjoyed the life of a smart young woman about London, lived for months on end with the David Garricks, was a pet of Dr. Johnson, wrote didactic books which went like hot cakes, made a fortune, produced religious tracts that sold by the million, gave her name to a model girls' school, became the elderly protégée of powerful bishops, was the center of an ecclesiastical controversy that rocked the church, and finally settled down as a lively and delightful saint living at Barley Wood, Wrington, Somerset.

Hannah's life was peculiarly interwoven with the lives of her four sisters. They were the environment which molded her personality. One cannot understand her character unless one is acquainted with these four vigorous women, nor can one understand the sisters until one knows something about the personality, principles, misfortunes, and achievements of their dominating father. The five daughters copied his traits, his tastes, his religion, and his profession. As he was prudent, conventional and friendly, so were they. Like him they were loyal to the Church of England but sympathetic toward other sects. As females they did not much concern themselves with politics beyond being Tories like him and passionately admiring royalty.

None of the sisters married, but each took the courtesy title "Mrs." when she reached middle age, according to the custom of the time, and they followed the father's example in living to a ripe age. They differed from him in another matter besides not marrying; for while he lost a fortune and his social rank, they made a fortune to replace the lost one and regained for themselves his early higher station. They won back all that had slipped from his grasp and more.

Not many facts are recorded about Jacob More beyond his successful fatherhood. He was born at Thorpe Hall, Harleston, Norfolk, about 1700, and grew up intending to enter the ministry and expecting to inherit an estate some twelve miles distant at Wenhasten, near the coast of Suffolk. This property was worth over eight thousand pounds a year and included a family mansion complete with library and ancestral portraits. A cousin, also named More, disputed Jacob's claim in court and won the case after long and costly litigation.

As the money which was to have paid Jacob More's university expenses had been spent defending his claim to the estate, he had to give up the idea of being a clergyman. He was, however, a well-educated man. As a boy he made his mark in the Norwich Grammar School, and he was evidently a bookish man for in his old age he amused himself with Latin verse.

Diversity of religious and political beliefs in his boyhood home made him unusually tolerant. His mother was a Presbyterian and her father had boarded a non-conformist minister in the days when the religious services of dissenters were held secretly in the dead of night, with sentries at the doors. Two of his uncles had fought with Cromwell. Jacob More was himself a high churchman, but he was friendly with dissenters and Catholics.

His mother had been born in 1666, the year of the great London fire, and lived into her ninetieth year. She must have been still living in Norfolk while Jacob's children were growing up in Somersetshire, but there is no record of their having seen her. She was a woman of unalterable convictions and terrible energy, rising at four o'clock in the morning even in winter and even when she was eighty years old. One of the stories handed down in the family was that, being subject to frequent and sudden attacks of pleurisy and being distant three miles from medical aid, she learned to bleed, in order to perform this operation on herself. She was vigorous, intelligent, and domineering.

When Jacob More was about thirty years old he migrated from Norfolk to Gloucester. We know nothing of his reasons for choosing this county for retrieving his fallen fortunes, but we do know that soon after his arrival he had as a patron Norborne Berkeley of Stoke Park, Stapleton. The place was also referred to as Stoke, Stoke House, and Stoke Gifford. This gentleman and his family were friendly and helpful to the Mores through several generations. Norborne

Berkeley became the fourth Lord Bottetourt in 1764, a title which was revived for him after having been in abeyance for about three centuries and a half. He died Governor of Virginia in 1770 and was buried at the College of William and Mary in Williamsburg. Other members of this noble family should be mentioned because they played so important a part in the Mores' welfare. Upon Lord Bottetourt's death his sister Elizabeth inherited his barony, being already married to Charles Noel (Somerset), fourth Duke of Beaufort. She is frequently mentioned in Hannah's letters simply as "The Dowager Duchess" and Hannah was accustomed to visit her at Stoke Gifford. The friendships did not end there, for the Duchess' son Henry (Somerset), fifth Duke of Beaufort, married Elizabeth, the daughter of one of Hannah's closest friends, Elizabeth Boscawen, widow of Admiral Edward Boscawen. The next generation grew up to be acquaintances of the then elderly Hannah rather than close friends. The Duchess of Rutland, granddaughter of the Dowager Duchess and of Mrs. Boscawen, is occasionally mentioned in Hannah's letters; and her children sometimes came to call on Hannah. From the closeness of this long-continued relationship between the families, it seems probable that Jacob More came to Stoke Gifford because he was already in some way known to Norborne Berkeley or was warmly recommended to his care by a mutual acquaintance.

At the time Jacob More left Norfolk the More family was related both to the gentry and to well-to-do farmers in Norfolk, having social connections which included Sir John Bloise and Sir John Rouse, proprietors of large agricultural estates; Reginald Rabett of Bramley Hall; and other notable families of the neighborhood.

Jacob More was the sort of young man whom older men like to assist, for he had a pleasing personality and was practical, conscientious, industrious, and friendly. His first position was that of supervisor of excise in Bristol. Later Norborne Berkeley obtained for him the headmastership of a foundation school four miles out of Bristol at Fishponds, in Stapleton. This school was established in the reign of George the Second and was still in existence in Victoria's reign! [1]

Many such free schools were established in England during the early part of the eighteenth century by landowners who felt responsible for their laborers. The condition of farm workers was deplorable and grew steadily worse as agriculturalists enclosed what had hitherto been common land, depriving the laborers of free pasturage and garden plots. When the spinning and weaving with which the women folk had supplemented the men's scanty wages went from cottages into factories, the poverty became terrible. Philanthropic people bestirred themselves to alter these conditions, and among the reforms they introduced throughout England, Scotland, Wales, and Ireland were free elementary schools, endowed or supported by annual subscriptions. The one at Fishponds was endowed. Such schools were under the supervision of trustees who were the heirs of the founders or members of the village government or the gentry of the neighborhood. These trustees chose the teachers and decided which pupils should be admitted. It seems probable that Jacob More was the first headmaster at the Fishponds school.[2]

The instruction in these institutions was far ahead of that in dame schools, but as a rule not as advanced as that of grammar schools where the pupils paid tuition. Courses were given in the four R's of the time—religion, reading, writing and arithmetic. Sometimes instruction in Latin was also available. The pupils were often provided with clothing, and crafts were taught as well as book learning. The pupils were apprenticed to village craftsmen when they reached the right age.

It is easy today to be contemptuous of eighteenth-century free education because its primary purpose was to convince the poor that God demanded of them contentment with lowly station, long hours of work, low wages, coarse food, and plain clothing. Any laborer in field or factory with exceptional ability was expected to use his good brain in making the most of what he had, not in obtaining more; and mutual benefit societies must be for sickness and not for the purpose of raising wages or improving work conditions. The free schools taught these doctrines to the pupils and to the parents. This limitation was in accord with the principles of government by which the country was at that time ruled. People were rigidly classified and their duties laid down. The gentry were under obligation to look after the laborers on their estates and expected, but not compelled, to distribute part of their riches among their dependents. If the rich evaded this duty they could look forward to punishment in the next world, while if the poor suffered over much, it would be made up to them in Heaven. This economic system worked badly, but it was the best that England had evolved and many wealthy and intelligent men and women spent their lives trying to make it work better. They exerted themselves in behalf of the poor, the sick, the insane, debtors, slaves, prisoners, and paupers. Social welfare work was being born. These were the tenets taught to the More sisters by their father; this was the system in which they were raised and in which they believed all their long lives.

Soon after his arrival in Gloucestershire, Jacob More married Mary Grace, daughter of John Grace, a farmer of Stoke. Very little is known about her, beyond the general statement that she was a woman of plain education, with vigorous intellect and sound judgment, anxious that her daughters should have the learning which had been denied her. The Graces probably belonged to that class of independent yeomen who were more common in the early part of the century than later on when large farms were eating up little farms, crowding out small freehold farmers and tenants.

One receives the impression, from the way Mrs. More is ignored by the early biographers of her famous daughter and not mentioned in letters, that Jacob married below his station. This would be a natural action for a penniless, disappointed man, lonely in unfamiliar surroundings, but from what one knows of Jacob More's prudence and conservatism one feels that it was probably as good a marriage as he could make under the discouraging circumstances of his position.

Although so little is said of the mother, we know that the relationship between Jacob More's family and his wife's kinfolk was intimate and lasting, for the Grace connection was generously remembered in the wills of both Hannah and her sister Martha.[3] Indirect evidence that the two families visited back and forth is furnished by the familiarity with the pastoral scene shown by Hannah in some of her *Cheap Repository Tracts*. It is otherwise difficult to account for her detailed information on farmers' problems and ways of life, for her own personal life was lived in her father's and her sisters' school homes, among the gentry in London, and as a retired gentlewoman at Barley Wood. Even remembering that her father's school was in a country district and that she was in and out of laborers' cottages in connection with her Sunday School work, one feels that her simple tales of joys and sorrows in farm families are based on a personal knowledge which she could have obtained among her mother's kinfolk. Her annals of the country poor are graphic word pictures of eighteenth-century English agricultural life. Hannah wrote them well because she knew her subject; at some time she must have been at home among farm people.

When Jacob More received the headmastership of the Fishponds foundation school he moved his family from Gloucester to that village. Here Hannah was born and here the sisters all lived until the older ones moved to Bristol to carry on a girls' boarding school.

CHAPTER II

The Sisters' Childhood

THE FIVE little More girls grew up in their father's school in Fishponds, a hamlet of Stapleton (a village of about twenty-two houses), in the parish of Martock, four miles out of Bristol. The building was a large two-story structure, with two huge chimneys, a wing at each end, and a thatched roof. The family life and the school teaching went on in the same building. We do not know whether it was a boarding or a day school, but it was probably, although not certainly, for boys only.

Hannah, the fourth child, was born February second, 1745. It speaks well for the parents' care of their offspring that in a period of high infant mortality they raised their five daughters. The names of the little girls were Mary, Elizabeth, Sarah, Hannah, and Martha. Mary and Hannah were called by their full names, the others becoming Betty, Sally, and Patty.

The girls early developed strongly individual personalities as if they sensed that, being so many and so near of an age, they must differentiate themselves. Certain qualities they had in common: ambition, industry, intelligence to a high degree, piety, and quick wit. The eldest, Mary, carried a heavy load of responsibility; Betty, gentle and helpful, interested herself in home crafts; Sally was the wag of the family, delighting and shocking the others with her high spirits and indiscreet remarks; Hannah was early marked as the genius of the family; and Patty was Hannah's slave—and tyrant.

The family adored Hannah. She was as spoiled as if she had been the eldest or the youngest, instead of the fourth of five. She was so delicate that no one dreamed that she would live into her eighty-ninth year—the oldest of a long-lived family. Looking back over her life, reading her letters and following her career, one sees what was hidden from her contemporaries, that her illnesses were usually caused by emotional upsets. As a child she was high-strung, easily stimulated, affectionate, and oversensitive to criticism. Such a child might well discover ill health as an ally against vigorous, well-meant management; for an oversusceptible child needs some weapon of defense against loving tyranny. A sick child cannot easily be opposed; a patient, uncomplaining child can only be loved and coddled. So Hannah, when hardly more than a baby, acquired invalidism as a defense against the normal harshness of the world.

The girls were trained in cooking, sewing, and other home crafts; housework was drilled into them as thoroughly as Latin conjugations. Even after they were well-to-do ladies at Barley Wood with a staff of servants to wait on them, any one of them could and frequently did take a hand in the kitchen. The girls were taught to use their needles as well as their pens and in their later, prosperous years they sewed and knit for the poor. No hands were allowed to be idle, even if they were tiny. There wasn't money enough to keep a slothful child.

One must not get the impression that all was stern duty in the More household. There was laughter and lively talk and entertaining of guests, and from earliest days each child felt herself an important member of the group. Mr. More was accustomed to gather the little girls about him for stories of Roman heroes, which he told first in Latin and afterward in English. One pictures the group in the evening before the great fireplace, mother at a table sewing by a working candle, Patty in her cradle, the other children entranced by the vigorous Latin phrases falling from their father's learned lips. The greater part of Mr. More's library had been lost while being transported by sea from Norfolk, the few Latin, Greek, mathematical, and geographical books which he carried with him for light reading on the journey being all he saved, but he preserved much of the lost library in his memory.

A handful of significant anecdotes showing Hannah's precocity was held in the family memory, but as in the case of many a famous person the recollection may have been determined by later achievements. Hannah, aged three, repeated her catechism so smartly that she received a sixpence from the clergyman; Hannah, aged four, wrote a poem on the Bristol road passing her father's door:

This road leads to a great city,
Which is more populous than witty.

Hannah loved to preach a play sermon from a play pulpit to a family audience; Hannah demanded foolscap writing paper instead of toys; Hannah told little Patty such wonderful stories in bed that the younger sister tumbled out to fetch writing materials lest the gems be lost.

The little girls grew up in the same house with their father's classrooms and, if the custom of the times was followed, were early pressed into service as pupil teachers. They were accustomed from infancy to the didactic sound of the teaching voice and the monotonous chanting of lessons; books were important and the written word was for instruction, not amusement. This may be the reason that in their later years they looked upon the whole world as one great schoolhouse, upon human beings as wilful pupils who would not learn their lessons, and upon themselves as ordained teachers. This attitude was especially strong in later life in Hannah and Martha, both of whom instructed the public through written and spoken words.

Jacob More began to train his daughters to be teachers while they were still young. There is no record that he ever exerted himself to arrange marriages for them. Perhaps he thought the lack of dowries an insurmountable obstacle; perhaps he did not want his daughters to marry. Hannah was once engaged, but the marriage never took place. Patty tried her best to prevent her friend Selina Mills from marrying Zachary Macaulay, on the ground that marriage was narrowing, and later on she was exasperated when the teachers in the village schools under her supervision persisted in falling in love.

The father could instruct the girls in most of the branches necessary to fit them to keep a school, but he did not speak French; so when Mary was twelve years old she was sent into Bristol for French lessons, three times a week, making the eight-mile journey on foot. The Bristol papers of that year advertise two schools teaching French. One in Clifton, kept by Mr. and Mrs. Lewis, offered courses in "genteel behavior, French, music, writing and arithmetic," Mr. Lewis teaching dancing and Mrs. Lewis needlework. Another school in College Green, the heart of Bristol, kept by Mrs. Beecher, a clergyman's widow, also offered French.[1]

What Mary learned in Bristol, the hard-working child, sometimes fainting at her tasks, taught her little sisters at home. She was twelve years old at this time which means, according to our method of reckoning, that she was in her twelfth year, for ages were then designated by the coming birthday instead of the past one. So eleven-year-old Mary drilled three even younger sisters in French verbs. Patty was too young, but doubtless she was encouraged to crow in French. Four pupils learned on one tuition.

Mr. More was not altogether easy in his mind about educating his daughters because he shared the general belief that female brains were more delicate in texture than male and easily wrecked by book learning. When he began teaching little Hannah Latin and mathematics, he was so alarmed at her quick comprehension that he stopped the lessons. Hannah was heartbroken and her mother joined her in begging him to continue. The father compromised on Latin, firmly refusing to subject the little girl to the excitement of further mathematics. Hannah always regretted not going on with mathematics and when she was an old lady said solemnly that the little she had learned had been of great advantage to her.

The effect of Mr. More's attitude was to incite Hannah to strenuous effort to prove she was as keen and robust as a boy, while at the same time she got the impression that she was smarter than most girls. Mr. More may have had an antipathy to female pedants, but he did his best to turn

Hannah into one. That he was not wholly successful was due to the fact that Hannah was not by nature a scholar. She was quick-witted, impulsive, and impatient of tediousness in any form. After she began writing books she rushed through work at astonishing speed. She leaped at a task and got it over as soon as possible. She was not good at a long pull.

Hannah, after she left her father's home to live with her sisters at their school, continued her Latin under James Newton, classical tutor at the Bristol Baptist Academy. Mr. Newton stated that although she studied with him less than ten months her talent and determination were such that she surpassed in her progress all others that he had ever known.[2] She studied also Italian and Spanish and attended the lectures of men who came over from Bath to repeat in Bristol their talks on literature, astronomy, elocution, religion, philosophy, and science. A fortunate chance had perfected her colloquial French before she left home, for a group of officers from French ships captured by the English during the Seven Years' War were interned in a stone prison in Fishponds, but enjoyed the liberty of parole. Mr. More opened his house to them, and as Mary, Betty, and Sally had by that time taken their French to the Bristol boarding school, it fell upon young Hannah to interpret. By this experience she gained poise and a facility in French conversation which stood her in good stead when she lived with the bilingual Garricks in London. Yet Hannah always distrusted the French and disapproved of French fashions, cookery, literature, and politics—a characteristic eighteenth-century antipathy.

CHAPTER III

The More Boarding School

WE DO NOT know what inspired the sisters to start a girls' school, beyond the fact that there were few even passable educational institutions for girls. Parents customarily employed governesses, supplementing the daughters' education by means of visiting masters. The Mores' school filled a need and was successful from the beginning. The opening of their boarding school in Bristol was announced in a Bristol newspaper of March eleventh, 1758:

> On Monday after Easter will be opened a school for young ladies by Mary More and sisters, where will be carefully taught French, Reading, Writing, Arithmetic, and Needlework.

The announcement was repeated the following week with the additional statement:

> A dancing master will properly attend.[1]

This young ladies' seminary, modestly started at Number Six Trinity Street, College Green, Bristol, was to become famous throughout England, and its reputation has lasted to the present day. The name "Hannah More School" was in use by a girls' preparatory school in Bristol as late as 1938, and another by the same name flourishes in Maryland, both namesakes of the institution which was carried on by the More sisters nearly two hundred years ago.

The original academy was opened and run by an extraordinarily youthful staff made up of Hannah's three older sisters, Mary, Elizabeth, and Sarah, aged approximately nineteen, seventeen, and fourteen. Younger Hannah and youngest Martha soon joined the teaching force. Although Hannah was released from actual teaching when she was twenty-two because of a proposed marriage, which came to naught, she continued to make her home with her sisters in the boarding school, moving with them to Bath when they retired, and finally settling with them in a permanent home, Barley Wood, a small but charming estate in Wrington, Somerset, some twelve miles from Bristol.

As the More family had no capital to start the Bristol boarding school, they raised funds by subscription. The solicitation of donations from wealthy families was an accepted method of financing an educational or philanthropic venture, and later on the sisters in their turn were patrons of many worthy individuals and causes.

The Mores had a talent for knowing the right people and conducting themselves in a manner pleasing to their social and financial superiors, being neither aggressive nor unduly modest. They were able to receive assistance gratefully and yet preserve their dignity. Patronage at that time corresponded to present-day scholarships and fellowships; it was one of the few ways talented, ambitious individuals of the upper middle classes, without money or influential connections, could rise above the station to which they were born.

The name of one of the patrons of the young ladies' seminary has been recorded for us: Mrs. Edward Gwatkin, of

Bristol, born Ann Lovell, co-heir with her brother of their father Captain Robert Lovell of Trefusus, Cornwall. We can venture a guess as to some of the other patrons. Among them were probably Norborne Berkeley, not to become Lord Bottetourt until six years later; his sister Elizabeth, already the Duchess Dowager of Beaufort; and Mrs. Boscawen, widow of the admiral, whose daughter Elizabeth was to marry the Duchess Dowager's son, the fifth Duke of Beaufort. Several links connect this group of More patrons: Mrs. Gwatkin's father's estate and the seat of the Boscawen family (later inherited by Mrs. Boscawen's son Viscount Falmouth) were both in or near Truro, Cornwall, suggesting a possible acquaintance or even friendship between the two women; Mrs. Gwatkin's son Lovell married, later on, a niece of Sir Joshua Reynolds. Most of the Mores' friends in the early days were of higher social rank than themselves.

The boarding school started under good auspices and at a propitious time. The middle class all over England was thriving and Bristol folk were especially successful. Bristol merchants, traders, and sea captains were well-to-do. The merchants imported goods independent of London, their cargoes coming direct to them from Wales, Ireland, the West Indies, Holland, Scandinavia, Russia, Newfoundland, and the Mediterranean, making the port of Bristol second in importance only to London.

The tremendously profitable slave trade added to the general prosperity. Ships made what was called the triangular voyage, taking English goods to the west coast of Africa, from there carrying slaves to the West Indies, and returning to England from there laden with sugar, rum, and tobacco. The city drew wealth also from the rich silver-

BIRTHPLACE OF HANNAH MORE

From a drawing by Rev. Henry Thompson (circa *1834), reproduced in his* Life of Hannah More.

HANNAH MORE (1780)

From an engraving by E. Scriven of a painting by Frances Reynolds. Reproduced by the kind permission of the Trustees of the Bristol Art Gallery.

THE CHEDDAR HOUSE IN WHICH THE MORES OPENED THEIR FIRST SUNDAY SCHOOL.

THE BLAGDON HOUSE IN WHICH ANOTHER SCHOOL WAS OPENED.

Both from drawings by Rev. Henry Thompson.

GARDEN OF GARRICK'S VILLA AT HAMPTON WHERE LORD MONBODDO PROPOSED MARRIAGE TO HANNAH MORE AND LATER TO GARRICK'S WIDOW.

From a sketch by Rev. Henry Thompson.

HANNAH MORE (1813)

From an engraving by E. Scriven of a portrait by Mr. Slater. Reproduced by the kind permission of the Trustees of the British Museum.

HANNAH MORE (1821)

From a painting by H. W. Pickersgill. Duplicate portraits were made, one for Lovell Gwatkin, Esq., and the other for Sir Thomas Dyke Acland. Reproduced by the kind permission of the Trustees of the National Gallery.

Coach hire several times	." 3".
2 Play tickets	." 8".
Mending Pr Stays	." 4".
	20" 5"9½
	20" 7".
	40"12"9½
Mantua Makers Note	1" 3"1

Recd. Febry 13th 1777 of Mr. Gegg
the full Contents of the above
Mary More

From these entries we can deduce the young lady's interests. Board must have included tuition as only dancing and music instructions are listed. Tea, entered by itself, comes to the astounding sum of one pound, eleven shillings, sixpence for six months. Bills from corsetmaker, shoemaker, dressmaker, and drygoods merchant indicate interest in fine clothes. "Yd ⅛ Muslin, Yd ⅛ do," and "¼ yd Muslin" were probably for those finely embroidered white collars, cuffs, and caps that gentlewomen stitched and wore. Three charges for dressing hair and pins, coach hire several times, and "2 Play tickets," suggest social outings. Missing any charge relating to sports, one remembers the dreary walks along Bristol roads which were the nearest these elegant damsels came to athletics. The expenditure of nineteen shillings and a sixpence for Young's Works (*Night Thoughts* was in the best-seller class) suggests that Miss Lintorn, like her young teachers, favored poetry.

A picture of Hannah among the school girls comes to us from Richard Polewhele, Devonshire clergyman, poet and prose writer, who when an old man set down for his children memories of his youth. Young Polewhele first visited Bristol with his mother in 1777, when he was still at the Truro school where John Wolcot (Peter Pindar) was teaching. Polewhele's portrait later painted by Opie shows small, high-set eyes, a long nose, a well-shaped mouth, and a complacent expression. Humility was never Polewhele's failing; he always fancied himself. During his Bristol visit he circulated among the notables, making the acquaintance of Catherine Macaulay, the historian, who was forty-five to his eighteen, and Hannah More, who was thirty-three. Both women were already famous, but that did not prevent the young sprig from patronizing them. Mrs. Macaulay was his favorite at this time. Describing her famous birthday party on April second, 1777, at which six gentlemen including himself read odes composed in the lady's honor, he comments:

"I was introduced also to the young dramatic poetess of Bristol, Miss Hannah More; who, whilst Catherine was receiving homage at Bath from greybeards and from boys, was herself enthroned amidst a crowd of boarding school misses, tutored to lisp, in soothing accents, her dramas and her praises."

When Mrs. Macaulay soon after married a man twenty-five years her junior, Polewhele was one of several men whose hearts suffered a sea change. His opinion of Hannah on the other hand grew more flattering as she became more famous.[5]

The more depressing side of what was considered necessary for a young lady's education is shown in a letter written by an elderly lady to Rev. Henry Thompson when he was collecting data on Hannah More for a biography. As

Barley Wood (1822)

From a water color by Captain John Johnson in the log of his sailing vessel that voyaged between Bristol, England, and St. Kitts in the West Indies in which he says: "Fair day—rode to Barley Wood to see Hannah More." *Reproduced by the permission of the Trustees of the British Museum.*

HANNAH MORE (*circa* 1830)

From a miniature, unsigned and undated, existing in duplicate in the possession of Cuthbert Becher Pigot, Esq., and of the Bristol Art Gallery. Reproduced by the kind permission of Mr. Pigot.

ad mines of the near-by Mendip Hills, the fertile agricul-ıral tracts of Somersetshire, and the wide sheep downs of /iltshire. The opulence and the free spending of the town indicated by phrases in common use like "Bristol milk" or sherry, "Bristol feast" meaning a banquet, and "Bristol lderman" to indicate a gourmet. Even today "shipshape, Bristol fashion" indicates special skill and efficiency.

Twelve stone and wooden bridges over the river Frome espoke enterprise; docks, cranes, and drawbridges were up o date; industry was shown by glass manufactories, foun-dries, chemical works, potteries, and textile factories. The cloud of smoke forever hanging over the city was counted a sign of prosperity. There were sidewalks, street lamps, water and sewer systems, churches, and hospitals. A city library and many endowed schools bore witness to culture.[2] Hotwells, the section in which were situated the medicinal springs, was fashionable as a health resort (although never as popular as Bath), supporting assembly rooms in which assemblies were held Mondays and Thursdays, the rules being copied from Bath and the master of ceremonies wearing a ribbon and a medallion. Lodging-house keepers were reported to have ac-cumulated fortunes during the summer and autumn seasons.

Bristol was connected with London by a good road over which the "British Flying Machine" made three trips weekly in summer in the incredibly short time of two days. Three coaches a week went to Bath and one to Gloucester. These traveling conditions made Bristol accessible from all sides.

In this prosperous, lively, cultured town, the three eldest More girls opened their academy at Six Trinity Street, Col-lege Green, near the Cathedral. The school made money from the start and four years later the sisters built at Forty-three Park Street, the first house on that steep thoroughfare.[3] In thirty-odd years they made enough money to retire in comfort.

A few anecdotes and bits of information picture for us life in this eighteenth-century finishing school which was famous in England while the American and later the French Revolution were going on across the waters. Here is the bill from June to December, 1776, for the tuition and extras of Martha Lintorn—incidentally a lifelong friend of the More sisters—written in Hannah's delicate, legible script and receipted by Mary More.[4] In a lower corner are faint penciled figures where Hannah calculated the pounds, shillings, and pence or someone checked her totals.

Rev.^{d} M-^{r} Gegg for Miss Martha Lintorn
To Mary More

	L S D
To half y-^{rs} Board, Miss Martha Lintorn from June to Dec-^{r} 1776	15″
Tea	1″11″6
Yrs Dancing	12″6
½ Yrs Musick	3″ 3″.
	20″ 7″
Stay Makers Note	1″13″6
Linen Draper's Note	3″. .″2½
Milliners Note	4″17″4
Yd ⅛ Muslin	.″ 7″4
Yd ⅛ do	.″ 8″5
5 yds Maneo	.″ 8″9
¼ yd Muslin	.″ 1″6
Mercers Note	4″19″6
Shoemakers Note	1″18″9
Dressing hair and pins	.″ 2″.
To do	.″ 2″.
To do	.″ 1″6
Youngs Works	.″16″.

he obtained some of his information from Mrs. Thomas Simmons, who, as Frances Lintorn, had been a pupil in the school, it is quite probable that the young lady referred to was either Martha or Frances Lintorn.

A young lady was placed with the Misses More for education. Her eldest sister (the writer of the letter) was invited to spend some time with them as visitor. She had attained much excellence in drawing and as often as her drawings were exhibited, they drew forth much admiration. One person there was always present, who observed a strict silence, much to the mortification of the young artist; and that person was Hannah More. One morning this young lady made her appearance rather late at the breakfast table. Her apology was this, that she had been occupied in *putting a new binding on her petticoat*.

Mrs. Hannah More, fixing her brilliant eyes upon her with an expression of entire approbation, said,

"Now, my dear, I find you can employ yourself *usefully*, I will no longer forbear to express my admiration of your drawings." [6]

CHAPTER IV

Social Life in Bristol

THE LIVELY, intellectual social life that went on at Forty-three Park Street was one cause of the school's success. Pupils could mention famous names in their letters home and distinguished visitors broadcast their approval upon their return to London. Mrs. Elizabeth Montagu after a visit to the school reported: "They are all women of admirable sense and unaffected behaviour and I should prefer their school to any I have ever seen for girls, whether very young or misses in their teens." [1]

The sisters realized that their personal acquaintance among notables—including speakers who came to Bristol from Bath to deliver courses of lectures, famous actors and actresses brought from London to appear in the beautiful King Street theatre, English nobility taking the cure at Hotwells, and neighboring country gentry, as well as a selected group of Bristol folk—was as important in establishing a profitable school as a good curriculum.[2]

As Jacob More had hospitably opened his school home in Fishponds to lonely exiled French officers, so his daughters welcomed to their school home desirable acquaintances as well as friends, and somewhat as Hannah had gained ease in colloquial French from the visiting officers, so now she increased her poise by continually meeting strangers.

The sisters had a rare gift of making friends and keeping them. Charles and John Wesley, who had one of their meeting houses in Bristol, found Mary especially congenial. Charles sent a message to Hannah when she was in the full swing of her London triumphs, advising her to remain in the fashionable world where she could influence the rich and the great to lead better lives. When Charles Wesley was an old man, Hannah had the delight of introducing to him William Wilberforce, the opponent of slave trading and her collaborator in promoting Sunday Schools. Young Wilberforce, coming to call upon Hannah in Bath, was ushered into a room where a group of people sat round a table at tea. The venerable Methodist saint rose and came forward to greet the young reformer and gave him his blessing. "Such was the effect of his manner and appearance," says Wilberforce, "that it altogether overset me, and I burst into tears, unable to restrain myself." [3]

Dr. James Stonehouse, later Sir James, who lived in the next house on Park Street, was the friend and counselor of the five women whom he named The Sisterhood. He had been a physician with a large practice in Northampton until a severe illness sent him to Hotwells, Bristol. After his recovery he took orders and later on came back to Bristol to live because his health was better in that city. While Dr. Stonehouse was a physician he had been concerned with the spiritual as well as the physical health of his patients, and now that he was a clergyman he had a practical interest in his parishioners' health and financial well-being as well as their spiritual needs. He was in advance of his times in sensing the close relation between physical and emotional health. The high-strung, ambitious Mores with their prosperity, their headaches, their driving energy, their passionate decorum, and their religious concerns could not at that time have found a better adviser. Dr. Stonehouse was especially appreciative of Sally, whose calculated naïveté was a thorn in her sisters' flesh, to the extent of collecting and writing down her witticisms under the title "Sally-isms." He encouraged Hannah in her early writings and exchanged Latin verses with her. Like all the men friends of the More sisters, he was a man of definite ideas and vigorous personality. It took strong individuality to hold one's own enough to enjoy the five lively, determined ladies. It is to be regretted that in his old age Sir James was persuaded to burn his autobiography because it related the sinfulness of his youth when he did things like learning French from Paris carriage drivers in order to perfect his profanity.

Another Bristol friend was Josiah Tucker, Dean of Gloucester Cathedral and Rector of St. Stephen's in Bristol, the sisters' church. He was a shrewd, kind old man who sent Hannah his very original pamphlets and apologized to her for marrying his housekeeper. Mr. Peach, given name unknown, a wealthy and learned linen-draper with a shop in Maryleport Street, a friend of Hume, the historian, during the years he spent in Bristol, is the only tradesman listed as a member of the More social circle.

All these men had wives, but the wives are not mentioned, although we have no reason for supposing that they stayed at home when calls were made on the Mores. Hannah wrote lovely obituaries for several wives but appears to have had no earlier interest in them. The More sisters, though anti-marriage, were men's women. Perhaps they had a surfeit of female society among themselves.

Among the lecturers who came to Forty-three Park Street were James Ferguson, the astronomer, and Thomas Sheridan, father of the famous playwright. Ferguson is said to have so admired young Hannah's early verse that he submitted his own writings to her criticism, while she imbibed scientific lore from his teaching. Sheridan, who gave a course on oratory, illustrating his points with readings from the scriptures and masterpieces of English literature, belonged to the old ranting school of actors and was known to the irreverent as "Old Bubble-and-Squeak," but to young Hannah he was soul-stirring. She expressed her girlish enthusiasm in a poem which asserted that he harmonized the ruffled soul, raised the mourning and the gay controlled, was as correct as science and as elegant as wit, as powerful as reason, as sweet as fancy, and so on. When a mutual acquaintance showed the verses to Old Bubble-and-Squeak, he was struck with the young lady's intelligence and said he would like to meet her. This was the beginning of an acquaintance between him and Hannah, which included his delightful wife, Frances Sheridan, playwright and novelist, and later his son and his daughter-in-law, the lovely singer, born Linley.

The election of Edmund Burke to Parliament from Bristol in 1774 was an exciting affair in which the sisters took part. When Henry Cruger, a Bristol merchant, stood for Parliament, Burke was rushed down from Yorkshire to stand with him, traveling in his chaise with post-horses and covering the two hundred and seventy miles in forty-four hours. The poll had then been open six days. Burke went directly to the Guildhall, sat on the platform for a few minutes to catch his breath, and rose to make a remarkably fine speech. During the entire month that the poll was open the excitement was intense and the Mores did their bit, mainly with verses by Hannah, who had already met Burke in London.

An electioneering party, parading the streets, halted in front of Forty-three Park Street, and, requested by their leader to give three cheers, responded with, "More, Sappho, and Cruger, forever!" Spritely Sally wrote to a friend: "It puzzled many of the gazing multitude, particularly the females, who wanted to know if Sappho was another candidate; but luckily our friend the alderman next door explained the mystery, and informed them that Sappho was nothing more than a harmless female poet, who formerly made verses, and the whole was a compliment to *you know whom!*" [4]

The charming Burke brothers, Edmund and Richard, were frequent guests at the house and when Edmund's success was assured, the Mores sent him a wonderful cockade composed of colors which in his famous essay he had classified as Sublime and Beautiful, entwined with myrtle, ivy, laurel, and bay, decorated with silver tassels, and accompanied by some of Hannah's fulsome verse. Burke wore the cockade on chairing day, when he received also from the sisters a wreath and a couplet. Burke too could weave words into pleasant phrases and he called the next day to thank Hannah for the cockade "in such terms [it is Mary writing to Mrs. Gwatkin] that never, no, never, were compliments dictated in such a charming manner before." [5]

The More sisters were good company, skillful in putting people at ease and in drawing out the special talent of each guest. They were themselves good talkers but they bridled their witty tongues to give others a chance. As a group they had a flair for meeting desirable individuals and turning casual acquaintance into enduring intimacy. They were born politicians, instinctively liking the right people. Each year their circle grew larger.

Even in their youth they were a remarkable group of young women. Mary, on whose shoulders rested the heaviest burden, was blunt, honest, and dictatorial, a disciplinarian of the now-I-am-going-to-be-frank sort, whose desire for others' well-being impelled her to point out their faults. She allowed no indulgences to herself or anyone else and she was called "The Man of the Family." Patty, the youngest, was a little like her eldest sister, domineering, loyal, and persevering, but with quick wit and droll tongue. It is difficult to understand why she was such a general favorite, for her letters and *Mendip Annals*, her journal, are censorious and dogmatic. Yet when Dr. Winterbottom came home on a visit from Sierra Leone where he was assistant to Zachary Macaulay he wrote back to his friend: "How can the men be so blind to Patty More's merits? It ought to have been a national concern, and so much goodness should have been married even though it had been enforced by an Act of Parliament." [6]

Mary and Patty were like their father's mother, that indomitable old lady in Norfolk; resolute, energetic, and authoritative. Betty was gentle, loving, and helpful; good at needlework and cooking; housekeeper at the school, and needlework teacher. She was the mediator and harmonizer and was called "The Wife of the Family" and "The Good Angel."

Since the two oldest played the roles of "The Man" and

"The Wife," the three youngest became something like foster children to the two who carried the responsibility. Sally decided to be merry and was the gayest one of the gay family, looking always on the bright side and making indiscreet remarks. Toward the end of her life she became something of an *enfant terrible*, driven too far by the need of achieving individuality. There was not a touch of the family priggishness about her and she might have been pleasantly sinful if she had had Hannah's chances in London. Sally wrote two novels, probably published anonymously, for no trace of them can be found. In her letters she tossed off phrases that bring pictures before one and the tracts she wrote in later life are lively and sometimes humorous.

All the girls suffered from their father's determination to impose one definite pattern on their differing individualities. Mary and Patty, following easily the Puritanic standard, had little consideration for sensitive natures. Betty slid from under and found refuge in effacement. Sally escaped by refusing to be serious; "mercurial" her sisters called her. Hannah was seriously injured by the rigid training. She was gentle and oversensitive like Betty but she did not take a back seat where she would be unnoticed. She had to have attention. Hannah was not so very, very good as her parents and sisters insisted she was. The struggle between the natural woman in Hannah and the unnatural pattern of determination, industry, and austerity forced upon her wracked her nerves. Hannah was a charmer. She pleased her sisters as much as she did outsiders and not all glamor girls can do that. The sisters set the stage for Hannah and gave her the leading role. Under these circumstances she developed self-confidence, graciousness, and modest ease in conversation.

She was vivacious, impulsive, and admiring. Above all she was sincerely appreciative of older people's achievements; a winning quality in young people. She was gay, high-spirited, and quick-tongued whenever people met her. They did not know that this light-heartedness alternated with periods of depression in private, when she withdrew from activity and gave herself up to headaches, colds, bilious attacks, and other functional illnesses. The doctors, the sisters, and all the friends were baffled by Hannah's illnesses and she was blistered, cupped, bled, and dosed for her nervous breakdowns.

These five highly individualistic sisters made up a delightful household of young people in which understanding and genuine kindliness softened shrewdness and ambition. The oldest was only twenty-eight when the youngest was sixteen. In spite of their strongly contrasting personalities they lived together harmoniously. Doubtless there were some quarrels and occasional bad tempers, but, bound together by family tradition and a common, active aim, they achieved a pleasant atmosphere.

CHAPTER V

Mr. Turner and Dr. Langhorne

HANNAH was released from schoolteaching and given leisure to become a woman of letters by an unusual circumstance. An annuity was settled upon her by a gentleman twenty years her senior who, in the phraseology of the day, repeatedly postponed fulfilling his matrimonial engagement with her. The name of Edward Turner is preserved from oblivion solely because he jilted Hannah More.

Mr. Turner had a fine estate, Belmont, near Wraxall, some six miles from Bristol in an especially lovely spot on the southern side of a hill, with a neat house against a background of tall elms, small oak, and twisted aged yews. Paths were cut through the ancient woodland and the views over the valley were delightful.[1] The owner of this charming estate had horses to ride and drive, a good income, a liking for young people, and a respectable housekeeper to act as chaperone. Hannah met him through his cousins, the Turner sisters, who attended the More boarding school and visited him in the holidays. The Turner girls were accustomed to invite Hannah and Patty, only slightly their seniors, to accompany them. The Lintorn girls, also pupils at the school, were likewise related to him and were probably among the guests.

Hannah and her host had many tastes in common: love of scenery, fondness for planning gardens, and appreciation of poetry. The lovely grounds of Belmont were the first on which Hannah exercised her ingenuity; later on she had a famous garden around her cottage, Cowslip Green in Wrington, and still later she and Sally and Patty designed and planted the grounds of the sisters' home, Barley Wood, where even yet the old terraces, walls, and plantations are to be seen.

At this period of Hannah's life she broke into verse at the touch of emotion and Mr. Turner adorned his woods with her poems neatly lettered on boards and nailed to trees. One set of verses set up at the top of a steep incline hymned the satisfaction enjoyed when one surmounts a sharp pitch of path or a difficulty in life, while verses recording Mr. Turner's grief at the death of a friend were engraved on a cenotaph. These quaint ornamentations were still preserved when Rev. Henry Thompson visited Belmont after Hannah's death. Two of Hannah's early poems are said to have been written during her visits to Belmont and a cottage in the grounds called "The Hannah More Cottage" is still pointed out as her writing room. *Inscription on a Beautiful Retreat called Fairy Bower* are lilting lines inspired by a near-by hill called Failand, a contraction of Fairyland. *The Ballad of Bleeding Rock or the Metamorphosis of a Nymph into Stone* was suggested by a rust-streaked rock in the grounds. It is an imitation of Ovid and records the desertion of a nymph by her faithless lover but, when Mr. Turner was likewise faithless, Hannah did not turn to stone; she sold the poem.

Of Mr. Turner himself, we know little beyond his peculiar

inability to turn his betrothal into marriage during six years of engagement. Hannah had a pleasing personality. She was attractive in appearance, with marvellous dark eyes, a slender graceful figure, and quick pretty ways. Her nature was friendly, affectionate and loyal, although she was a little spoiled by too much praise. It is unlikely that she pledged her hand to Mr. Turner without giving him her heart, although her love was probably decorous rather than intense. The slight, easy verse which she composed during this period of engagement to Belmont's master indicates that she was moving tranquilly from the shelter of her sisters into the care of a middle-aged man with a good income, a fine estate, and congenial tastes. The estate would, in a way, have regained for the whole family the security that Jacob More failed to inherit. Hannah's position as the wife of a country gentleman would have put them back in what they felt was their rightful rank. This was not to be.

Mr. Turner three times balked at wedding days. We do not know what excuse he gave for postponing marriage but he twice saved his face. The third time, no.

One of Mr. Turner's young cousins, the Frances Lintorn who married Captain Thomas Simmons of Bath, and was Hannah's lifelong friend, gave an explanation after Hannah's death: ". . . for the estate of matrimony he appears to have wanted that essential qualification, a cheerful and composed temper. The prospect of marriage, with the appendate of an indifferent temper, was gloomy enough, but there were other objections, on which it is unimportant to dwell." [2] Whatever these objections were, the Mores had overlooked them for six years.

At Mr. Turner's earnest request he met Hannah in a final

interview which was painful but decisive. He was frantic at the prospect of losing her and perhaps he was ill-pleased with his own conduct. He actually begged for another chance, sure that at the fourth try he could get himself to the altar. He declared that he would marry Hannah at any day and any hour. When it was clear that he would receive no fourth chance, he offered her an annuity, which she refused but which her sisters and Dr. Stonehouse accepted for her without her knowledge. The annuity accepted was two hundred pounds a year, a lesser sum than the repentant Mr. Turner offered. For a time Hannah refused to use the money, but time, her friends' persuasion, and her own practical sense overcame her humiliation and she became an independent gentlewoman with a fairly comfortable income of her own.

Pecuniary heart-balm was an accepted convention of the time. The beautiful and virtuous Miss Elizabeth Ann Linley, who married Richard Brinsley Sheridan, son of Hannah's friend "Old Bubble-and-Squeak," had three thousand pounds and a thousand pounds' worth of jewels already bestowed upon her by an elderly fiancé who withdrew his proposal of marriage.[3] When Hannah was a co-visitor with her at David Garrick's home less than ten years later, Hannah succumbed to that lovely lady's charm as did everyone who met her. A fascinating short-lived actress of extraordinary beauty, a Miss Hart, who married Samuel Reddish, the actor, was another young woman who had an income settled on her by an elderly admirer whose second thoughts were stronger than his love. Both of these ladies were on the public stage, so that their acceptance of compensation for disappointed love seems not as incongruous as it was in the case of Hannah More, a simple schoolteacher. Hannah, by accepting the annuity, laid herself open to criticism from those who did not like her and embarrassed those who admired her. The More sisters were neither wholly saintly nor wholly worldly, but practical.

Hannah is said to have made a resolution never to marry as a result of this humiliation. Perhaps this was the way she justified to herself the acceptance of the annuity. But there were other influences that turned her toward celibacy. Looking at the matter in the light of her lifelong aversion to marriage, one wonders if she may have had an extreme reserve, a marked distaste for the caresses of an intimate relationship, which increased the trepidation of the middle-aged bachelor. Although she had a number of later incipient love affairs, she carried none to the logical conclusion, but showed positive genius in turning men's awakened interest into lasting friendship. She was a man's woman who held men at arm's length. One reason for the enduring devotion she received all her life from middle-aged and elderly men may have been that they could trust her never to allow them to overstep the line of strict decorum.

Although we know that Lord Monboddo offered marriage and rumor had it that several others had similar inclinations, something prevented Hannah's accepting a husband. The five sisters had an anti-matrimonial bias in common. In the case of Patty this manifested itself in a determined effort to prevent the marriage of her friend Selina Mills to their friend Zachary Macaulay, and later in discharging women teachers in the charity schools which she and Hannah organized and supervised, when they engaged themselves to marry. The Mores seem to have been one of those families so firmly bound together that no member can break away from the clan to form an alliance with an outsider.

Mr. Turner never got over the breaking of his engagement to Hannah. His first glass of wine every day in company or in solitude was a solemn toast to Hannah More. He used to say sadly that Providence had overruled his wish to be her husband in order to preserve her for higher things.

The former lovers must have heard of each other from time to time through the Lintorns and the Turners, who continued close friends of the Mores. Mr. Turner and Hannah did actually meet in person some twenty years after they missed each other at the altar. The sisters were spending the summer at Hannah's cottage, Cowslip Green, Wrington, Somerset. A garden bloomed there, as a garden bloomed everywhere the More sisters lived, and Mr. Turner riding by stopped to admire the flowers. He was overwhelmed, so he said, to discover that this was Hannah's home. One suspects that he was riding by because his cousins had told him all about Cowslip Green. The sisters invited him in and put him at his ease. From that time on he was an occasional guest, dining with the family, interesting himself in Hannah's Sunday School and attending at least one of the big school picnics in the Mendip Hills. Hannah sent him a copy of each of her books as they came out and he left her a thousand pounds at his death. Neither Hannah nor her sisters held the past against him.

Hannah went to Uphill on the coast to recuperate after the mortifying crash of her long engagement. Her friends said she was recovering from an ague, for the convenient phrase "nervous breakdown" had not then been invented.

Disaster always made Hannah ill. She fell sick when she was distressed or scared or shamed or hurt or could not decide what course to pursue. So now at Uphill in 1773 she came back to health in high spirits, ready for some gaiety, and her partner in gaiety was Dr. John Langhorne, the poet, who was staying for his health at Weston-super-Mare near by. Dipping in the sea was a fashionable prescription and Weston was beginning to be a popular resort.

Dr. Langhorne, Vicar of Blagdon, was a figure in the literary world. He was not a university man although he was entered at Clare Hall, Cambridge, and a degree may have been granted him by the University of Edinburgh in recognition of his Scottish pastoral, *Genius and Valour*. Three years before Hannah met him at the seaside he had published his best-known work, a translation of Plutarch in collaboration with his brother William. He had married for a second time the year previous to his gay, though doubtless decorous, flirtation with Hannah. Dr. Langhorne's temperament was affectionate and impulsive like Hannah's. Charm and gaiety alternated with despondency, and somewhat as Hannah escaped the unendurable by retreating to a sickbed so he took refuge in alcohol. He lacked Hannah's strong will and rectitude, or perhaps it was four strong-willed sisters that he lacked.

Uphill was a village of a few cottages, occupied by fishermen and laborers, where the river Ax ran into the Bristol Channel.[4] Weston consisted of one irregular street half a mile in length, running through a woody vale beside a brook. Between the two villages stretched a three-mile curve of sandy beach covered with mollusks to be gathered for eating and lovely shell for fashionable art work. Among the rocks were wild roses and blue periwinkles and the *herbe de Saint Pierre* used in pickling.[5] At ebb tide the beach was firm and smooth and along this curved track rode the verse-writing rector of Blagdon and the young poetess of Bristol. Hannah sometimes rode on a pillion behind her servant.

If the two poets missed each other, they left verses in a cleft post which served as a private post office. Once Dr. Langhorne wrote on the sand with his cane:

Along the shore walked Hannah More;
Waves! Let this record last;
Sooner shall ye,
Proud earth and sea,
Than what she writes, be past.

Whereupon Hannah, with her riding whip, wrote in reply:

Some firmer basis, polished Langhorne, choose,
To write the dictates of your charming muse;
Thy strains in solid characters rehearse,
And be thy tablet lasting as thy verse.

Hannah wrote more elaborate verse on the incident later on, but her considered lines were not as pleasing as the improvisation.

The friendship between the two poets continued after their return to their respective homes in Bristol and Blagdon. The letters written by Dr. Langhorne to Hannah were spritely and the verses he sent her were gay. He reproached her for not letting him send his carriage to Bristol to bring her to Blagdon and when she consented he burst into song:

Blow, blow, my sweetest rose!
For Hannah More will soon be here,
And all that crowns the ripening year
Should triumph where she goes.

My sun-flower fair, abroad
For her thy noble breast unfold,
And with thy noble smile behold
The daughter of thy God.

Ye laurels, brighter bloom!
For she your wreaths, to glory due,
Has bound upon the hero's brow
And planted round his tomb.

Ye bays, your odors shed!
For you her youthful temples bound,
What time she trod on fairy ground,
By sweet Euterpe led!

Come, innocent and gay,
Ye rural nymphs your love confess,
For her who sought your happiness,
And crowned it with her lay.

The apostrophes to laurels and nymphs refer to Hannah's *Inflexible Captive* and *Search after Happiness.*

One trip to Blagdon vicarage was embalmed by Hannah in doggerel verse which she never printed. Someone saved it and Rev. Henry Thompson included it in his life of Hannah. The verse is very bad indeed, but the picture is delightful. Hannah and Sally on a Sunday May morning left smoky Bristol for the "verdure and freshness" of Blagdon, stopped at the sign of the Bell to freshen up and eat breakfast toast and tea, attended service to hear Dr. Langhorne preach, and went on to dinner at the vicarage with him and his wife where they "relished the wine and applauded the mutton."

Misfortune soon overwhelmed Dr. Langhorne. His second wife, like his first, died in childbirth within a few years of their marriage, and the husband, broken by successive griefs and heavy drinking, did not long survive her.

The type of man who attracted Hannah was now fixed. He was usually married, older than she, witty, and distinguished. The long list of her friendships included William Powell, the actor; John Langhorne; David Garrick; Dr. Johnson; Beilby Porteus, Bishop of London; Sir William Pepys, Master in Chancery; Horace Walpole; Rev. John Newton, Cowper's friend and mentor; and other erudite and prominent men. Patty in later years developed a kindliness toward curates, but Hannah insisted on distinction even after she was obliged to content herself with the devotion of men younger than herself because all her elders were dead. Her last close friend was William Wilberforce, M.P., antislavery advocate and friend of Pitt.

CHAPTER VI

Hannah's First Plays

BRISTOL was theatre mad. The enthusiasm was of long standing, for as long before as 1715 an anonymous shilling pamphlet on *The Consequences of a New Theatre to the City of Bristol* was "humbly submitted to the consideration of the wiser and more serious part of the inhabitants of the said city." The alarmed writer foretold that if the projected theatre were built no master would be able to maintain authority over his apprentices, no husband could control his wife, and no father could enforce obedience from his daughters. In spite of the warning, drama continued so popular and profitable that in 1766, not long after the Mores came to Bristol to live, the Theatre Royal was built on King Street; here Hannah's own plays were performed a few years later.[1]

The Theatre Royal, known also as the King Street Theatre, a building rich in carving, gilding, and painting, was the pride of Bristol, and was pronounced the most complete of its size in Europe. Before the theatre was finished, Garrick came to inspect and praise it, but Hannah did not meet him personally until she visited London about ten years later.

The opening night was a gala affair. As a license had not

been obtained, the performance was announced as "A Concert of Music and a Specimen of Rhetoric." Admission was free that night and servants came early to keep seats for their employers, who arrived at seven. The "specimen of rhetoric" was the play *The Conscious Lovers,* with prologue and epilogue written by Garrick, who was not himself present.

We may be sure that the Mores and perhaps their entire student body were there, for we know that they had a very special interest in drama, and William Powell, who took the part of Young Bevil, was their special friend. Martha Lintorn's school bill lists "2 play tickets" and Mary Robinson, later the actress "Perdita," tells in her memoirs how, when a pupil in the More school, she went to the theatre for the first time in company with the whole school to see Powell in *Lear.* Hannah wrote a prologue to *Hamlet* spoken by Powell at one of his benefit nights, when he was playing at the old Jacob's Well Theatre. His daughters were pupils in the More school, as were those of Mrs. King, Mrs. Pritchard, and other actresses appearing in Bath and Bristol.

William Powell was a fine actor. He was about medium height, carried himself well in spite of being round-shouldered, possessed a pleasing voice, and was extraordinarily emotional in his acting. Bristol people liked him socially as well as professionally and his sudden death after being connected with the Theatre Royal for three years was a shock and a grief to everyone. His death was supposed to have been caused by his rashly throwing himself naked in the cool green grass when heated by playing tennis. During his brief illness chains were stretched across King Street to bar traffic from the section where he lived near the theatre, and performances were omitted lest the sounds disturb him. His death came unexpectedly while Hannah was taking Mrs. Powell's place by his bedside. The actor is said to have raised himself in bed, crying out, "What is this I see before me?" A moment later he cried, "Oh, God!" and fell back dying in Hannah's arms.

The night following his death the play *Richard III* was attempted, but the actors were unable to perform their parts and the audience left in tears. The funeral, held in Bristol Cathedral with full honors, was interrupted by a strange incident. Ned Shuters, one of the members of the troupe, strangely dressed in a scarlet waistcoat, stalked solemnly up to the Cathedral door in the midst of the service, hammered loudly with his stick, and declaimed lines from *Romeo and Juliet*:

Thou detestable maw, thou womb of death,
Gorg'd with the dearest morsel of the earth,
Thus I enforce thy rotten jaws to open,
And in despite, I'll cram thee with more food! [2]

A benefit performance was performed some nights later for Powell's family, the play chosen being *The Roman Father*, a tragedy by William Whitehead in which Powell himself had appeared. The audience came dressed in black.

This was Hannah's first experience in losing a dear friend, but it was a grief many times repeated during her long life and always a devastating experience.

Bristol enjoyed a rich theatrical life, and sometimes upward of a hundred carriages waited before the playhouse. Much of the time a company performed at the King Street Theatre for an entire season, and other years the John

Palmers, father and son, managers of the Orchard Street Theatre, Bath, brought their troupe weekly to Bristol to repeat Bath successes. The acting was of a high quality, for constant interchange went on between the London stage and the provincial houses. Garrick, a close friend of the younger Palmer, was accustomed to send to him young talent to be tried out and trained in the provinces. Many famous actors went from the Orchard Street, Bath, and the King Street, Bristol, theatres to Drury Lane and Covent Garden. The plays included the Elizabethan and the Restoration dramas.

In such an environment it was natural enough that Hannah's first long piece of writing should be a play. It was natural also that the play should have been one suitable for production by the young ladies of the boarding school. *The Search after Happiness* was dedicated to Mrs. Gwatkin and the first published edition bears the date 1773, but the preface states that it was written when the author was sixteen, that is, ten years previous, when it was recited by a party of young ladies. The stated object was to promote a regard for religion and virtue in the minds of young persons and afford them innocent amusement and practice in recitation.

The poem is a delightful one with rhythmic meter and pleasing rhyme, a conversation rather than a drama, interspersed with melodious songs. The lyrics were printed in *Dodsley's Annual* with a hearty recommendation of the play as suitable for the perusal of elegant females because it conveyed important truths in elegant numbers.

It is pleasant to think of this play being given at Forty-three Park Street by excited young ladies in hoops and sacques and ringlets, before an audience of mothers and cousins and aunts, male relatives being rigidly excluded. The teachers must have been almost as nervous as the actors, for private theatricals were a daring venture even if cast and audience were all female. You get a reflection of this in the prologue and epilogue which in the original version are more naïve than as published in the *Collected Works.* Hannah rewrote some of her early work when she published it later on, remodeling it to her own elderly approval.

The prologue, spoken by one of the young ladies, begs indulgence for the young author:

With trembling diffidence, with modest fear,
Before this gentle audience we appear.
Ladies! Survey us with a tender eye,
Put on good nature, and lay judgment by.
No deep laid Plot adorns our humble page,
But scenes adapted to our sex and age.
Simplicity is all our Author's aim,
She does not write, nor do we speak for fame.
To make Amusement and Instruction friends,
A lesson in the guise of play she sends;
She claims no merit for her love of truth,
No plea to favour, but her sex *and* youth;
With these alone, to boast, she sends me here,
To beg your kind, indulgent, partial ear.
Of critic man *she could not stand the test,*
But you with softer, gentler hearts are bless'd.
With him she dares not rest her feeble cause,
A mark too low for satire, or applause,
Ladies, protect her—do not be satiric,
Spare censure, she expects no panygeric.

The didactic epilogue was certainly written by that same Hannah who would not admire a girl's drawings till assured she could sew a binding on a skirt. It was spoken by two young ladies. After the First Young Lady has asked the audience if they liked the play, Second Young Lady assures any who might feel critical that the actresses can also manage a house:

Child! we must quit these visionary scenes,
And end our follies when we end our teens,
These bagatelles we must relinquish now,
And good matronic gentlewomen *grow;*
Fancy no more on airy wings shall rise,
We must scold the maids and make the pies;
Verse is a folly—we must rise above it,
Yet I know not how it is—I love it.
Tho' should we still the rhyming trade pursue,
The men will shun us,—and the women, too;
The men, poor souls! of scholars *are afraid,*
We shou'd not, did they govern, *learn to read,*
At least, in no abstruser volume look,
Than the learn'd records—of a Cookery book;
The ladies, too, their well-meant censure give,
"*What!—does she* write? *a slattern, as I live—*
"*I wish she'd leave her books, and mend her cloaths,*
"*I thank my stars I know not verse from prose;*
"*How well these learn'd ladies* write,
"*They seldom act the virtues they recite;*
"*No useful qualities adorn their lives,*
"*They make sad* Mothers, *and still sadder* Wives."

Thus the accusation. First Lady presents rebuttal:

I grant this satire just, in former *days,*
When SAPPHOS *and* CORINNAS *tuned their lays,*
But in our chaster *times 'tis no offence,*
When female virtue *joins with female* sense,
When moral CARTER *breathes the strain divine,*
And AIKIN'S *life flows faultless as her line;*
When all accomplish'd MONTAGU *can spread*
Fresh gather'd laurels round her Shakespeare's head;
When wit, and worth, in polish'd BROOKE *unite,*
And fair MACAULAY *claims a* LIVY'S *right.*

Thus far to clear her from the sin of rhyme,
Our author bade me trespass on your time,
To show, that if she dares aspire to letters,
She only sins in common with her betters:

The second Young Lady goes on with the apology, mentioning the names of women who though writers were also excellent females, and ends by backing down on all possible claims which might offend, with the lines:

One virtuous sentiment, one generous deed,
Affords more generous transport to the heart,
Than genius, wit or science can impart;
For these shall flourish, fearless of decay,
When wit shall fail, and science fade away.[3]

Hannah believed destiny imposed one set of duties upon men and a completely different set upon women, although an exceptional woman might push her way a very short distance into what was essentially a masculine province.

The Search after Happiness: a Pastoral Drama takes place in the pretty-pretty country so dear to eighteenth-century versemakers:

Here lowly thickets, there aspiring trees;
The hazel copse excluding the noon-day beam,
The tufted arbor, the pellucid stream;
The blooming sweet-briar, and the hawthorne shade,
The springing cowslips and the daisy'd mead;
The wild luxuriance of full-blown fields,
Which spring prepares, and laughing summer yields.

Here, far from the gay misery of the thoughtless great, the walks of folly, the disease of state, four ladies of distinction seek wisdom. Urania, a widow with two children, who has retired to a cell in this lovely spot, advises each how to overcome her particular fault, whether envy, pedantry, novel-reading or laziness, and exhorts them collectively on the glory of modesty and humility in women and the impossibility of happiness this side of heaven.

The sentiments were platitudinous, but one must remember that they were written by a girl of sixteen for even younger pupils and well-known truths are often inspired statements to children. Indeed Hannah wrote simple admonitions all her life in novels, sermons, and tracts, and her books were best sellers. Every reader could recognize his neighbors' failings in her pages.

Hannah exchanged her amateur standing for professional status as a playwright when John Palmer, manager of the Theatre Royal in Bath, produced her tragedy *The Inflexible Captive*, later called *Regulus*. The opening night was April nineteenth, 1775, after she had made one visit and probably two to London and was acquainted with the Garricks.

The basis of the play was her own translation of *Attilio Regolo,* one of Metastasio's less well-known lyrical dramas. Regulus, a prisoner of war, was returned to Rome by the Carthaginians to negotiate peace, but he advised against accepting the proposed terms and honorably went back to Carthage to die. The play had already been published by S. Farley, in Castle Green, Bristol, 1774. It seems to have been tried out in Exeter shortly before it was put on in Bath and was probably given later in Bristol.

Garrick and his wife were present at the first night, the famous actor remaining backstage with his friend the manager. Garrick wrote the epilogue, a flattering eulogy on women's literary achievements, and Dr. Langhorne provided the prologue, a flowery trifle about wreaths immortal and the fair foundress of the scene tonight. The Mores had a gala night. Sally wrote; "All the world of dukes, lords and barons were there. I sat next to a baron and a lord. All expressed the highest approbation of the whole. Never was a piece represented there known to have received so much applause." [4]

The *Bath Chronicle* reported in the issue of April twentieth: "It was received with uncommon applause, and promises to be a favorite piece. . . . The whole was received with a warmth of applause that reflects great honor both on the Authoress and her friends." Later issues of the paper state that it was repeated May fourth and sixth.

Garrick wrote to George Colman, the day after the premier: "The Inflexible Captive has been played here with success, and I touched up Mrs. Didier with an Epilogue, which had a good reception. Henderson played Regulus, and you would have wished him bunged up with his nails before the end of the first act."[5]

John Henderson was a youth of talent whom Garrick had sent to Palmer for training and experience, and despite Garrick's impatient criticism he was a very good actor who later won London laurels. Dimond, who took the part of a consul, had been trained by Garrick. Rowbottom, Blisset, and Miss Wheeler, members of Palmer's troupe, were all good actors and Miss Mansell, later Mrs. Farren, was just entering a long, successful career. Hannah was fortunate in the cast.

CHAPTER VII

London and Doctor Johnson

WITH HER first visit to London Hannah changed from a girl to a woman. Under the adoring protection of her sisters she had held on to girlhood overlong, and at twenty-six sometimes behaved with a sweet girlishness which enchanted elderly gentlemen but indicated immaturity. London and the Dr. Johnson set gave her the self-confidence she had needed.

The first of a series of annual London visits covering some twenty-five years took place in the winter of 1773–4, or of '74–5; Hannah's habit of not dating letters makes it impossible to be sure of the exact date. Sally and Patty accompanied her and the three took lodgings in Henrietta Street, Covent Garden. They doubtless went from Bristol to London by stagecoach, as coach fare was under two pounds, while post travel with its hour rate, turnpike tolls, and tips to post boys cost more and the Mores had not yet accumulated their modest fortune.

The London which Hannah knew was a city of about five hundred thousand; the streets were paved with cobblestones; there was no sewer system; and though there was a primitive street-lighting system, night traffic relied chiefly on linkboys. Dr. Johnson was living in Johnson Court, Mrs. Elizabeth Montagu was in Hill Street, the Garricks had recently moved into the Adelphi, and the Bathursts had just built Apsley House.

This was an exciting time for bookish folk like the More girls to visit London, for literary life was in full swing. The novels of Richardson, Smollett, Fielding, and Sterne had been published; Johnson had produced his dictionary; Hume and Robertson were writing history; Walpole's *Castle of Otranto* and his *Mysterious Mother* were best sellers; Chatterton, Macpherson and Percy had revived interest in early literature. The drama was very much alive; Goldsmith's and Sheridan's masterpieces were being played, Garrick had brought Shakespeare back to the stage, although sometimes in altered versions, and the actors and actresses were excellent.

The sisters did the regulation sightseeing. Hannah stole two pebbles from Pope's grotto, a sprig of laurel and a pen—not the poet's pen but one belonging to Sir William Chesterfield who then owned the estate. She inspected Garrick's villa from the outside and approved the garden, not knowing that she would live in that villa and walk in that garden during long, long visits. She stayed at Hampton Court three days in one of the private apartments of the palace, but whom she visited we do not know. She was a conscientious sightseer but not enthusiastic. The theatre was more to her taste. She was lukewarm about Sheridan's *The Rivals,* which had been rewritten but not yet acclaimed. Burgoyne's *Maid of the Oaks* pleased her better. It was people, however, who stirred her interest most, and she had the chance of meeting many whom she had long admired.

The More sisters were introduced into London society by

Sir Joshua Reynolds and his sister Frances, also a portrait painter. Since Mrs. Gwatkin's son Lovell later married the Reynolds' niece Theophila, it seems possible that it was through her that the sisters were taken under the Reynolds' wings. The Reynolds had recently moved into a fine house on Leicester Square where they entertained in a friendly, absentminded fashion, knowing everybody and loved by all. The three sisters were cordially welcomed by the Reynolds' friends and held their own at dinners and evening routs; Sally was a beauty and a wit, Hannah was a bright-eyed genius, and Patty had the charm of youth as well as a quick tongue.

One of the first dinner parties Hannah attended was at the Hill Street home of Mrs. Elizabeth Montagu, widow of Edward Montagu and "Queen of the Blues." She had acquired literary standing a decade before through an essay defending Shakespeare from Voltaire's criticism and three dialogues contributed to Lyttelton's *Dialogues of the Dead.* On this slim output she was labeled "Our Modern Aspasia" and "Our Female Bride of Literature," but her family called her "Fidget." Though she was a scanty writer she was truly a Great Lady, with wealth, social standing, personal brilliancy, poise, and kindliness. Even after years of intimacy Hannah wrote to her with a certain formality that indicates an enduring awe. An oddity of the long friendship between them was that Hannah always thought Mrs. Montagu was about to die. After this first dinner party Hannah wrote home an enthusiastic description of Mrs. Montagu's animation and wisdom, but added sadly that her active spirits would soon wear out the frail receptacle that held them. Later on she was convinced that her friend was hastening to insensible decay by a slow but sure hectic, and when the lady moved into her magnificent Portman Square mansion Hannah lamented that she could enjoy it for only a very little while. Fortunately she lived for some twenty-five years to correspond with Hannah when they were separated and to entertain her at her country place, Sandleford Priory, near Newbury, when she traveled between Bristol and London.

The most fashionable hairdresser came to the Henrietta Street lodgings to prepare Hannah for the dinner. This was a concession to the importance of the occasion, for Hannah disliked the elaborate structures of hair, plumes, ribbons, and ornaments which women then carried on their heads. Her early portraits show hair drawn loosely away from her forehead and rolled in the back. In the Opie portrait the hair is powdered. In two of the early pictures and in all of the later she wears a turban or a cap. A lock of her hair, cut after it had turned white, and preserved in the Bristol Museum and Art Gallery (before its damage by enemy action), was of a coarse texture, and from the portraits one judges it was thick and heavy.

Hannah had already met enough of the dinner guests to feel at ease at the Montagu dinner. She had been presented to Dr. Johnson, Mrs. Boscawen was a friend of long standing, the Reynolds were present, and no one could be uncomfortable with plump Mrs. Elizabeth Carter, vastly learned, admired and loved. Hannah, looking at the greatness about her, felt herself "a worm, but a happy worm." She confided to Mrs. Boscawen that she did not repine at being the meanest person in the company. Social discomfort came to Hannah, in those early days, not when she was among her superiors, but when she had to associate with inferiors. Not till she was an old lady did she learn to enjoy the company of persons younger and less notable than herself. The change from being a protégée to being a patron was hard for her to make. She was rich in years and fame before she could accept the position of leader. At this dinner of Mrs. Montagu's, while she was still "a happy worm," Dr. Johnson startled her with a query as to how she liked Robert Jephson's tragedy *Braganza,* which ran for fifteen nights in February that year. Hannah, deciding it was less an evil to disagree with the rest of the company than to tell a lie, said she did not like it. Truth telling was rewarded by Johnson's reply, "You are right, Madam." [1]

It was Hannah's good fortune that society was taking notice of women who were merely intellectual and respectable; they no longer needed to be well-born or wealthy. Never before in any land had there been so diverse a group of intellectual women as in the coterie in which Hannah took her place. Mrs. Montagu was a *grande dame;* Miss Reynolds, a portrait painter; Mrs. Delany was the friend of royalty; Mrs. Boscawen, an admiral's widow; but Mrs. Thrale was a brewer's wife, Mrs. Carter, a schoolteacher, and Mrs. Garrick had been a dancer. Hannah entered this circle through Mrs. Boscawen's kindness, but she held her own by her wits and her charm.

Hannah's preference for older men and women had much to do with her social success. Her closest friends, Mrs. Garrick, Mrs. Montagu, and Mrs. Boscawen, were from twenty to twenty-five years her seniors. She enjoyed Mrs. Carter, twenty-eight years her elder; Mrs. Chapone, eighteen; Mrs. Vesey, thirty; and Mrs. Delany, forty-five. Her men friends also were her elders: Dr. Johnson was forty years older; David Garrick, twenty-eight; and Horace Walpole, twenty-eight. In her later life her close friends Beilby Porteus and John Newton were both her seniors.

Hannah was not particularly pleased with Mrs. Thrale, Fanny Burney, nor any other of the younger women except Mary Hamilton, the niece of Sir William Hamilton. She rather liked Boswell when she first met him, but later had an unpleasant encounter with him at a small, choice party at Bishop Shipley's where he was "disordered with wine" and was, she thought, impertinent to her.

Dr. Johnson made a good deal of Hannah. The friendship between the young woman and the elderly man was born in flattery and in flattery grew strong. Peppering with praise was a lively game openly played in the Johnson circle. You flatter, he flatters, they flatter; everyone flatters but me. I do not flatter; oh, no, not I. You like to be flattered, he likes to be flattered, she likes to be flattered, they like to be flattered; everyone likes to be flattered but me. I do not like to be flattered; oh, no, not I. A very pretty controversy has grown up as to whether or not Hannah's peppering was once too strong for the doctor's taste. Some of his other pets liked to think that he was disgusted with her.

The Reynolds were a little nervous when they first introduced Hannah to Dr. Johnson at their house. They warned her that he might be silent and depressed, but as it turned out he was in the best of spirits. When she entered the room he came rolling forward in his clumsy way with Sir Joshua's macaw on his hand and greeted her with verses of her own writing. It was a poem about not getting up in the morning written for Dr. Stonehouse. who called her a slug-a-bed. Remembering how Dr. Johnson struggled with inertia himself, one understands his amusement at the lines:

Soft slumbers now my eyes forsake,
My powers are all renew'd;
May my freed spirit too awake,
With heavenly strength endu'd!

Thou silent murderer SLOTH, no more
My mind imprison'd keep;
Nor let me waste another hour
With thee, thou felon Sleep.

Kind Miss Reynolds carried Hannah, Sally, and Patty to call on Dr. Johnson at Seven Johnson Court. They went in Sir Joshua's gaudy coach, a great vehicle with carved gilded wheels and panels painted to represent the seasons, attended by footmen in silver liveries. The call delighted the sisters, for they met Mrs. Williams, the blind poetess who was a member of the household, heard about the trip to the Hebrides and the book Johnson was writing on the subject, and listened to his recollections of Samuel Richardson. Although it was raining, the doctor insisted on accompanying his guests back to Fleet Street where the gaudy coach waited at the entrance to the court. One likes to picture the shabby, awkward old giant, always kind to young beauty, handing into the coach three happy girls and their pleasant hostess, with silver footmen hovering about, all in the rain.

The mutual admiration of Hannah and Dr. Johnson became one of the jokes of the older women who took Hannah to their hearts and petted her like a precocious child. When Dr. Johnson accompanied her home from one of Mrs. Montagu's parties, that lady declared that she was afraid to trust them together with such open affection on each side lest they elope to Scotland, and the gallant doctor made an appointment to drink tea with Hannah and Sally the following day in order to read Hannah's *Sir Eldred* aloud. This may have been the occasion when he set the seal of his approval on this poem by adding a verse of his own composition. Mrs. Montagu was so pleased with her teasing that she said, according to Sally: "If tender words are the precursors of connubial engagements, we may expect great things; for it is nothing but 'child'—'little fool'—'love' and 'dearest'."

Spritely Sally's letters home during this season and Hannah's during the following years make many mentions of Dr. Johnson. Sally wrote of one conversation she held with the great man:

> After much critical discourse, he turns round to me, and with one of his most amiable looks, which must be seen to form the least idea of it, he says, "I have heard that you are engaged in the useful and honourable employment of teaching young ladies," upon which, with all the same ease, familiarity, and confidence we should have done had only our own dear Dr. Stonehouse been present, we entered upon the history of our birth, parentage, and education; showing how we were born with more desires than guineas; and now, as years increased our appetites, the cupboard at home began to grow too small to gratify them; and how with a bottle of water, a bed, and a blanket, we set out to seek our fortunes; and how we found a great house, with nothing in it; and how it was like to remain so, till looking into our knowledge-boxes, we happened to find a little "larning," a good thing when land is gone, or rather none; and so at last, by giving a little of this "larning" to those who had less, we got a good store of gold in return; but how, alas! we wanted the wit to keep it—"I love you both," cried the inamorato—"I love you all five—I never was at Bristol—but I will come on purpose to see you—what! five women live happily together!—I will come and see you—I have spent a happy eve-

ning—I am glad I came—God forever bless you, you live lives to shame duchesses!" He took his leave with so much warmth and tenderness, we were quite affected at his manner.[2]

The great man kept his word and came to see The Sisterhood that same spring of 1776 on April twenty-ninth, during Hannah's absence in London. He had come over to Bristol from Bath with Boswell for personal investigation of the Chatterton mystery. The More sisters must have been able to give him first-hand information of the poet, for they were acquainted with the Chatterton family and were kind to Chatterton's mother. After the mother's death, Ann, the sister of the poet, lived with the Mores at Barley Wood.[3] Boswell does not mention this call on The Sisterhood in his life of Johnson. Boswell was one of the few people whom Hannah allowed herself heartily to dislike, and his critical references to her in the *Life* indicate that he returned her feeling.

When Hannah was sitting to Frances Reynolds for her portrait, Dr. Johnson, happening in, "stayed the whole time," Hannah wrote home, "and said many good things by way of making me look well." He promised to write something for Patty's memo book which was beginning to contain certain notable items thanks to Hannah's begging.

A delightful incident in their friendship occurred in 1782 when Johnson "gallented it" about Oxford with Hannah, showing her his own college, Pembroke, with particular delight. When they came to the common room they found a very pretty compliment arranged for them. A large picture of Johnson had been framed and hung that very morning with this motto: "And is not Johnson ours, himself a host. From Miss More's Sensibility." [4]

Whenever Hannah was in London she kept the family at home informed concerning Dr. Johnson's health and fluctuating spirits. At a dinner given by Dr. Porteus, the host asked Hannah to sit next to the doctor because she was so successful in drawing him out. The plan worked so well that by the middle of the meal Dr. Johnson was holding Hannah's hand, repeating passages from *The Fair Penitent*, and telling her that she should have married her fellow townsman Chatterton, "that posterity might have seen a propagation of poets." It was on this occasion that, urged by Hannah to take a little wine, he replied, "I can't drink a *little*, child, therefore I never touch it. Abstinence is as easy to me as temperance would be difficult." [5]

After Johnson had restricted his social life to small quiet gatherings because of his failing health, the friendship lessened in gaiety but increased in tenderness, and Hannah visited him at his home in Bolt Court, to which he had moved. After a day spent with him and Miss Williams at the Reynolds', she wrote home: "We did not part till eleven. He scolded me heartily as usual, when I differed from him in opinion, and, as usual, laughed when I flattered him. . . . I never saw Johnson really angry with me but once; and his displeasure did him so much honor that I loved him the better for it. I alluded, rather flippantly, I fear, to some witty passage in 'Tom Jones': he replied, 'I am shocked to hear you quote from so vicious a book. I am sorry to hear you have read it: a confession which no modest lady should make. I scarcely know a more corrupt work.' I thanked him for his correction. . . ."

CHAPTER VIII

David and Mrs. Garrick

HANNAH was attractive. There was something of the china shepherdess in her appearance; an innocent naughtiness lit up her countenance, quiet fun twinkled in her large dark eyes and a slight quirk twisted the corners of her mouth. In figure she was on the small side with just the right amount of plumpness. She dressed with marked simplicity, although sometimes in bright colors. Once she went to a party in a scarlet frock to find the other guests in court mourning, and when she was a very, very old lady she wore a lovely pea-green silk frock with an exquisite Chinese shawl. The embroidered linen caps which she wore in her old age were dainty and most becoming.

During these early years in London she enjoyed life to the full, only occasionally troubled by scruples which later came between her and social amusements. Her enthusiasms were poetry, the theatre, and conversation. She had no real liking for painting, an actual distaste for music, no desire for travel, and impatience with politics. An oddity of the letters which she wrote at this period is that she almost always wrote "I" instead of "we"; "I did thus and so," even when a sister was present; and Sally, writing home, wrote "Hannah did thus and so," although she herself was Hannah's companion. No trace of jealousy appears among the sisters; Hannah was the center of the stage while they were chorus and audience.

Hannah had started on her spectacularly successful career as an author. Her tremendous vogue is now forgotten, but everything she wrote was a best seller and editions were sold out before they were on the book stalls. No one could have dreamed that she would be so completely forgotten in a hundred years. Her preliminary triumph came with the publication in 1777 of two ballads. Her publisher was Thomas Cadell, London bookseller and publisher, and son of a Bristol bookseller. In his enthusiasm over his new client, he told her if she could find out how much Goldsmith had been paid for *The Deserted Village* she should receive the same. Goldsmith had been paid sixty guineas, but as Hannah did not know she was contented with forty pounds. The two ballads were *Sir Eldred and the Bower* and *The Ballad of Bleeding Rock.* Cadell was justified in his optimism for he and his son after him published all her best-selling books except the tracts and made a large amount of money for both author and publisher.

Sir Eldred shows Hannah's interest in the current revival of old English legends by Dr. Percy, Beattie, Chatterton, and others. Sir Eldred, a young and valiant knight, whose castle was the ancient glory of the north, loved Birtha, whose heart was a little sacred shrine where all the virtues met. Unfortunately, she forgot to tell her lover that she had a long-missing brother and when Sir Eldred came upon her embracing a strange knight in the garden, he promptly killed the intruder. The result of his jealous act was despair, madness, and death.

Dr. Johnson, reading the poem aloud, was so delighted that he wrote a stanza which was duly included:

My scorn has oft the dart repell'd
Which guileful beauty threw;
But goodness heard, and grace beheld,
Must every heart subdue.

The less popular *Ballad of Bleeding Rock* is a pseudo-mythological tale, written during her engagement to Mr. Turner. The all-too-appropriate theme is the death of a nymph when deserted by her lover, and the poem begins:

Where beauteous Belmont rears her modest brow
To view Sabrina's silver wave below,

Hannah must have recovered completely from the humiliation of being jilted to be able to offer these verses to the public without embarrassment.

The greatest happiness brought her by the success of *Sir Eldred* was the joy of hearing Garrick read it aloud at his house after "a snug little dinner in the library," where there was "much wit under the banner of much decorum." She wrote home:

"I'll tell you the most ridiculous circumstance in the world. After dinner Garrick took up the Monthly Review (civil gentlemen, by-the-by, these Monthly Reviewers), and read 'Sir Eldred' with all his pathos and all his graces. I think I never was so ashamed in my life; but he read it so superlatively that I cried like a child. Only think what a scandalous thing, to cry at the reading of one's own poetry! I could have beaten myself: for it looked as if I thought it very moving, which, I can truly say, is far from being the case. But the beauty of the jest lies in this: Mrs. Garrick twinkled as well as I, and made as many apologies for crying at her husband's reading, as I did for crying at my own verses. *She* got out of the scrape by pretending she was touched at the story, and *I* by saying the same thing of the reading. It furnished us with a great laugh at the catastrophe, when it would really have been decent to be a little sorrowful."

The same day held another delight, for she and Sally gave a wholly successful party in their lodgings that evening. The guests, arriving at seven, were Dr. Johnson; Frances Reynolds; Mrs. Boscawen; Rev. Josiah Tucker, Dean of Gloucester; and the Garricks. The party was a tremendous success. Johnson, often harsh toward Garrick who had been his pupil in the old Lichfield days, was this night in good humor.

"Garrick was the very soul of the company and I never saw Johnson in such perfect good-humor," Hannah wrote home. "Sally knows that we have often heard that one can never properly enjoy the company of these two unless they are together. There is great truth in this remark; for after the dean and Mrs. Boscawen (who were the only strangers) were withdrawn, and the rest stood up to go, Johnson and Garrick began a close encounter telling old stories 'e'en from their boyish days' at Lichfield. We all stood around them about an hour, laughing in defiance of every rule of decorum and Chesterfield. I believe we would not have thought of sitting down or parting, had not an impertinent watchman been saucily vociferous. Johnson outstayed them all and sat with me a half an hour." [1]

The triangular Mr. Garrick–Mrs. Garrick–Miss More friendship was in full swing by the spring of 1776, and after Sally went back to Bristol Hannah moved to the Garricks' where she lived for three months. The later part of her visit was extended in order that she might see the actor perform his most famous roles for the last time, for he had now definitely announced his retirement after nearly thirty-five years of acting. Though he had appeared as many as a hundred times a season during his vigorous youth, twenty times was now too much for him and only the excitement of acting gave him false strength to sustain his great art. Garrick had put on flesh although he was still extraordinarily graceful. His face was seamed and his first entrances on the stage in the roles of youthful lovers came as something of a shock, but in a few minutes he had his audiences hypnotized into seeing him young and handsome. His magic was eternal.

It is no wonder if Hannah's head was a little turned by Garrick's friendship. He was the brilliant manager of a famous theatre, the greatest living actor, and a playwright of no mean skill. In his private life he was on intimate terms with members of Parliament, well-known writers, and lords and ladies of high degree. He was a wit about town, a welcome guest in great houses, and a popular host in his own home. Withal he was a man of probity and standing with whom a respectable young lady from Bristol could associate without risk of censure. Hannah More and David Garrick had a number of traits in common; both had raised themselves from obscurity by their own efforts and both had social talent with which to supplement their professional work. They were equally impetuous, vivacious, and high-spirited. Garrick had the kindlier nature, even though Hannah was more religious; it is true Garrick had a quick temper and was irritable and sometimes unjust, while Hannah controlled her temper, but she lacked his impulsive, outgoing friendliness. Both were money-makers, generous, and full of affection toward their friends.

Mrs. Garrick had come to England as a *danseuse* from Vienna. La Violette was her stage name; Eva Maria her baptismal name. Rumor had it that the Empress Maria Theresa had been so disturbed by the Emperor's admiration of the lovely girl that she had sent her to London to the care of Lady Burlington, wife of Richard Boyle, fourth Earl of Cork and third Earl of Burlington. The Burlingtons took her into their home and treated her like a daughter. Lady Burlington was accustomed to accompany her charge to Drury Lane when she danced there, waiting in the wings with a *pelisse* to wrap around the dancer when she came off the stage. La Violette became the rage and the toast of the town. It is worth mentioning that only admiration and praise is recorded of her; she was a charming woman and a wise one.

Mrs. Garrick never learned to pronounce the letter "t," and the resulting accent delighted her husband and friends. But she had good command of her adopted language, for she once sent Hannah the verse:

This essence of roses,
The sweetest of poses,
Was given by dear Hannah More.
Near my heart I will wear it,
No movement shall tear it
From thence with the weight of proud ore.

All reports agree in describing her as attractive, discreet, and very lovable. These qualities she never lost and she was attended by love and admiration all the years of her long life. When Hannah was an old lady she told the Misses Roberts, who immediately wrote it down in their memo book:

> Although she [Mrs. Garrick] was a woman of such correct and elegant taste in dress, that Ladies of the highest Rank would sometimes request her to come and look at them when dressed for Court that she might rectify anything that was amiss, by her judgment, yet she did not by any means make her own dress a matter of any importance but on the contrary was very indifferent to it; Dr. Johnson who was sometimes more observant of these matters than would have been supposed, once gave it as a test that [Mrs. Garrick] was a very good dresser, that people did not remark what she had on, meaning that everything was in such good keeping as to prevent any part of her attire from being too prominent.[2]

At Garrick's special invitation, Hannah remained in London until she had seen him in all of his most famous parts. Dr. Stonehouse, the Mores' next-door neighbor, wrote Garrick: "I am glad you kept her to see Hamlet. Had you not in a manner compelled her to stay, such is her fear of intruding, that she would have left London without seeing what she so ardently desired—"[3]

Contemporary theatrical histories, autobiographies, and letters record the tremendous excitement of those last weeks of Garrick's stage career. Admirers came even from the Continent for the final performances. Garrick himself could not always obtain seats for his friends, but he got Hannah into the pit although duchesses and countesses were crowding into the top galleries and important persons were turned away at the door. During this period when he was the most important man in the world, Hannah was living in his house, dining with his friends, spending week ends with him at the Hampton villa, seeing him daily as if he were an ordinary person.

Hannah did not remain in London for Garrick's final performance. She was not present at that memorable last appearance when the audience cried "Farewell! Farewell!" and Mrs. Garrick sobbed in her box, while the players who had crowded into the rear of the stage made way for the old actor walking slowly from the stage, looking backward as if he could not bear to leave.

Hannah had left earlier and was in Bristol, watching the papers for the final announcement of Garrick's retirement. Her first letter to him brought a charming, hasty note scratched on a bit of paper, saying that Mrs. Garrick was keeping her letter for him to read after he had got over the strain of playing King Richard at the King's Command—a play too strenuous for his failing strength—and telling her how they missed her. This was the beginning of a lively correspondence which went on whenever the friends were separated. The first letters Hannah wrote him were self-conscious literary efforts, but her formality broke down before his lively, careless style, punctuated with dashes and scattered with abbreviations which were already passing out of style, and she was soon writing with an easy gossiping pen. To none of her many correspondents during her long life did she write with equal freedom and delight. She wrote to David Garrick as a woman writes to a dear friend whom she is sure of pleasing, and if her remarks were often trivial and sometimes snobbish, they were free from the artificiality which beset her when she tried too hard to measure up to somebody's standard.

Hannah worked during the summer of 1776 on her most successful play, *Percy*, sending the acts to the Garricks for criticism. Mrs. Garrick was considered an excellent judge of drama. By the following December Hannah had progressed to the point where Garrick wrote her: ". . . the 3 [acts] will do and well do—but the 4th will not stand muster—that must be changed greatly but how I cannot yet say. . . . Mrs. Garrick who has been very ill and attended by Dr. Cadogan has read you too with care—she likes the first 3, but can hardly believe you touched the 4th. . . ." [4] Not until the following winter was the play completed and produced.

The year 1777 was the most exciting of Hannah's life, for it included three stays in London, a long visit to her father's relatives in Bungay, Suffolk, with a coach trip through Norfolk; the publication of the *Ode to Dragon* which had been in circulation, handwritten, for some time; the publication of a volume of essays; some minor incidents like the visit to the opulent Wilmots and the brush with Mrs. Brooke; and finally the production of *Percy* at Covent Garden Theatre. Mr. Turner was correct when he said that Providence had reserved Hannah for a happier fate than marrying him, and he might have added that his annuity had enabled her to grasp this fate.

Hannah's letters to her family written from Bungay furnish some information concerning her father's family. She visited some cousins by the name of Cotton, but as she called a number of relatives "cousin" we do not know the exact relationship, nor do we know any given names. Jacob More's sister had married a Mr. Hayle of Needham, but no one by that name is mentioned in the letters. The Cottons lived in a large, well-furnished house outside Bungay, and Mr. Cotton was a well-to-do man, generous to the church. Mrs. Cotton's parents lived "very genteely" and one of her sisters was married to "a man of very good fortune," while another was the wife of Lord Hume. Most of the Cotton cousins were farmer folk and toward them Hannah condescended, but she spoke handsomely of the "Brockish cousins," praising the husband for taste, manners, and absorption in the study of divinity. This cousin may have been Lawrence Gibbs who was the Brockish incumbent at that time,[5] or perhaps his curate. None of these relatives are mentioned in Hannah's later letters nor do any of the names occur in her will.

The Bungay visit included not only being feted by the family connection but also making an excursion with Mr. and Mrs. Cotton, swinging round a circuit of one hundred and sixty miles "comfortably in their chariot." The tour included the towns of Norwich, Durham, Swaffham, and show places like Walpole's Houghton Hall, and Mr. Coke's Holkham Hall. Hannah had an eye for scenery and appreciated park, wood, and water views and landscape gardening; she leaped at any library that came her way, but her conscientious admiration of the Walpole picture collection at Houghton Hall was stereotyped. The same circuit was travelled by François de Rochefoucauld some seven years later when he was in England studying agriculture. It was a section of great farms where wealthy owners were conducting large-scale experiments in cattle breeding and increased crop production and, although Rochefoucauld found their work of vast importance, Hannah saw only scenery and big houses. Perhaps cousin Cotton chose the route, for although Hannah came of farming folk on both sides, the great adventure of agriculture then going on meant nothing to her. Nor did she show any interest in the technique of farming later on when she wrote of farmers and their help in the *Cheap Repository Tracts.* She loved her flower garden and knew about kitchen gardens, but crops and herds were always outside her curiosity.

When Hannah stopped in London on her return trip from Bungay, she went directly to the Adelphi and found there a coach waiting to carry her to Hampton where she was welcomed and put in her old chamber. Again she was in the midst of that life which was so delightful to her, jaunts and dinners and reading aloud, with Garrick keeping everyone in high spirits. She went with Mr. and Mrs. Garrick to visit the Henry Wilmots at their magnificent Farnsworth Place (later called Farnsworth Park) in Hampshire in the midst of old Windsor Forest. Henry Wilmot was the youngest brother of the better-known Right Honorable John Eardley Wilmot, Knight, Lord Chief Justice. John Wilmot and Garrick and Johnson had been schoolmates in Mr. Hunter's school in Lichfield, but Garrick's friendship was with the younger brother. This Henry, for years secretary to Lord Chancellor Camden (another friend of Garrick), made a fortune as a lawyer and entertained lavishly both at his town house in Bloomsbury Square and at his inherited estate in Hampshire.

Eleven visitors were at Farnsworth Place this time and Hannah commenced with all of them friendships which they handed down to their grandchildren. She met the Bathurst family here and was thereafter a frequent dinner guest at Apsley House, then newly built at Hyde Park Corner, and she visited many times at their country seat, Cirencester Park, in Gloucester. In later years Lady Bathurst used to bring her four daughters who, like the More sisters, lived and died unmarried, to call at Barley Wood, and Hannah called the group "Lady Bathurst and her fair train."

Dr. and Mrs. Kennicott, he a famous Hebrew scholar and she famous for having learned that language for the wifely purpose of reading to him, were among those present and before many years Mrs. Kennicott had become "little Kenny" to Hannah and her house in Oxford one of Hannah's favorite visiting places. Hannah mentions "two or three other very clever people" who probably included the Wilmots' daughter, Mrs. Seton, and also a delightful sister, Mrs. Morris. Through the Wilmots Hannah became well acquainted with Lady Julianna Penn, wife of the second son of William Penn whose first wife had been a Bristol woman. Mr. Wilmot was the Penns' personal solicitor, as well as his agent for the affairs of Pennsylvania until the American Revolution. Hannah's charm enabled her to hold her own in such a circle and to form a remarkable group of friends.

This same year Hannah drew her pen in defense of Garrick when he was caricatured in *The Excursion*, a novel by Mrs. Frances Brooke, the wife of Rev. John Brooke. Mrs. Brooke was ill-favored in appearance, being short, fat, and squint-eyed, but her ugliness was considered agreeable, she was well bred, and a good talker. Her success with her novels, especially *Emily Montague*, made it exasperating to her that Garrick rejected her plays and her opera. The refusal of a manager to produce a play was not accepted as final at that period. The writer often brought pressure to bear through some influential nobleman or a public personage who must not be offended, so that a manager was sometimes obliged to take back his rejection and produce a drama against his own judgment. Mrs. Brooke had not been successful in her attempts to override Garrick's adverse decisions. When she applied to Dr. Johnson to judge her *Siege of Sinope*, he replied that if she read it very carefully she could herself tell if anything was amiss. "But, sir," replied the lady, "I have no time. I have already so many irons in the fire." "Then, Madam," roared the doctor, "the best thing I can advise you is to put your tragedy along with your irons." [6]

In Mrs. Brooke's novel a pompous theatrical manager was obviously a caricature of Garrick. Hannah sharpened her quill in his defense. Her review, published in Griffith's *Monthly Review*, August, 1777, is an attack on the novel and a passionate eulogy of Garrick.[7]

The *Ode to Dragon*, written the previous year, had received so much praise that Hannah now published it in a delightful, thin volume, with beautiful type on heavy paper. Dragon was a dog of parts. Before he settled down to being guardian of the Hampton villa, he travelled back and forth to town with the Garricks and even appeared with spectacular success on the Drury Lane stage. The ode is in Hannah's happiest vein and laments Garrick's retirement from the stage. She changed it for inclusion in her *Collected Works* and not for the better. The last verses in the original form read:

Peace! To his solitude he bears
The full-blown fame of thirty years;
He bears a nation's praise;
He bears his liberal, polished mind
His worth, his wit, his sense refined;
He bears his grove of Bays.

When others drop the heart-felt tear,
Because this Sun has left his sphere,
And set at highest noon;
I'll drop a tear as warm, as true,
I loved his beams, as well as you,
And mourn they set so soon.

But all in vain his orb he quits,
Still there, in Memory's eye, he sits,
And will till Time be done:
For he shall shine while Taste survives,
And he shall shine while Genius lives,
A never-setting sun.

CHAPTER IX

Percy, A Tragedy

PERCY, A TRAGEDY IN FIVE ACTS, was produced at Covent Garden Theatre, December tenth, 1777. Hannah, without even one sister, stayed in lodgings in Gerrard Street, until she came down with one of her illnesses, when Mrs. Garrick installed her in the Adelphi.

Garrick threw his tremendous energy into the production, aiding his friend Thomas Harris, the manager, and writing both prologue and epilogue. Hannah wrote home in fine spirits that he demanded payment for his verses because Dryden always got five guineas, but had generously offered to compromise on a handsome supper with a bottle of claret. Hannah haggled, holding steak and porter sufficient payment. While they wrangled toast and honey came up from the kitchen and on that they compromised.

The background of *Percy* is the feud between the Douglas family, living on the Scotch side of the border, and the Percys who were Earls of Northumberland and Lords of the Marches for the English realm. Thomas Percy gave Hannah her theme in his *Chevy Chase.* The wild and mountainous Northe Countrye with its solitary shepherds and wandering harpers appealed strongly to the English eighteenth-century imagination, for English culture was now so firmly established that primitive ways seemed romantic.

A note in the first edition of *Percy* gave credit for some of the incidents to "The French drama, founded on the famous story of Raoul de Coucy," a crusader who on his deathbed directed that his heart be sent back to his lady love. The lady's husband, intercepting the gift, served it up to her for dinner. Hannah changed this gruesome incident, having Percy return alive, to be killed before the lady's eyes by her jealous husband.

Garrick was familiar with Belloy's play, *Gabriella de Vergy,* for the author had read it to him in Paris in 1765 and Garrick had written Colman about it, praising it highly. When the drama was produced in Paris twelve years later, Garrick's friend Mrs. J. H. Pye wrote him of its success, but did not send him a copy because, she said, he already had one.[1] Hannah may have seen this copy, but she borrowed little from it but inspiration.

The theme of Hannah's play is that revenge is a boomerang. The motivation seems today far-fetched and the action melodramatic, but the play was a tremendous success. Earl Percy loved Elwina, daughter of Lord Raby who, feeling that his hunters had been insulted while chasing the deer on Cheviot Hills, refused Lord Percy's attempts to propitiate him, broke Elwina's engagement to Lord Percy, and forced her to marry Percy's enemy Earl Douglas.

Elwina explains the situation to Percy in a clandestine interview after his return from the Crusades:

But who shall tell the agonies I felt?
My barbarous father forced me to dissolve
The tender vows himself had bade me form—
I struggled, fainted, and complied.

Elwina conducts herself with punctilious and exasperating virtue, prating to both husband and lover of wifely duty and unsullied fame. "She who ne'er could love shall yet obey thee," she assures her husband. The exasperated husband kills the lover, the wife drinks poison, the husband stabs himself, the father repents his blind obstinacy and the curtain falls.

The cast was good. The part of Earl Percy was taken, according to the printed version, by Lee Lewis; Earl Douglas by Mr. Woughton; Earl Raby, Mr. Aiken; Edric, Mr. Whitefield; Harcourt, Mr. Robson; Sir Hubert, Mr. Hull; Elwina, Mrs. Barry; Birtha, Mrs. Jackson. Lee Lewis, Francis Aiken, Hull, and Whitefield were all actors of reputation whose names appear with commendation in theatrical reviews of the period, and Mrs. Barry was a great actress. The new plays of the season, preceding the production of *Percy,* had been failures; Home's *Alfred* at Covent Garden had been withdrawn after three nights; *The Roman Sacrifice* by William Shirley and Cumberland's *Battle of Hastings* at Drury Lane were both unsuccessful. London, ready for a novelty, went wild over *Percy;* even men shed tears in abundance over Elwina's fate.

With Mr. and Mrs. Garrick, Hannah attended her first London production, sitting in a dark corner of the manager's box. Later that same evening she wrote home from Garrick's study:

"He himself puts the pen in my hand, and bids me say that all is just as it should be . . . Mr. Garrick's kindness has been unceasing." [2]

This was the happiest moment of Hannah's whole life. She had achieved a triumph never to be repeated, for her friend David Garrick was to die before her next play came on the boards. Without him there was no joy for her in the theatre.

In the midst of praise and parties and happiness Hannah was taken ill in lodgings with one of those visitations, severe, intermittent, and indefinite, which gave her friends frequent anxiety. If one examines the long series of illnesses extending from the time Hannah was a little girl to a few years before her death in her eighty-ninth year, one detects, in spite of the vagueness of the information afforded, a recurrent pattern.

The course of this particular breakdown was typical. On a Tuesday, not yet sick, she dined with the Wilmots. She dined with the venerable Mrs. Delany on Wednesday, in company with her much-loved Mrs. Boscawen, much-admired Mrs. Carter, and one very agreeable man, name not stated. On Sunday morning Lady Bathurst found her in bed.

"'Tis well I was ill or I should have had a fine trimming, for she makes breakfast for the chancellor every morning before nine, during the whole winter." [3] She was, however, well enough to go that Sunday evening to dine at the Garricks' with the "Sour-crout Party," a weekly dinner of men, taking its name from the principal dish. On the following morning Mrs. Garrick found her so ill that she begged to send a doctor and a dinner, but the sufferer refused both. Nevertheless, Garrick stopped on his way to a club dinner at the Turk's Head to leave a hot minced chicken in a stew pan, a canister of tea, and a pot of cream. Hannah was deeply touched by their solicitude.

The Garricks came to see the invalid every day, finding her

always patient and cheerful to the point of gaiety. All her life her friends remarked her sweet reasonableness under suffering; she was a model invalid. Garrick arrived one morning in a violent hurry, announcing that he had just ordered mourning for himself and his wife and settled with the undertaker; he wanted a few hints as to what Hannah wished on her tombstone. Hannah retorted that he was too late as she had commissioned Dr. Johnson to write her epitaph but as she thought Garrick would praise her more she would be glad to change.

As it was obvious that Hannah could not take proper care of herself in lodgings, Mrs. Garrick adopted her into her own family, where her niece Betty Fürst was already spending a year. From that time on, Hannah always stayed at the Garricks' home when she was in London. So far as one knows she was never again in lonely lodgings.

The next few weeks were heaven on earth to Hannah: her name was on every London tongue; her sisters made a trip from Bristol to share her triumph; congratulations poured in; the Earl of Northumberland and his son Lord Percy delegated Dr. Percy to convey thanks for the honor she had done them by the play and to regret that gout had kept them away; the second Lord Lyttleton was said to attend every night; Mrs. Boscawen sent the dramatist a laurel wreath which led to the exchange of complimentary verses; most of the critics were friendly and the magazines praised the play.[4]

The Ladies' Pocket-book, in 1778, included her in an engraving of The Nine Muses, the others being Miss Carter, Mrs. Barbauld, Angelica Kauffmann, Mrs. Sheridan, Mrs. Lennox, Mrs. Montagu, Mrs. Macaulay, and Mrs. Griffith, all women better known than she. It is no wonder that Hannah's head was a little turned by the notice she received.

Percy ran twenty-two nights, a spectacular success at a time when playgoers were so few that the drama had to be changed frequently. It was revived off and on until 1815 and perhaps later, being played at Drury Lane and the Haymarket as well as Covent Garden. Mrs. Siddons added Elwina to her roles and played it in Bath in 1778–9, three times in Bath and Bristol in 1780–1, again three times in Bath the following season, and four times in Drury Lane in 1785–6. There may have been more than these recorded appearances. Mrs. Barry chose the play for her benefit in Bristol. The drama was translated into French and was played in German in Vienna.[5]

Among the most fulsome admirers of *Percy* was William Heard, the son of a Piccadilly bookseller and the author of two plays that failed. His poem, *Impromptu, On Seeing Miss More's Tragedy of Percy*, ends:

> *Each auditor with loud applause,*
> *Confessed the fair had won the cause,*
> *And cried, MORE, MORE, yes MORE!*

This poem was in a volume entitled *A Sentimental Journey to Bath, Bristol, and their Environs*,[6] and dedicated, "As a Testimony of Respect for Refined Genius, Exalted Sentiment and Unaffected Manners the Following Sheets are Inscribed to Miss Hannah More by Her Most Obedient Humble Servant, the Author."

The title poem of the volume contains compliments to Hannah with footnotes which display the writer's learning:

From Tindal's charming villa we descend,
To where resides the poet and the friend,
Where genius lives; where taste and wit combine;
Where fancy wantons with the tuneful Nine.
Oh, More! *I must paint thy generous heart,*
Must catch a grace beyond the reach of art,
Devoid of pedantry, thy numbers flow,
And sweet instruction with delight bestow:
The rough unpolished manners you refine,
For sense & sensibility are Thine . . .

Ver. 469 From *Tindal's—Mr. Tindal's seat is called the* Fort, *alluding to the remains of an* Entrenchment *built by t.* Royalists, *in the reign of Charles I.*

Ver. *ibid.*—We descend—*Park Street*

Ver. 473 —*Oh,* More!—*Miss H. More*

Ver. 376 —And sweet instruction—*Delectando pariterque monendo.*

Two others of Heard's poems on Hannah outdo even this in flattery; one of them "Supposed to be written where Miss More frequently walked," and the other addressing her as "Hail heaven-born nymph withall divinely fair." Hannah and her friends were obviously pleased, for the list of subscribers printed at the end of the volume includes six copies to the Mores, six to various Garricks and four to the Stonehouses.

The first edition of *Percy* sold out in a fortnight. From stage production and printed copies Hannah cleared nearly six hundred pounds by March, putting the money into five per cent securities.

Mr. and Mrs. Garrick divided their time between their

town house and their villa. Laetitia Hawkins remembered from her childhood how happy Garrick always seemed when he came over from his country home to her father's near by. He was low of stature, well shaped, with a dark complexion and brilliant black eyes never at rest. He was accustomed to wear a dark blue coat, buttonholes bound in gold, and a small cocked hat laced with gold. The children were glad when he came, for gaiety always accompanied him. Sometimes he perched on the table while he talked and sometimes he chased the boys round and round the grounds. At Hampton he threw off the stress and worries of theatrical life and enjoyed himself. Hannah More in her old age told the Misses Roberts how he dealt with a Mr. Roffey, a neighbor who had settled near by chiefly with a view to cultivating an acquaintance with the actor. Garrick protected his valued privacy by saying frankly to Mr. Roffey: "Let us come to an explanation. I cannot play at cards and you cannot play at books. We therefore do not suit each other; so let us be good civil neighbors without exchanging visits." [7]

The garden of the villa, sloping to the Thames, was inconveniently located across the road from the house, but Garrick tunneled under the highway and his novel underpass was much admired. The family spent a good deal of time under the trees in the garden by the river and there entertained friends at tea. In this romantic spot old Lord Monboddo, who came galloping down from Scotland on horseback each year, made to Hannah a formal declaration of love and asked her hand in marriage. She declined the offer. On their return to the drawing-room, the eccentric old man told Mrs. Garrick what had occurred, saying; "I am very sorry for this refusal. I should have so much liked to teach this nice girl Greek." The old gentleman, who sometimes wore a pompadour-pink coat and a large white "grizzle" wig, was a kind, erudite, unexpected sort of person who roused great amusement by his theory that the orang-outang was man in a state of nature. Everything he did was odd, even the manner of his proposals of marriage. He was evidently not heartbroken at Hannah's refusal, for he also made Mrs. Garrick an offer after Garrick's death. While walking in the grounds with him Mrs. Garrick asked him if the gardens were not very complete. He replied that it was a perfect Paradise, lacking only Adam; Mrs. Garrick's Italian name was Eve. Lord Monboddo later made Mrs. Garrick a formal offer of marriage in a letter written in such odd style that she could not resist showing it confidentially to her friends.[8]

The villa at Hampton was charming, the grounds delightful, the host and hostess cordial and affectionate, and the social life was the quietly gay variety which Hannah most enjoyed. The Garricks took her with them when they went out to dinner or on longer visits. When they went over to Richmond to dine with Sir Joshua Reynolds, the guests included Edmund, Richard, and William Burke, as well as Gibbon. Hannah made friends wherever she went and soon had an excellent social connection of her own. Garrick always had an eye on her to see that she received due attention and was placed in no awkward situation. During their visit to the Garricks' friends, the Henry Wilmots of Farnsborough Place, Hannah was embarrassed when they prepared to have music on Sunday afternoon. Garrick, remembering that Sunday music was against her conscience, turned to her saying; "Nine, you are a Sunday woman; retire to your room. I will recall you when the music is over."[9]

How strictly one should observe the Sabbath to keep it completely holy was something of a puzzle to Hannah. When she first came to London and was newly out from under the eyes of Mary the mentor, the solicitude of the other loving sisters, her father's paternal authority, the excellent advice of Dr. Stonehouse, and the sharp eyes of sixty boarding-school misses, Hannah went on the loose in a very mild way; very mild, indeed. She kept a Sunday engagement with Mrs. Montagu, but tasted wormwood in the cup of pleasure; she attended the opera and heard her still small voice saying; "What doest thou here, Elizah!"; she dined at Mrs. Boscawen's with Mrs. Montagu, Mrs. Carter, and Mrs. Chapone on a Sunday and squirmed in justifying her conduct in the letter home. In the Garricks' household such matters seemed unimportant either way and she was free to act as she chose without either censure or applause. Garrick did not try to fit her to a pattern, and she was at ease in his home. He was a wise man as well as a great actor, conventional in his personal conduct, revolutionary in his art, tolerant in his beliefs, and respectful of other persons' individuality. Hannah was like a person who doubts his own existence when he cannot see his reflection in some mirror. Reflected in Garrick's approving eyes, Hannah dared be herself. For the three years of her close friendship with him, she rested from the conflict of trying to be what other people wanted her to be. Rested, that is, as much as was possible for an oversensitive nature harried by the devotion of four sisters, the rigorous training of her youth, the solicitude of elderly friends, and the boarding school in the background.

City life was as delightful as the country periods. The block of houses called the Adelphi had been recently built by Robert Adam on the Thames Bank and the Garricks' house had been furnished by Chippendale. The drawing-room was a stately apartment, lofty and well-proportioned, the windows draped in green silk, spaced with pier glasses, comfortable with carved sofas and chairs upholstered in green. It was a gracious room. The dining room, where literary breakfasts as well as formal dinners were held, was especially lovely with its curtains of crimson tammy, a heavy lustrous silk, carved mahogany chairs upholstered in red Morocco, mahogany sideboard and side tables, and large mahogany dining table which could be one long board or three separate tables.[10] The carved marble fireplace and the lovely ceiling painted by Angelica Kauffmann are preserved in the Victoria and Albert Museum. The terrace in front of the house overlooked the Thames and from the front windows one could see the sailing craft and watermen's row-boats passing up and down, laden with merchandise and with passengers going from one river stairway to another.

When Hannah was at the Adelphi she had three rooms to herself, and she was free to work or loaf, to see her own friends, or to join the family. Garrick was himself a hard worker, writing hours on end and seeing his friends chiefly at meals. He was especially fond of gathering people about him for late breakfasts. To the Adelphi came such men as Richard Owen Cambridge, who admired Hannah's *Ode to Dragon,* although he had in general a natural aversion to odes as some people have to cats; Lord Camden, former Lord Chancellor, whom Hannah would have taken for an elderly physician although she detected something of genius about his nose; and many Lords and Ladies; in fact about every-one who was prominent in the political or literary world. No actors nor actresses were invited, but plenty of bishops. The gentlemen brought their wives, but men's wives did not usually interest Hannah and the greater number of her personal women friends were widows or elderly spinsters. When the Garricks entertained French scholars, wits, and distinguished travellers, Hannah, thanks to her early experience translating for the French officers interned at Fishponds prison, could hold her own with ease and spirit.

The evening life was fully enjoyable when there was no company beyond perhaps one or two old friends. Garrick's willingness to read aloud was one of his engaging traits. He would read Shakespeare, perhaps, or Pope's *Essay on Man*, pausing to discuss the best way of accenting a line. A good bit of highly complimentary verse-making went on and sometimes they played simple games like "cross purposes," "crooked answers," or "what's my thought like." Hannah thought there might be wiser parties in the world but none more cheerful than these intimate gatherings at the Garricks' house in London.

We leave the record of this happy winter with the account of the last party attended with David Garrick. "I dined with the Garricks on Thursday," she wrote home shortly before returning to Bristol. "He went with me in the evening, intending only to set me down at Sir Joshua's, where I was engaged to pass the evening. I was not a little proud to be the means of bringing such a beau into such a party. We found Gibbon, Johnson, Hermes Harris, Burney, Chambers, Ramsey, the Bishop of Asaph, Boswell, Langton, and so forth; and scarcely an expletive man or woman among them. Garrick put Johnson into such good spirits that I never knew him so entertaining or more instructive. He was as brilliant as himself, and as good humored as anyone else." [11]

It may be that Garrick's feeling for Hannah was no warmer than his affection for his friend's daughter, Miss Cadogan, or for his brother George's daughters, Bell and Kitty, whose support he assumed, or his wife's niece, Betty, to whom he left a legacy, but Hannah's adoration of him went far beyond that of a niece for an indulgent uncle. Her long engagement to Mr. Turner, her vigorous flirtation with the popular Dr. Langhorne, and her later long-continued friendships with Bishop Porteus, Horace Walpole, John Newton, and William Wilberforce, besides lesser intimacies with many other notable men, indicate an affectionate, outgoing disposition that turned naturally toward men. Her association with David Garrick pleased her mind, her ambition, her vanity, and most of all, her heart.

CHAPTER X

Garrick's Death

GARRICK's letters to "My dearest Hannah" and "My dear Nine" during the summer and fall of 1778 were full of friendliness and gossip. She was in Bristol working on her play *The Fatal Falsehood* (first called *The Bridal Day*) which, like *Percy*, travelled act by act to the Garricks in London, but was unfinished at the time of the actor's death. Garrick's health had been failing for a long time so that his friends had become somewhat accustomed to his illness. His serious attack at Broadlands, the Hampshire home of his friend Lord Palmerston, Henry Temple, the second viscount, was followed by apparent recovery and Hannah's annual visit was scheduled for January. His death came as a terrible shock to her. She wrote immediately to his friend and solicitor, Albany Wallis, asking him to ascertain if Mrs. Garrick would like her to come immediately to London:

The anguish of my heart on the great, the irreparable loss we have sustained will, I am sure, to so feeling a mind as yours be apology enough for my troubling you now when you are oppress'd by so many troubles.—Oh Sir! what a friend have I lost! My heart is almost broken! I have neither eaten nor slept since. My tears blind me as I write—But what is *my* loss, what is *my* sorrow? It is quite lost in the idea of what our beloved

Mrs. Garrick suffers. . . . Ask her, dear Sir, if she will allow me to come to her—I cannot dry her eyes but I can weep with her.—I can be of no service perhaps but there is a sort of mournful consolation in the company of one who knew, who loved, who mourns, and who will forever mourn the first of men —I write nonsense—I don't know what I write![1]

Upon receiving Wallis' reply that Mrs. Garrick wanted her, Hannah went immediately to London, staying with Dr. Cadogan, Garrick's physician, a former Bristol man. The actor's body lay in state within the black-draped Adelphi home until February first, while Mrs. Garrick lived in a friend's house. When she met Hannah, Hannah wrote home, ". . . she ran into my arms, and we both remained silent for some minutes; at last she whispered, 'I have this moment embraced his coffin, and you come next.' "[2]

Mrs. Garrick was not present at the impressive funeral ceremony at Westminster Abbey, for it was not customary for wives to take part in funeral rites, but Hannah and Miss Cadogan, who had been a favorite with Garrick, received a ticket of admission to the Abbey. The two women went first to Charing Cross to view the procession, the tolling bells of St. Martin's and the Abbey, Hannah wrote home, falling upon their stricken hearts. They made the mistake of giving up their ticket when they reached the Abbey and by some mischance were shuffled with others into a tower staircase with locked doors at each end. They ran up the stairs to beat upon the upper door and down the stairs to beat upon the lower door. At length their hysterical outcries brought a man who, learning their identity, took each of them by the arm and got them not only into the Abbey proper, but into a little gallery in the south transept, now called "The Poet's

Corner," directly over the open grave, where they could see everything.

The funeral procession, leaving the Garrick house in the Adelphi at quarter after one, was two hours in reaching the Abbey. In it were thirty-three mourning coaches drawn by six horses each, besides porters, pages, and horsemen. Riding horses were adorned with sweeping black velvet saddlecloths, riders carried black scarves and staffs; there were black feathers, the pennon, the escutcheon, and, following the other coaches, Mr. Garrick's empty coach. The hearse, preceded by six pages, was "full drest, with the body in a coffin, covered with crimson velvet, gilt furniture, nails, &. on which were the arms of the deceased, with this motto underneath, Resurgam, and his name, his age, and the day and year of his death."

"An Old Comedian," who wrote this description in a small book on Garrick,[3] went on to say: "The concourse of people of all ranks who assembled along the Strand, Parliament Street and other places leading to the Abbey, to pay their last tribute to the deceased favorite, was greater than ever was remembered on any occasion; and not a face was seen, that did not wear its portion of the general concern."

The great west doors of the Abbey were thrown open, the organ played and the choir sang Handel's anthem. As Hannah, high above the open grave, watched the crowd enter and approach the grave, she must have felt that the honor paid to the great actor was commensurate with his fame. The pallbearers were: The Duke of Devonshire, Lord Camden, Lord Spencer, Lord Ossory, Lord Palmerston, Hon. Mr. Richard Rigby, Sir W. W. Wynne, Rt. Hon. Mr. Stanley, Albany Wallis, Esq., and John Paterson, Esq. The chief mourners were Hannah's friends whom she had come to know through living with the Garricks: Richard Brinsley Sheridan; the three nephews, Rev. Carrington, Nathaniel and David Garrick; his niece Arabella's husband, Captain Schaw; Dr. Cadogan; and Mr. Lawrence, Garrick's apothecary. Butler, the Drury Lane carpenter, and Fosbrook, the bookkeeper, were in the group. Hannah knew also the members of the Literary Club, who attended together, and among those grouped as intimate friends were many others whom she had come to know well.

The Bishop of Rochester, Dean of Westminster, awaited the crimson-velvet-covered coffin at the west door. The choir in hoods and surplices accompanied it to the grave, singing as they went. After services the coffin was let down into the grave, directly below where Hannah stood with Miss Cadogan. The funeral has been criticized as ornate and tawdry, but it was according to the custom of the time and its theatrical showiness was suited to the famous showman. Although David Garrick was often petulant and unreasonable in business matters, in crises he never failed his friends nor belied his own spirit. He was a great actor and a great man. After the ceremony was over, when the crowd was dispersing, the man who had rescued Hannah and Miss Cadogan from the enclosed stairway sought them with an invitation from the Bishop's wife to come to the deanery to rest. She took them to her own dressing-room and tried to comfort them but they could not talk for sobbing. So she kindly left them to themselves and sent them wine and refreshments to help them recover themselves.

There was a rumor of Garrick's having remembered Hannah in his will. He had intimated this in the letter he wrote her when he was so ill at Lord Palmerston's, and Sir John Stonehouse wrote a friend immediately after Garrick's death that he heard a legacy had been left Hannah,[4] but Garrick's will made no small bequests and Hannah's name is not mentioned. He may have given Mrs. Garrick a list of mementos to be distributed among his friends, for Hannah in her old age was fond of displaying as a legacy from him an inkstand made from the famous mulberry tree, as well as the shoe buckles which were a part of the costume he wore the last night he played. As a matter of fact she was given the buckles earlier for she had them with her when she visited Mrs. Barbauld on her way from Bungay to London in 1777 and Mrs. Barbauld wrote her famous couplet:

Thy buckles, O Garrick, thy friend may now use,
But no mortal hereafter shall stand in your shoes.

A provision in Garrick's will made his wife custodian of their two homes, thus indirectly affording Hannah a domicile for many London seasons. Mrs. Garrick had brought her husband six thousand pounds at their marriage, and six thousand pounds he left her by will. In addition she received a life tenure of the houses at Hampton and in the Adelphi, the horses, carriages, and household furniture, with a yearly income of fifteen hundred pounds, provided she spent her time in England. If she went to the Continent for any length of time, she forfeited income and property. She was to acquiesce in writing within three months of his death, or lose everything. She agreed to the provisions.

Mrs. Garrick was severely criticised on her management of her financial affairs; first for not paying funeral expenses out of her income; second for allowing Albany Wallis to erect the memorial in Westminster Abbey, instead of doing it herself (Garrick had previously placed a memorial in the Abbey for Albany Wallis' son); later on for claiming part of a residue of the estate as next of kin; for letting the Hampton House get out of repair; and finally for distributing twelve thousand pounds among her foreign relatives thirty-five years after her husband's death. In everything except money matters she was highly praised.

After Garrick's death, Hannah was like a soldier in battle who fights on, not realizing that he is mortally wounded. Although it was her habit to make something of a to-do over her troubles, she met this terrible bereavement in a different fashion. Her direct reactions were curiously stereotyped. Writing home after his funeral, she said: "I can never cease to remember with affection and gratitude so warm, steady and disinterested a friend." She goes on in a rather conventional style: "I can most truly bear this testimony to his memory, that I never witnessed, in any family, more decorum, propriety, and regularity than in his; where I never saw a card, or even met (except in one instance) a person of his own profession at his table." [5] Then she speaks of Mrs. Garrick's elegance of taste, correctness of manners, and original turn of humor, ending with laudatory comments on Garrick's intellectual pursuits and taste and the high tone of conversation at his house. These were the prescribed sentiments of bereavement. It was as if, while she had been able to express her innocent love for him freely during his lifetime, she felt self-conscious about it after his death; as if decorum decreed that only his widow had the right to mourn.

Yet she cried out, on hearing later of the death of James Harris, Garrick's friend, whom she knew but slightly: "Poor

Hermes Harris is dead. Everybody is dead, I think; one is almost ashamed of being alive!"[6] Once she wrote home, apropos of nothing at all: "Poor Dr. Schomberg is dead; Beauclerk is dying; what terrible depredations have been made in that society in a very little time."[7] Dr. Ralph Schomberg was Garrick's personal friend and one of the doctors who attended his deathbed, but Hannah did not like him very well, and Beauclerk was merely an acquaintance of Hannah. It was Garrick, their common friend and fellow-member of the Turk's Head Club, whose death Hannah was really lamenting.

Dr. Johnson's grief produced a perfect epitaph for Garrick: "His death eclipsed the gaiety of nations and diminished the stock of harmless pleasure." When Boswell later picked the sentiment to pieces, Johnson explained: "I could not have said more or less. It is the truth; *eclipsed*, not *extinguished*; and his death *did* eclipse; it was like a storm." So far as Hannah was concerned "extinguished" was the better word. Her gaiety flickered for a time and went out, and though she continued in London social life for some years, spontaneous enjoyment had gone. Garrick's death broke the pattern of Hannah's life.

CHAPTER XI

Life with Mrs. Garrick

HANNAH stayed with Mrs. Garrick after the funeral and endured with her the simple, inescapable reminders; the rooms in the Adelphi that were so empty, Dragon the house dog at Hampton rushing to greet their sad arrival, and the silent meals. Mrs. Garrick showed a gentle fortitude at which Hannah marveled. The husband and wife had loved each other devotedly and together they had taken young Hannah into their hearts. These three people each had unusual capacity for generous affection and loyalty. During Garrick's life Hannah cared more for him than for his wife, but after his death she added the love she had borne him to the lesser love she already felt for his wife. It is a mistake to believe that two women cannot love the same man without being jealous of each other; the love may be a bond between them. Moreover, Hannah, as the widow's closest friend, could join her in sorrowing openly as she could not in her own right.

Lady Sarah Lennox wrote to Lady Susan O'Brien, two months after Garrick's death:

> There is a poor widow whose situation seems to me upon speculation as the most lamentable I know, & that is poor Mrs. Garrick, whom I cannot think of without the most true concern. In the first place, I believe that if it is possible to give the name

of love to an attachment at the end of above 30 years, she was in love with her husband, but this I am sure of, he was the whole and sole occupation & business of her life. To nurse him when sick & admire him when well, has been her employment so long, that she must now feel the most forlorn & helpless of all creatures. She has no children to occupy her mind, no relation that she is attached to, & scarce a real friend, tho' she has numerous acquaintances; she has led a life of company & business, the *spirit* of her society is lost, & business she cannot have, for both her houses in town & country are so well compleat she has not a chair or table to amuse herself with altering; half or 3 parts of her income are appropriated to keep up the houses, so she has nothing on earth to do but to *vegetate* without any views, any enlivening hope, without any motive of exertion of mind.[1]

Mrs. Garrick's plight was not as hopeless as Lady Sarah pictured it. She had beloved relatives who came over from the Continent in droves after Garrick's death and she had within herself resources with which to meet her tragedy, among them the consolation of her religion. She was a Catholic and more at ease in her religion than was Hannah with her intense awareness of human sinfulness. Mrs. Garrick attended services in her own church but, Hannah once told the Misses Roberts, often went to Protestant churches when in the country, had constantly by her a Church of England prayerbook, the prayers in which she very much admired and commonly used, and several times expressed her regret that she had not been born in a Protestant country, for then she would have been of that religion, but she thought it right to continue in the religion in which one was born.[2] Theological argument never arose to divide the two women for both had tolerance for sectarian differences.

A common passion for reading was a help during the dreary first winter. After breakfast, Mrs. Garrick and Hannah separated, each going to her own room to read and write and work. At four they dined. Each had her book, which she read without restraint, as if alone, without apologies. At six they had coffee. A dowager or two of quality sometimes came to tea at eight. At ten they had salad and fruit.

They had their program of duties and mild pleasures; the sad business of looking over Garrick's papers and realizing the generosity with which he had given and lent money; dividing his books and handing over to the British Museum his collection of old plays; walking the swept gravel paths of the garden where the white snow contrasted with the golden fruit within the orange house; and feeding the birds three times a day. (When Mrs. Garrick was away from Hampton the birds were put on board wages, a small loaf being bought for them each day.) Hannah adapted herself with difficulty to the solitude. She wrote home:

> Her garden and her family amuse her; but the idea of company is death to her. We never see a human face but each other's. Though in such deep retirement, I am never dull, because I am not reduced to the fatigue of entertaining dunces, or of being obliged to listen to them. We dress like a couple of Scaramouches, dispute like a couple of Jesuits, eat like a couple of aldermen, walk like a couple of porters, and read as much as any two doctors of either university.[3]

During this period of overwhelming grief Hannah wrote in her poem *Sensibility:*

> *Say, can the boasted pow'rs of wit and song,*
> *Of life one pang remove, one hour prolong?*
> *Presumptous hope which daily truths deride;*
> *For you, alas! have wept—and Garrick dy'd!*
> *Ne'er shall my heart his loved remembrance lose,*
> *Critic, guide, guardian, glory of my muse!*

Oh shades of Hampton! Witness as I mourn,
Cou'd wit or song elude his destin'd urn?
The living virtue still your haunt endears
Yet bury'd worth shall justify my tears.
Garrick! those powers which form a friend were thine
And let me add, with pride, that friend was mine.
With pride! at once the vain emotions fled,
Far other thoughts are sacred to the dead
Who now with spirit keen, yet judgment cool,
The unequal wand'rings of my muse shall rule.
Whose partial praise my worthless verse ensure?
For Candor smiled when Garrick would endure.
If harsher critic were compelled to blame
I gained in friendship what I lost in fame,
And friendship's fostering smiles can well repay
What critic's rigour justly takes away.

Hannah's restless energy, which came and went but always came again, could not long content itself with walks and quiet talk and writing. Mrs. Garrick kept herself, Hannah wrote home, as secret as a piece of smuggled goods and neither stirred out nor let anyone in; an old woman crying fish or the postman ringing at the door were events in the quiet day. Although it was Hannah's firm conviction that she loved solitude, she really couldn't stand it. Her social talent was based on an active liking for people, provided, of course, that they were intelligent, respectable, and had social position.

One event broke the monotony of the first melancholy spring after Garrick's death: Thomas Harris, who had produced *Percy* at Covent Garden Theatre, persuaded Hannah to allow him to produce immediately the play on which she had worked before Garrick's death, *The Fatal Falsehood*, originally called *The Bridal Day*. Garrick had criticised the first two acts, but the play needed more of his expert revision. In this melodramatic tragedy Orlando, though pledged to Emmeline, loved Julia, the betrothed of his friend Rivers, and was incited by the villain, Bertram, to destroy Rivers. Bertram was himself accidentally murdered by Orlando, who stabbed himself on discovering what he had done. Emmeline went mad. A happy ending was procured by Rivers and Julia rushing into each other's arms.

The drama was pretty bad but it was well produced. Hannah was as fortunate in her cast as she had been in the production of *Percy*. Wroughton, Lee Lewis, and Francis Aiken, who had all three appeared in *Percy*, took the roles of Orlando, Rivers, and Bertram. Emmeline was portrayed by the popular Miss Younge from Drury Lane and Julia by the excellent actress, Elizabeth Hartley. The author's prologue was spoken by Hull and Sheridan's epilogue by Lee Lewis. The first night went off brilliantly and the critics were kind, but the play ran only four nights. The reason given was that the season was too far advanced. Some of the sisters who had come from Bristol for the event wrote home to the others that Hannah was mighty indifferent to the whole affair. The drama was later presented in Bath and Mrs. Siddons added it to her repertoire, although it was never as popular as *Percy*. Mrs. Siddons' partiality for Hannah's plays is the best testimony we have of the current esteem in which they were held. The very incomplete records of those years mention Mrs. Siddons playing *Percy* in London, Bath, and Bristol eight times and *The Fatal Falsehood* in Bath three times. As the records of the Bath and Bristol theatres are wholly lacking for some years and incomplete for other seasons, we are justified in assuming that these were not the only productions of the plays.

The Fatal Falsehood was sufficiently applauded the opening night to send Mrs. Hannah Parkhouse Cowley into a rage. She burst out in the *St. James Chronicle* with an accusation that Hannah had stolen the plot from her unpublished play *Albina,* and further intimated that there had been similar plagiarism in *Percy.* Mrs. Cowley's most popular play had been *The Runaway,* produced by Garrick at Drury Lane. After his withdrawal from management she offered her work to Harris at Covent Garden Theatre, sending him the manuscript of *Albina* which Garrick had already refused. Mrs. Cowley admitted that she did not know that Miss More had seen the manuscript, but stated that it had been in Mr. Garrick's hands while Miss More was living at Hampton and in Mr. Harris' hands at nearly the same time as *The Fatal Falsehood.* In the preface to the published edition of *Albina,* she asserted that *The Fatal Falsehood* had every essential circumstance in plot and character of *Albina.* "By some wonderful coincidence," she concluded, "Miss More and I have one common flock of ideas between us."

Hannah, ultra-sensitive to criticism, was outraged by the accusation. She denied it. Mrs. Cowley reiterated the charge. The public prints enjoyed the controversy. *The Gentleman's Magazine* published jocose verses on the quarrel.[4] Hannah wished to make an affidavit, but Cadell persuaded her to let the uproar die down from lack of fuel, so she contented herself with a coals-of-fire revenge, requesting Cadell to buy a ticket for Mrs. Cowley's benefit night and charge it to her or else subscribe for a printed copy of *Albina* without Mrs. Cowley's knowledge.

For several years Hannah had been rewriting Bible stories in dialogue form. She now published *Sacred Dramas.* The critics, usually enthusiastic about her writings, were lukewarm in their praise, yet the book ran into nineteen editions and was even translated into the language of the natives of Ceylon. Although the plays were intended for reading and not for stage production, Tate Wilkinson of the York Circuit relates in his *Wandering Patentee* a curious attempt to produce *Daniel in the Lions' Den.* A gentleman "of distinguished fortune, character and tastes" altered the play for the stage in so perfect a manner "as to please the most devout ear, and indeed impossible to offend the most rigid, as improper for the stage." A genteel audience at Doncaster at the time of the races on Saturday, October twelfth, 1793, received the drama with applause. At Hull, however, the following month, the announcement that the play was to be performed threw the religious people of the town into a frenzy and the preachers so "barked at and tore to pieces" the proposal of putting Biblical characters on the stage that Wilkinson abandoned the attempt.

Hannah More gradually turned against the stage. She resolved never again to enter a theatre. This resolution she kept even when Mrs. Siddons was acting the part of Elwina in *Percy* in London. As early as during Garrick's farewell season, Hannah had stated: "I find my dislike of what are called public diversions greater than ever, except a play; and when Garrick has left the stage, I could be very well content to relinquish plays also, and to live in London, without ever again setting foot in a public place." [5] Now that Garrick had left the stage forever, Hannah turned against the theatre. There was some talk of her editing Garrick's dramatic writings for Cadell and Davies, but it came to nothing.

In her old age Hannah regretted that she had ever written for the stage, and when she republished all her plays in her *Collected Works,* she introduced them by a preface in which she denounced drama, accusing it of dissolving the heart with amatory scenes, warping the mind with corrupt reasoning, and inflaming the mind with seducing principles. But she never turned against David Garrick, playwright and actor. She said in the same preface, when speaking most bitterly against the English stage: "Mr. Garrick did a great deal toward its purification. It is said not to have since kept the ground it then gained." Inconsistently, in her old age, she projected, but did not write, a series of plays for use in converting the heathen in Ceylon who had taken so kindly to her *Sacred Dramas* as to write them on palm leaves.

As Hannah's restlessness grew Mrs. Garrick encouraged her going out alone and Hannah spent delightful hours with the venerable Mrs. Delany, now domiciled with the royal family at Hampton Court. Later, with Mrs. Garrick, she visited the elderly Duchess of Portland at Bulstrode. Young Mary Hamilton, the charming niece of Sir William, invited her to breakfasts at the Court of St. James's where Miss Hamilton was in attendance upon the princesses. Mary, an especial pet of Mrs. Garrick, was the only young friend with whom Hannah was on an easy footing.

Mrs. Garrick, gradually emerging from her retirement, gave her first dinner party at the Adelphi, some two years after Garrick's death. The occasion is described by both

Hannah and Boswell. Only those who had been dear friends of David were present. Mrs. Boscawen, who shone with mild luster, and Elizabeth Carter, who wore the title of "Mrs." as the symbol of advancing years, were the two ladies invited to dinner. The gentlemen were Dr. Johnson, Boswell, Sir Joshua Reynolds, and Dr. Burney. Additional guests came in for the evening. David Garrick's portrait hung over the chimneypiece and the guests kept glancing up at it. It seemed almost as if their dear David were there with them and they were quietly happy to be again together in his home. Boswell whispered to Mrs. Boscawen: "I believe this is as much as can be made of life." They united to make the occasion easy for Mrs. Garrick.

When Johnson and Boswell left the house, they stopped by the rails of the Adelphi and looked over the Thames. Boswell recalled with emotion the two friends who had lived in the Adelphi before their deaths, David Garrick and Topham Beauclerk. "Ay, Sir," said Johnson tenderly, "and two such friends cannot be supplied."

Hannah wrote home: "The day and the evening turned out very pleasant." [6]

Slowly Mrs. Garrick took up her social life again. She kept her box at Drury Lane although most of her time was spent at Hampton. She would not marry again in spite of at least two excellent offers; one from Lord Monboddo and also one from Albany Wallis, her husband's close friend and her own trustee, an eminent solicitor, who left a large fortune at his death in 1800.[7]

The social life of Mrs. Garrick and Hannah, now that they had no longer a man to take them about, was largely in the company of the *Bas Bleu*, made up of elderly ladies who talked better than they danced and elderly gentlemen who could overlook a woman's age and wrinkles if she had a good brain served by a lively tongue. Hannah's poem, *The Bas Bleu,* has preserved for us a fine picture of this distinguished group.

There was no formal Blue Stocking Club where a learned lady could be put up for membership. Certain women were definitely in; certain others were out; while many were borderline members. Among the hostesses were the rivals, learned Mrs. Elizabeth Montagu, Hannah's lifelong friend, and spritely Mrs. Thrale. Each had or had had an elderly, wealthy husband and each had a talent for bringing famous persons about her. Mrs. Thrale had Johnson for a sponsor and Fanny Burney for a pet. Mrs. Montagu had had the devotion of the first Earl of Bath and Lord Lyttleton, and after their deaths had Sir William Pepys and a covey of lesser men, with Hannah More as a protégée. Another hostess was Mrs. Ord, widow of William Ord of Whitefield, Northumberland, whose special talent was the ability to mix different groups harmoniously. Mrs. Vesey, rattlebrained, deaf, sallow, wrinkled, and dearly loved, was the best hostess of them all, although she sometimes forgot to invite the guest of honor and always overcrowded her rooms. Horace Walpole called her parties "Babels" or "Chaos," but he enjoyed them. In all these houses Mrs. Garrick and Hannah were welcome guests. Among women whom Hannah came to count as her friends were learned Mrs. Carter, plain-featured Mrs. Chapone, beautiful Mrs. Crewe, Fanny Burney, Lady Bute, daughter of Lady Mary Wortley Montagu, eccentric Miss Monckton, and Mrs. Boscawen with her two daughters, the Duchess of Beaufort and Mrs. Leveson. Mrs. Siddons was received later on, but she was the only actress to crash the gate.

The men who attended the Conversation Parties were a sort of Gentlemen's Auxiliary, and glad they were to be allowed to come. Dr. Johnson was, of course, the big fish for whom all hostesses angled and Boswell came with him when he was in London. Old Bubble-and-Squeak Sheridan would come if Johnson was not to be present, while his son Richard Brinsley Sheridan would come anyway. Sir Joshua Reynolds was sometimes present. Edward Gibbon was too important to omit but the ladies did not much like him. James (Hermes) Harris was admired for his Greek and disliked for his manners. John Home, the popular playwright, was always welcome. Richard Owen Cambridge had a passion for knowing people which made him love parties. Horace Walpole was popular with the ladies because he liked them so well. Sir William Pepys was famous for his long nose, fashionable dress, shrewdness, and drollery. Charles Burney, Fanny's father, overcame the social handicap of being a musician. James Beattie was a favorite. Edmund Burke stole away from parliamentary meetings to come. Pascal Paoli, the Corsican, was brought into the circle. Giuseppe Marc Baretti came with the Thrales.

In April of 1784, the year Dr. Johnson died, Hannah received a note from him, which she prized because "It was a volunteer and not an answer," saying that he longed to see her in order to praise her poem *The Bas Bleu* as much as envy could praise. Miss Monckton, that eccentric hostess who did not bother to introduce her guests to each other, but strove mightily to prevent their forming a circle, took

Hannah to Bolt Court to gather in the praise awaiting her. Hannah wrote home: "He received me with the greatest kindness and affection, and as to The Bas Bleu, all the flattery I ever received, from everybody together, would not make up his sum. . . . He said there was no name in poetry that might not be glad to own it. You cannot imagine how I stared; all this from Johnson, that parsimonious praiser! I told him I was delighted at his approbation and he answered quite characteristically, 'And so you may be, for I give you the opinion of a man who does not rate his judgment in these things very low, I can tell you.' "[8]

Dr. Johnson had never been a "parsimonious praiser" of Hannah's work. It seems to us today that he erred on the side of overadmiration, but in the case of *The Bas Bleu* he was moved less by the versification than by its tender recollections of friends they both loved, many of whom they had already lost.

Hannah was puzzled and distressed by Dr. Johnson's dread of dying. She herself had a solemn enjoyment of deathbeds and looked forward with interest to her own. She did not understand the fear of death. After Dr. Johnson's death she persuaded herself that faith had subdued his fears and she wished that she might have heard the dying discourse of so great and good a man. In the years following she cherished the memory of having attended church with him the last time he took communion.

The elderliness of Hannah's friends is always noticeable. Among her favorites in London was General Oglethorpe, founder of the Georgia colony, in his late nineties, but still a famous host and storyteller. Her friends Mr. and Mrs. Soame Jenyns, gay and gallant, made up one hundred and sixty-five years between them. Richard (Leonidas) Glover, past eighty, was always ready to oblige by singing his ballad *Hosier's Ghost*. Lord Monboddo, a youngster not yet seventy, liked to shock her with his ridiculous theory that men and monkeys were kinfolk. The writers, actors, painters, divines, physicians, and scholars of this group did not retire from social life until they lay down to die.

The effect on Hannah of intimate association with such elderly persons was to set her in old ways of thinking. Intellectually she belonged to a generation already past, so that later on, when she came in contact with Southey, Coleridge, De Quincey, Cottle, and others who sojourned in Bristol, she was prejudiced against their ideas. She carried the age of Johnson over into the time of Shelley and Byron.

CHAPTER XII

Cowslip Green and Barley Wood

ALTHOUGH it is Hannah's name by which the Bristol school is designated, she had the least connection with it of any of the five sisters. She did not join the teaching group until several years after the older sisters had promoted the institution and had firmly established it, and she gave up her active connection at the time of her engagement to Mr. Turner. After she accepted the annuity from him she looked upon writing as her profession. The school continued to be her home and it is probable she had minor duties, as Miss Lintorn's bill is in Hannah's handwriting. She may even have taught some classes, but she was always free to go to London for her long yearly visits, and her literary output was soon too great to leave much time for teaching. Her London connection was invaluable in spreading the fame of the school.

Her sisters were able to give up their school and live on their incomes after a little more than thirty years of work. They retired earlier than they had intended because of ill health. Hannah's letters record her sisters' disorders with the same gusto she shows in talking about her own ailments, although she goes less into details; two are in bed or four are confined to their rooms or Patty has fainting fits or someone must go to Bath to drink the waters. Even taking into account Hannah's exaggerated interest in sickbeds and deaths, one sees that the sisters were not robust women in their middle age. The strain of carrying on a large and successful boarding school was excessive even though there were four of them to divide the responsibility.

Notice of the school's change of management was carried in *The Bristol Journal* for January second, 1790:

> Selina Mills, many years teacher at the Misses Mores' boarding school, begs leave to inform her friends and the public that she has taken the large and commodious house, now occupied by the Misses More (who retire from business) where she and her sisters propose to carry on the boarding and day school for young ladies on exactly the same plan and with the same masters. The school will open on Monday the 14th instant. The terms for boarding are reduced to 20 guineas. S. Mills returns her sincere thanks to the Misses Mores' friends for the great encouragement she has received from them.

The Mills sisters carried on the school until in 1799 Zachary Macaulay returned to England from his governorship of Sierra Leone, at which time Selina retired from teaching to marry him. Her sisters may have continued the school for a time; there is no record of when it was dissolved, leaving its famous name to be handed down from school to school.

The More sisters retired to Bath where they built one of the early houses in Pulteney Street, Number Seventy-six, close by Laurel Place, a fine large house in excellent taste. This section of Bath, sometimes called The New Town, was then being developed on the Pulteney estate and was designed by Thomas Baldwin, following plans of John Wood and his son John Wood. Pulteney Street was one hundred feet wide, and the houses were built with exteriors which harmonized, the interior planning and decoration being left to the owners and long-lease renters.

Hannah did not like living in Bath. It had grown to be a large city and apparently a noisy one with carts rattling over rough pavement and hucksters bawling through the streets. Hannah arranged a retreat from city noise by building a cottage in Wrington. Four houses were built by the More sisters, singly or in partnership. The school in Park Street, Bristol, was the project of the older sisters. The house in Bath was a family affair. Now Hannah built Cowslip Green, a modest cottage in Wrington, Somerset. Later she built a large house, Barley Wood, not far away, where, after the Bath house was given up, the five sisters all lived together.

Wrington at this time was a market town pleasantly situated in a fruitful valley between the high land of Broadwell Down on the northeast and Mendip Hills on the southwest, twelve miles distant from Wells and eleven miles south from Bristol. It contained some one hundred and sixty-three houses, and had about eight hundred and fifty inhabitants. The town was very irregularly built; the houses low and thatched, darkened by penthouses projecting over the doors and shops. A small Tuesday market was held and the remains of a cross were to be seen in the market place.[1] The church had, and still has, one of the most beautiful towers in the country, with a clock and six bells. De Quincey, whose mother built a villa in the Vale of Wrington, describes the landscape as a beautiful series of downs, like vast lawns, eaten close by sheep, on which you might roam on horseback for miles.

In the Mores' time the land was chiefly pasturage. A crop cultivated in considerable quantities was teasel, a strong, thistle-like plant formerly used in scratching newly woven cloth to raise a nap. There was also a good deal of dairy farming. The women and children occupied themselves with spinning and knitting.

Cowslip Green was a one-story thatched cottage. The drawing-room looked to the south, across the valley to the Mendip Hills. Hannah had great fun building and her friends were interested in the project. Walpole sent her all the Strawberry Press editions for her library and Mrs. Montagu presented her with a set of painted wooden chairs. Although it was a small house, sometimes a goodly number of people were able to pack themselves away in it. Mrs. Garrick visited her. Mrs. Montagu found it a great novelty to dine in a thatched cottage. Little Kenny (Mrs. Kennicott) had a glorious time broiling chops out-of-doors on knitting needles and training the roses and honeysuckle. Friends staying at the Hotwells drove over. William Wilberforce, who determined the course of Hannah's later life by inciting her to organize Sunday Schools on the pattern of those of Robert Raikes, came with his sister, or came alone, staying as long as a month, and on his honeymoon brought his bride for a few days. Hannah reported to Mrs. Garrick that the new wife was not a beauty, but very pleasing; a pretty, vivacious woman of the spritely, lively temper that Mr. Wilberforce liked. He was in poor health but high spirits and "very much in love as ever you saw a poor gentleman." [2]

For a while Hannah was happy in her charming cottage. She rode horseback through the lovely countryside and visited spots of rocky grandeur in the Mendip Hills, coming home loaded with watercress from the brooks and wild flowers dug for her garden. She had a genuine love of the countryside at a time when few appreciated its beauty. When she was staying alone at Cowslip Green, where, she wrote Mary Hamilton, the nearby farmhouses were a protection by night and a source of cream and eggs by day, she entertained the rector at tea in the "root house" covered with blue periwinkle and sweet honeysuckle, and in the evenings walked in the moonlight accompanied by a little dog and two cats.[3] This root house was not, as its name suggests, a storage house for vegetables but a rustic bower formed of tree roots wrenched from the soil by ox teams when the garden was cleared.

Gardening was an endless delight to the Mores. Hannah and Patty and Sally spent happy hours digging in the earth. When Hannah wrote *Coelebs* she had the heroine hang her watch on a tree lest she spend too much time working in the vegetable garden. Hannah herself worried lest she do wrong in loving her garden too well.

Trouble with the farmer next door began early. Hannah found him dishonest and slovenly and wondered if he did not carefully cultivate thorns and thistles in the adjacent fields. He built pigsties where they would most annoy her. The quarrel grew and the situation became unendurable. Hannah loved cottage simplicity and boasted about living on nothing in a country where nothing was to be had, but she was chagrined by filth. She was desperately ashamed when the rich Henry Thorntons and the Wilberforces visited her, for, as she wrote Mrs. Garrick, the unfriendly farmer next door had carried out his threats, not only by building pigsties under her nose but by draining "a certain Edifice" into the boundary ditch. Hannah could no longer entertain her friends at tea in the flowery root house because of objectionable sounds and sights and smells.[4]

Moreover the cottage was too small. The sisters were there much of the time and visitors had to be packed in carefully. Hannah had become acquainted with the Henry Thornton family, friends of the Wilberforces and the Macaulays, and when this group of Clapham Sect friends met at Cowslip Green to discuss good works, the cottage was too small to hold them. On one occasion Dr. T. S. Whalley and his wife, coming merely to call, suffered so serious a carriage accident that the cottage was turned into a hospital with the sisters in day and night attendance on Mrs. Whalley, who was too badly injured to be removed to her nearby home. Moreover, the little house could not be properly heated for cold weather. Hannah decided to build a bigger, better house.

The sisters were in sympathy with this plan. It may be that they were disappointed in their life in Bath. The city was a fashionable spa and they were not fashionable women. They were of far less consequence in Bath than they had been in Bristol and Hannah, who attracted interesting London visitors, hated Bath and stayed there as little as she could. She remained at Cowslip Green in the winter until she was frozen out and she went to London early each spring. Since Hannah would not live in Bath, the other sisters joined her in Wrington.

A beautiful, high piece of land with a fine outlook was found about a mile away. The new house was begun in April, 1800. The sisters began to plant trees before the masons had finished. The building was ready for the roof in August.

Then came the delays. The builder died, leaving no accounts at all to show what he had so far expended. The executors did not know what to do, but an agreement was reached after two different surveyors had estimated the value of the land, the materials, and the work. Hannah was deeply distressed at the delay and at the additional costs, but matters were finally straightened out and the sisters moved in.[5]

The house was two stories high, built of stone, and topped by a thatched roof. A rustic veranda which ran around the first story was before many years a trellis draped with roses, honeysuckle, jasmine, woodbine, and clematis. The sisters never lost interest in improving the grounds and before long the acres were lovely with laurel, larch, cypress, chestnut, and other trees and shrubbery. The grounds did not entirely escape the popular artificial touch for there was an urn in commemoration of the celebrated John Locke who was born in the village of Wrington, contributed by Mrs. Elizabeth Montagu, and another to the memory of Hannah's friend Beilby Porteus, Bishop of London. One hears also of "a Druidical Temple made of knots of oak," probably a summerhouse made of oak roots like the one in which Hannah served tea at Cowslip Green, but no shell and pebble grotto or sham Gothic ruin spoiled the lovely simplicity of the grounds.[6]

A pleasant social life went on among the gentry of the neighborhood. John Scandreth Harford, who inherited Blaize Castle, still a show place, was a great friend of the Mores. He is supposed to have been the model for the tiresomely perfect hero of Hannah's novel *Coelebs*, and he was one of the men who rallied round when Hannah in her old age was obliged to leave Barley Wood because of the strange perfidy of her servants. To him we are indebted for a description of a morning call which he made to present Rev. Walter Trevelyan, Vicar of Henbury, to the ladies of Barley Wood. Soon after the two gentlemen were ushered into the vacant breakfast room, a lady with bright blue eyes and a benevolent expression entered, hands thrown up in an animated manner, exclaiming, "I am not Hannah More!" This was Patty, the youngest, now in her early sixties. Another lady sailed in. "That is not Hannah More!" cried Patty. It was Sally, the wit and once the beauty of the family. A third time the door opened, to admit a lady "whose brilliant eyes lighted up a pale and sensible face." "This is Hannah More!" She was an alert old lady with bright, sparkling eyes and an intelligent expression, wearing an elaborate white muslin cap and a white fichu.

By the time the party sat down at the breakfast table, they had been joined by the two oldest sisters. Mary, addressed as "Mrs. More," and nearly eighty, was stately in appearance and reserved in address and deportment. She wore a high cap surmounting a ruff of white hair. No personal description is given of Betty, beyond her being good-natured and hospitable and pressing the guests to eat all the good things on the table.

The ladies were frank and cordial and kind and set the guests at ease. Hannah was careful that Mary, who was deaf, should lose none of the conversation. All showed a proud, loving deference to Hannah, who on her part made "no effort to shine; but again and again pointed and bright things fell from her lips in the most easy and natural manner." [7] They were surprisingly different, considering how much they were alike.

Lady Waldegrave, Elizabeth Laura, married to her cousin the fourth Earl of Waldegrave, who through her uncle the Earl of Orford had become a great friend of Hannah, lived near Wrington, and her mother the Duchess of Gloucester came to call on Hannah when visiting her daughter and corresponded with her when they were separated. John Hiley Addington, M.P., living at Langford Court, was one of her associates and his frank appears on some of her correspondence. Dr. and Mrs. T. S. Whalley, living in fantastic Mendip Lodge, designed like something out of the *Arabian Nights* and perched on a hilltop within sight of Barley Wood, brought their visitors to call on the Mores—among them Mrs. Siddons and Anna Seward, "The Swan of Lichfield," who was as critical of Hannah's pious personality as the latter was of her romanticism. Although Mrs. Siddons was a friend of Mrs. Garrick, Hannah never warmed up to her, but she spoke of her with deep respect.

The sisters dined at four and saw friends after five. They were conveyed to their own calls in a comfortable, low-hung chaise that held three. De Quincey describes their arrival at his mother's villa in a plain-looking, well-cushioned carriage as ample and roomy as the ladies themselves, drawn by sleek, dull horses at four miles an hour, with a sleek, dull coachman holding the reins. In the drawing-room Mrs. Sally was exuberant in spirits, mirth, and good nature. Mrs. Patty was distinguished for drollery. Mrs. Hannah was soft, delicate, and agreeable, and, De Quincey thought, in youth must have been pretty. Her eyes only were too bright for absolute repose of face. Hannah's eyes are mentioned in every description of her appearance, as well as her good breeding and quiet poise.

The young writing set that Joseph Cottle, the Bristol publisher, drew about him found Barley Wood less to their taste than did the older generation. It is true that when Coleridge was in Bristol in 1794 he wrote a play, with Southey and Robert Hall each furnishing an act, on the death of Robespierre, which was dedicated to Hannah More, but later relations were not so cordial. The play was never produced. When Coleridge called at Barley Wood with Cottle in 1814 he had, according to his habit, talked for two hours when a lady of title was announced. Hannah deserted the poet for the lady, leaving him to her sisters, and he resented what he considered a slight. Cottle had a similar experience, yet he always writes kindly of all the sisters. Both Patty and Hannah left small bequests to several members of the Cottle family and Patty left to Mr. Cottle himself a portrait of John Henderson, a brilliant, short-lived protégée of the Cottles and the Mores.

De Quincey, who gives us a picture of Hannah from the viewpoint of his generation, was bitter and inaccurate in the anonymous article he wrote immediately after her death, but his signed later article is less acrimonious.[8] His mother had built herself a villa in the Vale of Wrington and was a friend of the Mores. De Quincey himself disliked the sisters but he frequented their informal salon because he met there famous persons whom he wanted to know. On one occasion Mrs. Siddons read the sleepwalking scene from *Macbeth* and something from Milton. De Quincey at Hannah's request read Byron. Sometimes he could get the sisters to talking about Dr. Johnson and his friends and that was worth a young man's hearing. He was horrified at the disapproval of poetry which Hannah developed in her later years and he said he found it impossible to have any real conversation with her because she twisted every subject to her own viewpoint. The young writers whom Cottle gathered about him in Bristol annoyed Hannah as much as she exasperated them.

Little Tom Macaulay, eldest son of Zachary and Selina Mills Macaulay, had a second home at Barley Wood. A delightful relationship existed between the little boy and his parents' friend Hannah More, beginning when, aged four, he opened the door of his father's house in High Street, Clapham, London, to admit Hannah. He informed her that his parents were out but that if she would be so good as to come in he would bring her a glass of old spirits. It seems that he had been reading *Robinson Crusoe* and learned about old spirits from him.

His mother was still Patty's especial friend and she concocted for Hannah the beautiful frilled fine linen cap in which she sat for her Pickersgill portrait. From Hannah's reference to Tom in her letters to his father it is clear that she fully appreciated the extraordinary ability of the boy who was to become the famous Lord Macaulay. She guided his reading, gave him guineas to spend for books, listened with delight to his verse, and encouraged him in projects which were good for his delicate health. When he received honors at Cambridge she exulted in his triumph. A friend who was staying with her, probably one of the Misses Roberts, describes how Tom read aloud his second prize poem, *Evening*, in Hannah More's upstairs sitting-room, lounging over a chest of drawers in an ungraceful position and delivering the lines very badly.[9]

When Macaulay, like De Quincey, was asked to write a

sketch of Hannah's life and influence, he refused on the ground that she had been too dear to him for him to pen the criticisms which must needs be contained in an honest appraisal of her writings. Many years later he visited Barley Wood with the sisters' friend, John Scandreth Harford, whose brother William had bought the place. He told Mr. Harford about the many happy weeks he had spent in that home when he was a child and he talked with him about the five sisters. "The bright sisterhood," Macaulay called them.

CHAPTER XIII

The Milkwoman, the Mad Maid and the Kidnapped Heiress

DELIGHT in unusual personalities combined with zeal in doing good led Hannah to discoveries of merit in unexpected persons. She was frequently disappointed in her protégés, for, while she chose them for their talent, she judged them by their conduct. She expected them to act by her own rigid code and was constantly pained to find that highly endowed persons are not necessarily industrious, respectable, and grateful. There was John Henderson, a brilliant, erratic youth whom she, Cottle, and other patrons sent to Oxford, where he scintillated instead of studying; and there was fascinating Harriet Hester in London who was always on the verge of abandoning atheism and her current lover but never did; and other fiery brands that would not burn like working candles.

Ann Yearsley, the fierce, gifted Bristol milkwoman who wrote good verse, was Hannah's first experience in the difficulty of making geniuses do what is best for themselves. This woman, dubbed Lactilla from her occupation, was desperately poor, passionately attached to her six children, mad over books, starved for appreciation, impetuous, excitable, and frantic with frustrated talent. At a critical period when her mother was perishing of hardship, she herself pregnant, and her husband unable to support the family, a Mr. V— looking into a stable discovered the family huddled together, starving. He gave immediate help, though not soon enough to save the old mother. This was probably Richard Vaughn, Esq., of Bristol, for in the list of subscribers bound in the first volume of Yearsley poems, according to the custom of the time, the Vaughn family is down for five copies.

When the talent and the need of the unfortunate woman was brought to Hannah's attention she flung herself enthusiastically into a scheme for raising money by publishing the best of Mrs. Yearsley's poems, with the assistance of Mrs. Elizabeth Montagu. Mrs. Yearsley, then only twenty-seven, had been married at seventeen against her inclination to a man who had six pounds a year. The money vanished, the unsatisfactory husband remained and six children were added. She had found solace in reading Milton, Dr. Young and Virgil's Georgics. Hannah gave her Dryden and Ossian and hired a little maid to take care of the babies while she was out selling milk.

Hannah spent hours selecting the poems to be printed, editing them, arranging with Cadell for their publication and correcting proof sheets. Mrs. Montagu busied herself with the subscription list to such good purpose that, after all expenses were paid, £350 were invested in Five Per Cents, bringing in an income of about £18 a year, besides £20 for immediate spending.[1]

The first edition, brought out with so much care by Hannah, is still a charming volume. The faded pasteboard covers are marbled in pale shades, the corners tipped with leather and the leather back gilt-tooled. It contains one hundred and twenty-seven pages of heavy linen paper, with beautiful hand-set type and wide, restful spaces between the lines. Immediately after a condescending preface written by Hannah comes a list of the subscribers secured by Montagu and More to cover the cost of publication. One learns much from such lists and this one is especially impressive. The A section begins with Her Grace the Duchess Dowager of Athol; the B's are headed by Her Grace the Duchess of Beaufort, followed by duchesses, marchionesses, and countesses; the C's start with four countesses followed by an earl; and the other letters compete. Right Honorables, bishops, ladies, and sirs are thick as blackberries. The list is a roster of the *Bas Bleu* and their friends. Among the local gentry one finds five members of the Gwatkin family and—Mr. Turner. His relatives the Simmons and the Lintorns took four copies, too. Bristol folk remembered that they had not done right by their Chatterton.

This noble volume came into the wretched cottage of the indigent Yearsleys. The house, if like those of most poor laborers earning their nine shillings a week, was a one-room home, with one or two or no small windows, sparsely furnished with a table, a chest, a few stools, perhaps one chair, one large bed and shakedowns and trundle-beds for the raft of children. It differed from other cottages in containing a copy of the Bible, Young's *Night Thoughts* and a few books lent by interested gentry.

Can you see Lactilla, late at night, when the rest of the family are asleep, giving her the only privacy she knows, sitting at the table with a tallow dip, turning those lovely pages, reading in ecstasy the words she had written in despair? It was to her as if the heavens had opened and out of heaven had leaned a friend, Hannah More, whom she named Stella.

The first poem is *Night; To Stella.* There are two other poems to Stella and references to her throughout the volume which give the impression, not of a sycophant, but of a vehement woman romantically in love with an ideal, not actual, friend. Mrs. Yearsley's verse is filled with wild strength, overwhelming desire to perfect her talent, passionate appreciation of beauty, pride, and tumultuous struggling toward a goal but vaguely seen. Her crude genius was very far removed from Hannah's highly trained talent. The women were so different in every way that a rupture was inevitable and, given Mrs. Yearsley's nature, a violent rupture.

The outbreak came over money. Mrs. Yearsley wanted all the money earned by the book placed in her own hands; but Hannah, who with Mrs. Montagu was trustee of the fund, refused. Hannah was bringing out a second edition and the income from investment in addition to what the milkwoman earned at her trade and her husband's meager earnings would, she explained, provide an income sufficient for their low social status. Mrs. Yearsley had other plans. She did not feel that she best performed the duties of a mother by peddling milk, collecting hogwash, and putting her children to work. She was determined to improve her family's education and status. It was reported too that she wore fine gauze bonnets, long lappets, and gold pins.

Unfortunately, Hannah was absent from Bristol when matters came to a crisis, and Mrs. Yearsley came to the house demanding her money. Mary, accustomed for years to making wise, arbitrary decisions for her pupils, treated the rebellious woman as she would have treated a school girl and pointed out a path of docility, gratitude, and submission. The Mores themselves could tolerate an immense amount of condescension from benefactors, for while they were not themselves truly submissive nor docile, they were good-mannered, and they paid with gratitude for favors received. The rage with which Lactilla met their dictatorial kindness convinced them that she was drunk or mad. Elizabeth, the gentle one, who spent her life smoothing over roughnesses, tried in vain to keep peace.

The breaking of the ill-fated friendship seared Lactilla's soul and seriously injured Hannah's pride. Mrs. Yearsley did not rest until she had all her money—which finally came to £600—in her own hands to spend on her children. A part of it she used to apprentice a beloved son to an engraver, and part to start a circulating library at the Hotwells. Some of the townsfolk sided with Mrs. Yearsley against the Mores and Cottle wrote sympathetically of her work and personality. She brought out several more poems, a two-volume novel on the Man in the Iron Mask, which she sold for two hundred pounds, and a play, *Earle Godwin,* which was acted in Bath and Bristol. The later part of her life was shadowed by domestic griefs as well as by disappointed ambitions.

Louisa, the Mad Maid of the Haystack, was perhaps the most satisfactory of Hannah's protégées because being a Beautiful Maniac not even the Mores could expect her to reform. Since she disappointed no hopes, she could draw on their pity till her death.

Louisa came into Hannah's life indirectly through Mr. Turner. One of his cousins, while visiting him at Belmont, rode through the neighboring village of Flax Burton and there came across a beautiful, demented woman, about twenty-five, actually living in a haystack. She had decorated the surrounding bushes with trinkets and when discovered was walking wildly round and round her strange dwelling. The cousin learned that benevolent ladies of the neighborhood had tried confining the lovely lunatic in St. Peter's Hospital in Bristol, where she had been so wretched that they allowed her to return to her free haystack home. Trouble and misery dwelt in houses, she declared, and there was no happiness but in liberty and fresh air. The kind ladies, though they themselves preferred a roof, even if it did cover trouble and misery, gave in to her and clubbed together to buy the haystack.

Mr. Turner's cousin made an appointment with Louisa to come to Belmont the next morning, and to her surprise Louisa actually came. Mr. Turner addressed her in various languages to determine her origin—as she was clearly foreign—and the poor woman burst into tears on hearing German. John Wesley, later on, tried the same experiment with the same result.

Mr. Turner's cousin wrote to the Mores about the unhappy woman. They visited her and had her placed in Mr. Henderson's lunatic asylum at Hannam, near Bristol. The expenses were paid by the sisters, Lord and Lady Bathurst, and other persons of the neighborhood. Louisa must have been a lovely creature. John Wesley wrote of her:

March 25, 1782—Friday—I opened the new house at Freshford. In the afternoon I called at Mr. Henderson's at Hannam, and spent some time with poor, disconsolate Louisa. Such a sight, in the space of fourteen years, I never saw before. Pale and wan, worne with sorrow, beaten with wind and rain, having been so long exposed to all weathers, with her hair rough and frizzled, and only a blanket wrapped round her, native beauty gleamed through all—Her features were small and finely turned; her eyes had a peculiar sweetness; her arms and fingers were delicately shaped, and her voice soft and agreeable; but her understanding was in ruins. She appeared partly insane, partly silly, and childish. She would answer no question concerning herself, only that her name was Louisa. She seemed to take no notice of any person or thing, and seldom spoke above a word or two at a time. Mr. Henderson has restored her health, and she loves him much. She is in a small room by herself, and wants nothing that is proper for her.[2]

Thursday, Sept. 15, 1785. . . . I went over to Hannam once more and saw poor disconsolate Louisa, still wrapping herself up naked in her blanket, and not caring to speak to anyone; the late pretty tale of her being the Emperor's daughter, is doubtless a mere catch-penny; and her four and twenty examinations are as credible as Mahomet's journey through seventy thousand heavens.[3]

Legends clustered around Louisa, assisted by the cunning of her disordered mind. She told an attendant that her father's carriage was drawn by eight horses; that Bohemia was papa's own country; that she had escaped with a lover from a convent in Schleswig where her father had confined her because she would not marry his candidate. It was reported that a young man from abroad arrived at the lunatic asylum in a travelling carriage. Louisa uttered a piercing shriek. The young man cried, "It is herself!" and sprang back into his carriage.

The following lines by Mrs. Yearsley were written while she was still friendly with the More family:

Beneath this stack Louisa's dwelling rose;
Here the fair maniac bore three winter's snows;

Here long she shiver'd, stiffening in the blast
The lightenings round their livid horrors cast;
The thunders roar, while rushing torrents pour,
And add new woes to bleak affliction's hour!
The heavens lour dismal, while the storm descends:
No mother's bosom the soft maid befriends;
But frighten'd o'er the wilds she swiftly flies,
And, drenched with rains, the roofless haystack tries.
The morn was fair, and gentle—I sought
These lonely woodlands, friends to sober thought.
With solitude the slow-paced maid is seen
Tread the dark grove and unfrequented green.
Well S(tella) knew their lurkings: Phoebus shone,—
While, musing, she pursued the track alone.
O thou kind friend! whom here I dare not name,
Who to Louisa's shed of misery came;
Lured by the tale, sighed o'er her beauteous form,
And gently drew her from the beating storm;—
Stand forth—defend for well thou canst; the cause
Of Heaven, and justify its rigid laws.
Yet own that human laws are harshly giv'n,
When they extend beyond the will of Heav'n.
Say can thy pen for that hard duty plead,
By which the meek and helpless maid's decreed
To dire seclusion,—snatched from guiltless joys,
To where corroding grief the frame destroys?
Monastic glooms, which active virtue cramp,
Where horrid silence chills the vital lamp?
Slowly and faint the languid pulses beat,
And the chilled heart forgets its genial heat;
The dim sunk eye with hopeless glance explores
The solemn aisles and death-denouncing doors,
Ne'er to be passed again;—now heaves the sigh,
Now unavailing sorrows fill the eye.

The verses are somewhat critical of the More's action in shutting up poor Louisa where she would be safe but unhappy. One section of the poem is a long description of the mental horror of Louisa in the insane hospital. Coercion of any kind was abhorrent to Mrs. Yearsley's turbulent spirit.

A piece entitled *A Tale of Real Woe*, written by Hannah for the *St. James Chronicle*, was translated into German and circulated in Vienna and the story was also printed in France without result. In 1785 an anonymous French pamphlet, without name of publisher or place, told the story of Mlle. La Fraulein, supposed to be the illegitimate daughter of Emperor Francis I, who was persecuted by Maria Theresa until she lost her mind and wandered through the countryside. It was thought possible that Louisa was this unfortunate, who had somehow reached England. The death of "The Lady of The Haystack" in Guy's Hospital, London, is recorded in *Dodsley's Annual Register* for 1801, with the statement that the More sisters continued to support her after others had lost interest.

As Hannah grew older she was more cautious about helping picturesque unfortunates though she could never resist putting a smart lad in the way of picking up some education. Her gifts to educational and religious foundations increased as her personal interventions lessened. She spread her philanthropy over a wide area instead of concentrating it on individuals. It was safer that way.

By chance rather than by choice Hannah became involved in the romance of an heiress kidnapped from the boarding school the year after it was taken over by Selina Mills.[4]

Clementina Clerke, a Scotch orphan who had inherited

from her uncle Ogilvie property in the West Indies yielding an income of six thousand pounds, had a guardian living in Clifton who, on the advice of the Mores, placed her under Selina Mills' care.

As young Clementina, in her fifteenth year, took her daily promenades in and around Bristol with her schoolmates, she was ogled by Richard Vining Perry, a Bristol apothecary. Clementina was a small girl with a fair complexion, light hair, and dark blue eyes. She wore "Bombazeen Mourning with a Black Beaver Hat." Perry was "a Young Man of Genteel Appearance, fair Complection, light Hair tied behind, about Five Feet, Seven Inches high, of much Volubility of Speech." As this was the period of the macaroni, the buck, and the beau, the adventurous Perry was probably dressed in gaily-hued kneebreeches, swallowtail coat, ornate waistcoat, and a drift of white cambric neck-cloth, with a smart chimney-pot hat. He must have looked wonderful to a little girl in black bombazine. Perry induced Betty Baker, a servant at the school, to slip notes to Clementina, begging her to elope with him. Whether she consented or was tricked into leaving the school was later disputed, but even if she agreed, an heiress of fifteen, unacquainted with the world, could hardly realize the dangers of a clandestine marriage to a man with whom she had never spoken.

By her folly the artless little girl not only involved herself in an unhappy marriage, but unwittingly handed over her large property and income to Perry. A spinster retained the right to her possessions, but a married woman's property must needs be safeguarded by settlements carefully drawn up by lawyers before marriage, settling her property on offspring and determining the division of the income. Unless there were such settlements, the husband took all. If, however, Miss Mills could get the child back and show that she was kidnapped against her will, the property could be saved to her; although of course her reputation would be lost. Miss Selina and the More sisters were no match for The Villain with his fingers on a fortune. The weekly local papers reported the affair with zest and Hannah wrote hysterical accounts to her friends.

Bath Chronicle, Thursday, March 31, 1791, p. 2, col. 1.

. . . The affair was managed in the following manner:— A carriage, horses, and livery servant, were procured, so as to look exactly like those of the lady's guardian; they drove up to the Boarding-School, the servant producing a letter in the name of the guardian, well counterfeited, requesting that Miss Clerke might be suffered to spend the evening at his house at Clifton; that a relation of hers who was just arrived, and under the necessity of leaving town that evening for London, might have the pleasure of seeing her. The young lady was accordingly permitted, with her maid, to pay this visit, but instead of visiting Clifton, she found her way to Stokes-Croft, to the house of her admirer, where they remained till eleven o'clock at night; when they set out in a chaise and four accompanied by her maid and a gentleman of his acquaintance.

Weeks, of the Bush tavern, Bristol, Miss Mills, and her brother, went in pursuit of Miss Clerke. They were met by Mr. Perry, and the young lady at Carlisle, on their return from Gretna Green, posting fast for London.

Perry showed a pistol to the pursuers and went on toward London. Selina rushed to Bath, rousing the Mores at two in the morning, and with Mary More set off immediately for London. The elopement took place on the nineteenth of March; Mary More, Selina Mills, and perhaps her brother reached London the following day and put the matter into the hands of Sir Sampson Wright, magistrate of the Bow

Street Public Office, successor to Sir John Fielding. They took a miserable lodging convenient to the Bow Street Office, where they lived in great discomfort and anxiety. Toward the end of the month Hannah joined them and Mary was prostrated by the strain.

Posting bills were put up in Bath and vicinity and notices inserted in the London papers, offering a reward of a hundred guineas to anyone who would secure and take care of Miss Clerke so that she could be returned to her friends and apprehend Richard Vining so that he could be brought to trial. Lawyers in Bristol and in London warned against the publication of bans or the solemnizing of marriage between the couple. Perry countered with a newspaper notice signed by Clementina Perry and addressed TO THE PUBLIC:

> As it has been maliciously reported that I was taken away from Miss Mills's School by my Husband by force, and without my consent, this is to inform my Friends and the Public, that it is utterly false, and without the smallest foundation in Truth; and whatever Advertisements have or may appear, stating any such thing, are destitute of truth: and I beg my Friends and the Public not to credit any such injurious Report, to the Honour of my Husband, and the Happiness of myself.

The search in London went on for weeks. Hannah and Selina and a lawyer went from one lodging house to another under the pretense of wishing to engage rooms, while a hackney coach full of police waited at a distance. Hannah, utterly terror-stricken by the rumor that Perry never sat without a pistol on the table, was upheld by her persuasion of the child's innocence. "It was the most timid, gentle, pious little thing! How far the endearments and flattery of a wretch, who they say is specious, may have corrupted her in five weeks, I tremble to think," Hannah wrote Mrs. Kennicott.

The search was not given up until the child's friends were certain that Perry had taken her out of England. The *Bath Chronicle* continued to regale its readers with tidbits; reporting that a reconciliation had taken place between Miss Clerke and her Bristol friends and contradicting the statement the next week; reporting that the statement was false that Mrs. Perry was dead as she was in perfect health in Zurich in Switzerland; and two years later announcing the birth of a daughter to Mrs. Clementina Perry, wife of Mr. R. V. Perry, surgeon, late of Bristol.

It took three years to bring Perry to trial in Bristol. The result was a complete triumph for him; he had on his side a pretty little wife completely under his thumb and probably by this time in love with him, for he sounds like an engaging scoundrel, and he had also her fortune which enabled him to retain as his counsel brilliant Thomas Erskine. Moreover Betty Baker, who had been the go-between, was mysteriously missing when called as a witness. Mr. Erskine's speech was reported in *Felix Farley's Bristol Journal*, April 19, 1794:

> Mr. Erskine, leading Counsel for the Prisoner, then addressed the Court in a strain of that eloquence for which he is so eminently distinguished, and painted in the most lively and affecting colors what must be the dreadful situation of Mrs. Perry and her infant, thirteen months old, which was then in Court with her, if the Husband and father should be found guilty of the crime laid to his charge; but that, he observed, was impossible, the very existence of the little innocent proved it to be so.—He then called on Mrs. Perry, as an evidence for her husband. The Counsel for the prosecution strenuously objected to the admission of her testimony, contending that neither law nor precedent would warrant its being received.

Mr. Erskine in very strong language reprobated this doctrine, positively asserting that both by law and precedent it must be admitted; that it was most material towards proving or disproving the facts alleged against the prisoner; that deprived of it, impartial and substantial justice could not be obtained, and that rather than forego the advantages of it, he would sit in that Court 'till the day of resurrection. After very long and elaborate pleadings on this point, the Recorder admitted Mrs. Perry's testimony to be taken, observing, that as the Counsel for the prosecution were at liberty to have brought her forward on their part, it was but just that the prisoner should have the same privilege.

Young Mrs. Perry asserted that she had known clearly what she was about when she eloped, that she had known Mr. Perry a month and conceived an affection for him although they had never spoken, and that she was perfectly satisfied in every respect. Mrs. Perry's testimony exculpated her husband so completely that the jury delivered their verdict "not guilty" without going out of court. Mr. Perry reached his hand over the bar to his wife, who kissed it with marks of affection. When he left the bar the two embraced tenderly, to the delight of the spectators, who had received the verdict with tumultuous exultation. The onlookers took the horses from the Perrys' carriage and drew them through the principal streets of Bristol with loud acclamations.

The outcome of the marriage was as disastrous as the little girl's friends had foreseen. The surgeon discarded his girl wife and kept her fortune. She died poverty-stricken in Bath about 1812, while he was living magnificently in Jamaica where the property was situated, having taken the name of Ogilvie in recognition of the uncle from whom Clementina had inherited the fortune.[5]

The inability of the child's friends to protect her interests did not suggest to Hannah the desirability of a change in women's legal status. When Mary Wollstonecraft's *Vindication of the Rights of Women* was published the same year that Clementina was lured away, Hannah refused to read the book. She commented; "Rights of Women! We will be hearing of the Rights of Children next!"

CHAPTER XIV

Bishop Porteus and Horace Walpole

One can trace the successive interests of Hannah's life through her writings. Her playlet *The Search after Happiness* won her the warm approval of her family and the patrons of the school. *The Inflexible Captive* started as a language exercise. Her early verse was written to please this person or that one. *The Legend of Bleeding Rock* and inscriptions to be placed in the Turner grounds marked her engagement to an elegant estate and its owner. After she had visited London, she wrote *Sir Eldred of the Bower* in order, as she put it, to deserve the praise she had received, and by so doing received much more. *Percy* and *The Fatal Falsehood* were inspired by her devotion to Garrick. *Sensibility* and *The Bas Bleu* were for the elderly ladies and gentlemen who petted her after his death. *Sacred Dramas,* begun years before and finished during her retirement with Mrs. Garrick, was prophetic of her later absorption in religion. For Bishop Porteus' entertainment she wrote *Bishop Bonner's Ghost* and to Horace Walpole she dedicated *Florio: a Tale, for Fine Gentlemen and Fine Ladies.*

Hannah first met Beilby Porteus when he was Bishop of Chester and private chaplain to George the Third. She wrote home after this meeting that she found him perfectly to her taste and she never changed her mind. The bishop likewise found Hannah perfectly to his taste. After he was Bishop of London, stately Fulham Palace became one of Hannah's homes away from home and her yearly visit there was timed to include the annual house party of bishops.

Bishop Porteus was a thin-faced man with heavy eyebrows, silent in company but silver-tongued in the pulpit. He was distinguished for sweetness of disposition, charm of manner, and application to work. Every morning he rose very early in order to have a day long enough to include his many interests. Sunday schools, Sunday observation, foreign missions, abolition of slavery, were some of the causes for which he worked, in addition to the duties of his diocese.

Hannah's verses, *Bishop Bonner's Ghost*, were apropos of one of his hobby projects. An incident occurring during one of Hannah's visits to the palace furnished the theme. At six o'clock one morning energetic Bishop Porteus started to cut a path through a thicket in the palace garden toward a dark recess containing a stone chair known as Bishop Bonner's Seat. Bishop Bonner had been a stiff-necked old prelate in Queen Mary's time, noted for his persecution of Protestants. Hannah imagined that the old tyrant resented Bishop Porteus' invasion of his retreat. The poem is Bonner's bitter reproach to Porteus at letting light in where darkness had reigned. The verses, footnoted in pseudo-scholarly style, made a great hit. Horace Walpole was especially delighted with the poem. He begged and received the privilege of printing two hundred copies on the Strawberry Hill Press. Hannah appreciated the honor. Only a few copies remain today, rare items in a collector's list.

At the same time that Hannah was extending her acquaintance among the clergy she was cementing a friendship with that sacrilegious charmer Horace Walpole. She made Dr. Porteus and Mr. Walpole acquainted through *Bishop Bonner's Ghost,* and received Mr. Walpole's thanks for "your pimping between us." Mr. Walpole loved to startle the gentle lady. His letters to her continually scold her in a caressing fashion. When, for instance, he sent her money for a man who had been cut down alive after he had hanged himself, he writes:

> It is very provoking that people must always be hanging or drowning themselves, or going mad, that you forsooth, Mistress, may have the diversion of exercising your pity and good-nature, and charity, and intercession, and all that beadroll of virtues that make you so troublesome and amiable, when you might be ten times more agreeable by writing things that would not cost one above half a crown at a time. You are an absolutely walking hospital, and travel about into lone and bye places, with your doors open to house stray casualties. I wish at least you would have some children yourself, that you might not be plaguing one for all the pretty brats that are starving and friendless. . . .

The Walpole-More letters are witty, kind, and affectionate. When he addressed her as "Dear holy Hannah" he wrote the words with a smile which was not a sneer. He ended one letter: "Adieu, thou who mightest be one of the cleverest of women if you did not prefer being one of the best."

Hannah allowed him and him only to have her portrait by Opie, painted for Mrs. Boscawen, copied by Roberts. It hung at Strawberry Hill and was reproduced in the first edition of Walpole's letters. The elderly cynic had no influence over the earnest soul of Hannah and she in turn moderated none of his acid urbanity. He had an amused understanding of Hannah which her serious friends did not attain, seeing her in truer proportion than those who admired her more. He detected the woman under the saint and she saw the kindly soul beneath the cynic. The friendship was a credit to both.

For Horace Walpole Hannah wrote the most charming of her frivolous poems. It has a moral, but the lesson does not overshadow the story. The swing and lilt of the verses are delightful. *Florio: A Tale, for Fine Gentlemen and Fine Ladies* was the swan song of the Hannah whom Garrick had known. Although she kept on writing for many years, her output was planned to call sinners to repentance and there was no laughter in it.

The dedication to the Honorable Horace Walpole states that *Florio* was written to amuse a few moments of his tedious indisposition and be a paltry return for the many hours of agreeable information and elegant amusement which Hannah had received from his spirited and very entertaining writings. She signed the dedication:

I have the honour to be,
Sir,
Your much obliged,
And most obedient
Humble Servant,

HANNAH MORE.

January 27,
1786

Florio has a singsong meter and clicking rhymes. The polished, artificial verse is a happy form for the theme

—the metamorphosis of a macaroni into a country squire.

Florio, a youth of gay renown
Who figur'd much about the Town,
Had pass'd, with general approbation,
The modish forms of Education;
Knew what was proper to be known
Th' established jargon of Bon-ton;
Had learnt, with very moderate reading,
The whole new system of good breeding:

. . . .

His mornings were not spent in vice,
'T was lounging, sauntering, eating ice:
Walk up and down St. James's Street,
Full fifty times the youth you'd meet:
He hated cards, detested drinking,
But strolled to shun the toil of thinking.

Florio was not, however, destined to remain a silly, worthless creature for he had a good heart, sense, spirit, taste, and zeal, besides being handsome, generous, and the heir to a large estate. He had been influenced by bad companions. Florio's father had left him a fortune on condition he marry Celia, the daughter of a country squire, as soon as mourning clothes were laid aside:

Florio, reluctant, calls to mind
The orders of a Sire too kind:
Yet go he must; he must fulfill
The hard conditions of the will:

Fortunately, it was Spring:

When freed from winter's icy chain,
Glad Nature revels on the plain;
When blushing Spring leads on the hours,
And May is prodigal of flowers;
When Passion warbles thro' the grove,
And all is song and all is love.

Florio was bored by the quiet life in Celia's home; especially by the plain food:

One dish there was which never fail'd,
Celia with this each guest regail'd;
'Twas simple mutton, roast or boil'd,
Sole dish French cookery has not spoil'd.
Tho' rich in game, and stor'd with fish,
She ne'er forgot her standing dish,
Florio in secret would repine,
For Florio now but liv'd to dine;

Florio was tempted back to town, but having tasted the simple life of the country he no longer liked the town; accustomed to Celia's mutton, he turned from French cookery:

And when he cast his eyes around,
And not one simple morsel found,
O give me, was his secret wish,
My charming Celia's Standing Dish!

His eyes now opened to the rottenness of town life, he rushed back to country joys, Celia, and a saddle of mutton.

He drank port, avoided French phrases, and listened to the old squire's tiresome prattle.

Abroad, with joy and grateful pride,
He walks, with Celia by his side:
A thousand cheerful thoughts arise,
Each rural scene enchants his eyes;
With transport he begins to look
On Nature's all instructive book.

. . . .

Till Florio with a sigh, confest
The simplest pleasures are the best!

This eulogy of country life was written the year after Hannah built Cowslip Green and was a statement of her unchanging preference for rural surroundings.

CHAPTER XV

Hannah's Changing Interests

THE FOCUS of Hannah's attention shifted during a period of about ten years from enjoyment of London society to concentration on humanitarian projects. She felt her way slowly into this second phase of her life, losing her interest in superficial social relations and drawing into the scope of her benevolent activities the ignorant, the underprivileged, the enslaved, the heathen, and other unfortunates.

The change which took place in her personality is indicated in her portraits. The woman painted by Frances Reynolds the year after Garrick's death is a lively, pleasant girl with merry eyes and a sensitive mouth, looking younger than her years. Although her profession is symbolized by the pen in her hand, she looks more like a schoolgirl than a full-fledged dramatist. Opie's picture, painted six years later, shows a mature woman. She is dressed in a voluminous dark silk gown with a full white neckpiece. The small face is framed in a mass of powdered hair drawn loosely back and tied with a ribbon in a sort of bun; the forehead is high and delicately rounded; the nose is distinctly on the firm side; the mouth is ready to smile; the eyes are dark, lively, and quietly amused. There is the faintest suggestion of Mona Lisa. The effect is French, which is odd, for Hannah heartily disliked the French and all their ways.

Changes in the circumstances of her life caused the alteration in her personality. The successive deaths of Garrick, her father, Dr. Langhorne, Dr. Johnson, and others not so close but yet members of her London circle, saddened her and made her more susceptible to the influence of deepening friendships with the evangelical men and women of the Clapham Sect and other progressive religious groups.

Jacob More's death occurred almost exactly four years after Garrick's, while Hannah was on a winter visit to Mrs. Garrick. The blow was heavy, though not unexpected. We know little about the father's life after the children left home, for the letters which they must have written their parents have not been preserved for us. An early biographer of Hannah states that as soon as the Bristol school was on a paying basis the daughters bought a home for their father in the Stoney-Hill section of Bristol and provided female servants to attend him. As the girls' mother outlived him, one assumes that she shared this home.

One mention of the father before his death we find in Hannah's letters to her sisters in 1781: "Tell my father I am quite delighted with his verses, and particularly that he could write them in so good a hand; I have put them among my curiosities. I do not think I shall write such good verses at eighty-one." [1] This was probably a metrical translation of Latin verses which Dr. Robert Lowth, Dr. Porteus' predecessor as Bishop of London, had sent to Hannah at a dinner party, entitled *Hannae Morae. Virgini Plae Eruditae, Eleganti, Ingenio, Fecunda et Sapientia Pariter Illustri.* Hannah naïvely handed the lines to a gentleman to be read aloud to the company and was embarrassed at their complimentary tone.

Jacob More's death was announced in *Bonner and Middleton's Bristol Journal,* January eleventh, 1783:

On Sunday morning died at his home on Stoney-Hill, in an advanced age, Mr. More, father of the Miss Mores, in Park-street; whose extensive knowledge, integrity of heart, and cheerful piety, deservedly gain'd him the affection of his family and the esteem of his friends.

Hannah, who at that time was visiting Mrs. David Garrick, wrote to Martha:

Hampton, Jan. 9, 1783.
It was so unusual for me to receive a letter two days following, that when Sally's came on Wednesday, I had so strong a presentiment of its contents, that I did not open it for a long time; but I laid it down very deliberately, and went and did several things which I thought too well I should not be able to do after I had read it. Yet, notwithstanding all this preparation, I was just as much shocked at reading it as if I had expected nothing like it. I could not get quite through it for hours after, and yet there is no cause for grief, but much for joy, much cause to be thankful, and I am *very* thankful that he was spared to us so long—that he was removed when life began to grow a burden to himself—that he did not survive his faculties—that he was not confined to the miseries of a sickbed—but above all, that his life was so exemplary, and his death so easy. I wish I had seen him. Yet that is a vain regret. I hope he did not inquire after me, or miss me. Mrs. Garrick was very much affected, as my father was a very great favorite of hers.

Hampton, Jan. 28, 1783.
Since my dear father's death, I have never yet had resolution to go out of doors, so much as to walk around the garden, in almost three weeks. . . .

On May 5th of the same year she wrote from London:

Is it not very melancholy when you go to see our solitary

mother? I endeavor to think of it as little as I can, but in spite of all my endeavors it mixes with all my thoughts.[2]

Among the men and women whose influence on Hannah's development became ever stronger were John Newton, co-author with Cowper of *Olney Hymns*; the group that met at Sir Charles Middleton's to work for the abolition of slavery; and the men of the evangelical party including Zachary Macaulay, Wilberforce, and the Thorntons. Speaking rather generally, because the groups were overlapping, we may say that John Newton encouraged Hannah's spiritual development, the Middletons fortified her opposition to the slave traffic, Wilberforce and his friends supported her Sunday School work, while Macaulay kept alive her sense of responsibility for foreign missions.

The intimacy with John Newton was carried on almost entirely through correspondence. When Hannah More wrote a letter it was keyed to the personality of the recipient. To Horace Walpole she was a serious but witty lady interested in world events. With Dr. Beilby Porteus, she discussed philanthropic topics. To Sir William Pepys she was a bookish friend. She put the accent on religion when writing to any of the Clapham group. Reports on Sunday School work filled her letters to Wilberforce. From John Newton she asked advice about her soul.

John Newton is best known as the author of the hymn, "How Sweet the Name of Jesus Sounds," and as the curate of Olney who befriended the poet Cowper. He was a man of intense affections and his letters to Hannah More show more of the loving side of his nature than its harsher aspects. The two began corresponding when they were in different sections of London in 1787 and continued until a few years before his death in 1803.

Mr. Newton was an extraordinary person. He had violent emotions with tremendous persistence. When his attention focused itself on an object, a person, a desire, nothing diverted it. His early life, passed at sea, was a nightmare of press gangs, floggings, fevers and recklessness until he worked his way up to be master of a slave ship. He had religious services for his slave cargoes and allowed no blasphemy among the sailors. During these turbulent years he taught himself mathematics and languages from books which he carried in his pocket.

He fell in love with Miss Catlett, aged fourteen, during a stay ashore in England and after serving an impatient probation married her. He was passionately attached to her all their married life. While tide surveyor in Liverpool he went on with his self-teaching and mastered Greek and Hebrew because he wished to be a clergyman, but he applied without success to the Archbishop of Canterbury for ordination. Six years it took Mr. Newton to obtain ordination, though it was a foregone conclusion that even bishops must go down before that will power. When Hannah met him he had been for some years rector of St. Mary Woolnoth, London.

His picture shows a heavy, fleshy face, more like a slave trader than a man of God. One would put him down as narrow, dogmatic, and domineering and he was all that, but he was also affectionate, charming, and heavily playful. These pleasanter qualities come out in his relation to his wife, to Cowper, and to Hannah More. He was delightful with women, although pontifical. When his wife was on her deathbed, he detected in her a strong reluctance to dying and pestered the poor creature to bear witness as befitted a dying Christian. Instead of testifying, she stroked his face and called him by her pet name for him, "My pretty dear." The old slave trader was deeply loved.

The early letters which passed between Mr. Newton and Hannah give a delightful picture of two decorous, middle-aged persons, attracted to each other, and getting acquainted with the restrained elegance of their day and class. Hannah was already familiar with Newton's book *Cardiphonia* and had recommended it to Dr. Stonehouse. Mr. Newton's first letter begins, "My dear Madam," and is taken up chiefly with explanations that his admiration and his wife's justify his using that "familiar style of address." In a postscript he tells her that he is sending her a copy of the preface he wrote for the first volume of Cowper's poems, which the booksellers were afraid to bind up with the poems lest it should operate like a death's-head at a feast and, by its gravity, hinder the sale it was designed to recommend; but, says Mr. Newton, "I am not afraid to send *you* a copy."

Hannah replies with a "My dear Sir" and calls his attention to her having adopted his friendly mode of address. She goes on to explain why she feels justified in such cordiality and to regret that she does not know him and his wife better. Next, Mr. Newton writes of his disappointment at not seeing her at a party. She thanks him for the affectionate interest he takes in her welfare and asks his prayers that she may obtain more firmness of mind, a more submissive spirit, and more preparedness for death and the evils of life. In this letter, written three weeks after their first meeting, she tells him that she is looking forward to seeing him at Cowslip Green. Hannah More moved with rapidity as well as dignity.

From Cowslip Green Hannah asks advice as to whether her passionate love of gardening is evil because it takes up so much of her time and thoughts. Mr. Newton tells her that he has been dreaming of her hermitage and if it were not for his work he would like to live near her that he might enjoy her garden.

The friendship had gone on for three or four years in a mild and pleasant fashion, when the two had a falling out. When Hannah sent him an anonymous copy of her *Estimate of the Religion of the Fashionable World*, he immediately guessed the author, as did all her friends, and made the mistake of referring to the book as hers when they were both in company with two friends who were also in the open secret. Hannah's odd reluctance to admit that she had written what everyone knew was hers made an embarrassing situation. The blunderer was so overwhelmed by contrition at his awkwardness that he wrote an apology Saturday so that he would have it off his mind during the Sunday sermon and sent the letter on Monday morning. Hannah instantly sat down and wrote an apology in her turn. The little flare-up and the reconciliation brought them nearer together.

The long-talked-of visit to Cowslip Green occurred the year after Mrs. Newton's death. The widower, now sixty-six years old, was very lonely. His letters suggest that his heart may have been turning toward Hannah, but Hannah was not a marrying woman.

When he asked whether he should come in August or September, Hannah chose August because it was sooner and determined to get all her "little affairs" and "little schemes" out of the way to have time to enjoy her guest. The friendship had been working up to a pitch that suggests a coming romance, but the two were chaperoned at Cowslip Green by Hannah's sisters and by Mr. Newton's adopted daughter, Miss Catlett, his wife's niece. Still, a man of his determination could have—maybe did—put through a proposal. If so, he was refused.

The visit was a great success. The lonely man got plenty of comforting. Trifles amused them all: a thunderstorm so frightened Miss Catlett that she hid in a closet; a little sick maid received spiritual comfort from the divine. Mr. Newton went away leaving his pipe in the currant bush and no hand was presumptuous enough to remove it. Lizzie, the little maid who had been sick, often cried, "Oh, dear, I hope no one will break Mr. Newton's pipe." They called it a "venerable relic."

Mr. Newton's bread-and-butter letter contained the verse:

In Helicon could I my pen dip,
I might attempt the praise of Mendip.
Were bards a hundred, I'd outstrip 'em,
If equal to the theme of Shipham.
But harder still the task, I ween,
To give its due to Cowslip Green!

A month later he wrote; "Oh my dear ladies! O Mendip! O root-house! O chamber of peace! O ye walks and seats! If I never visit you more, I shall think of you and pay you a mental visit often and often. Surely no pipe in Somersetshire is so honored as that which dwells (there may it long dwell) in your black currant bush. I thank Lizzie for her care of it."

Patty received as a souvenir for her album a verse written by the poet Cowper at Mr. Newton's request. It reads:

In vain to live from age to age,
We modern bards endeavor;
In Patty's book I wrote one page,
And gained my point forever.
William Cowper.
Exemplar verum.
Witness, J. N.

Mr. Newton must have talked of the More sisters to Cowper with enthusiastic friendliness for the poet wrote at least three versions. Mr. Newton passed them on to Patty via a letter to Hannah, explaining that delivery had been delayed because he had said that the paper must not be doubled and Cowper had patiently waited for a friend who would transport the sheet without folding it.

Patty's album already contained notable manuscripts which Hannah had obtained for her in London. Lord Bathurst contributed two letters from Voltaire; Bishop Lowth, when Bishop of London, had given "a handsome piece of writing" in exchange for a copy of an unpublished poem of Hannah's ("for I am too much of a Bristol woman to give something for nothing," declared Hannah) and someone had produced a piece of laurel gathered from Virgil's tomb. Dr. Johnson had promised to write a contribution, but whether or not he did is not known.

As the memory of the visit faded, Mr. Newton's letters grew less interesting. They become very serious and so general in tone that they sound toward the end of the correspondence like parts of sermons. Once he gave a characteristic picture of himself: "The old man of seventy-six is still favored with perfect health, and can still preach as loud, as long, and as often as formerly. . . . Oh how great a debtor to grace is the poor African blasphemer and profligate."

During the later half of her life Hannah's taste for bishops grew upon her. In her early London days she had rather scorned the princes of the Church. She had once written home about a Garrick dinner, mentioning favorite guests by name and lumping the others under the casual phrase, "The rest were chiefly old doctors of divinity." Old doctors of divinity were among her dearest friends not many years later, as well they might be, for they were amiable, intellectual, delightful gentlemen. They were godly men of the world.

One friend of long standing was George Horne, successively President of Magdalen College, Dean of Canterbury, and Bishop of Norwich, who was considered more socially gifted than learned in spite of his spending twenty years on a commentary on the Psalms. One of his pleasing innovations while he was President of Magdalen was to preach on St. John the Baptist's Day from the stone pulpit in the Quadrangle, which was decorated with green boughs in memory of the preaching in the wilderness. For his little girl Hannah wrote *An Heroic Epistle, To Miss Sally Horne,—Aged Three Years*, inscribing the jingle on the blank pages of *Mother Bunch's Tales*, showing the superiority of these tales to other histories. Bishop Horne on his part made a hit with some verses recording Hannah's good temper when Bamber Gascoigne, Esq., clumsily overturned a cruet of vinegar on her beautiful gauze apron as she and Mrs. Garrick were eating oysters at an oyster club with some learned gentlemen, names not given.

It was at the home of Dr. Jonathan Shipley, Bishop of St.

Asaph, that Hannah spoke sharply to Boswell, "disordered with wine." Bishop Shipley was, or had been, more radical than most of Hannah's associates, for he was a friend of Benjamin Franklin and had sided with the American colonies against the King of England. Dr. Shute Barrington, another friend, bishop successively of Llandaff, Salisbury, and Durham, living to be ninety-one years old, was a pleasant man, conservative, and pious. He made unfortunate improvements to Durham Cathedral, but he believed in the education of the poor and gave away most of his fortune in charity. Hannah, who seldom cared for wives, liked Mrs. Barrington as well as she did the bishop and visited them every spring after her yearly stay with Mrs. Garrick.

The prelates of Gloucester and Bristol and Bath and Wells were helpful to her in her later period when she was establishing Sunday Schools and by the time she was an old lady she could have toured England staying only at bishops' palaces, a very welcome guest.

Hannah knew the Middletons from her early days in London, when they were Captain and Mrs., through the years when the captain became Sir Charles, a Member of Parliament, a Rear Admiral, a Vice Admiral, and finally Baron Barham of Barham Court. The intimacy increased when Hannah's thoughts turned strongly to humanitarian problems. Lady Middleton, the daughter of James, Lord Gambier, and aunt of Admiral James Gambier, was a charming woman with serious interests and a decided talent for painting. Her close friend Elizabeth Bouverie [3] lived with her in London during the winters; summers the Middletons moved with her to her beautiful estate, Barham Court, Teston,

Kent. Mrs. Bouverie was unmarried, "Mrs." being a courtesy title. Both ladies were of retiring disposition, but they entertained noted persons at Barham Court. When Mrs. Bouverie died, Mrs. Middleton having predeceased her, she left Barham Court to Sir Charles. To Hannah she left an annuity of one hundred pounds a year.

The Middleton family was drawn into the movement for the abolition of slavery through the rector of Teston, Rev. James Ramsey, a former navy chaplain. William Wilberforce, encouraged by Pitt, brought before Parliament in 1788, '92, and '96 bills prohibiting the slave trade, but it was not abolished until 1807. In 1833 slavery in British dominions was made illegal. During these years of struggle, abolitionists, including Wilberforce and Pitt himself, met at Barham Court to develop their plans. Hannah was invited at the same time. Her long poem *The Slave Trade* was highly praised as a contribution to this cause, which she had had at heart ever since the day young Zachary Macaulay bade the sisters goodbye as he left for Sierra Leone.

Usually accompanied by Patty, Hannah made an annual round of visits which was a calendar of her chief interests during the latter half of her life. She commenced with a long stay at Mrs. Garrick's London and Hampton homes. Then followed brief visits to Bishop Porteus at Fulham Palace, Lambeth; Bishop Barrington at Mungewell, near Oxford; Mrs. Boscawen at St. Clair, Kent; and occasionally Mrs. Boyle Walsingham at Thames Ditton and Lady Spencer at St. Albans, the latter two being among Mrs. Garrick's particular friends. On her way home she broke her journey at Mrs. Elizabeth Montagu's estate, Sandleford Priory, near Newbury; and she was likely to spend a few days with the

Dowager Duchess of Beaufort at Stoke Gifford, or her daughter the Duchess of Beaufort at Badminton, or the Bathurst family at Cirencester. The last three, while not active in humanitarian work, were generous in contributions to work which engaged Hannah's sympathies, besides being family friends of long standing.

CHAPTER XVI

The Sunday School Movement

THE STRONGEST of the factors which determined the serious tone of Hannah's later life was the Evangelical Movement. She came under the influence of that ardent, humanitarian fellowship through her association with the group commonly known as the Clapham Party or the Clapham Sect, a circle of men who took their name from the circumstance that the leaders were neighbors in Clapham, a suburb of London.

The Evangelical Movement was an effort to rouse the Church of England from the somewhat lethargic state into which it had fallen. A sort of spiritual coma had followed the ferocity of the earlier struggle between Catholics and Protestants and the fury of the Puritan revolution. The Church was recovering from the weariness of past violence. This apathy was sharply broken by the inspired preaching of Whitefield and John and Charles Wesley, who roused the lower classes to a disconcerting spiritual activity. The governing class in general hated a religious zeal which might easily interfere with their comfort, but the younger clergy in the church woke up and laymen took fire from them. Reforms began in the church which were most disturbing to people who disliked change.

The Clapham Sect were leaders in this effort to turn the flood of religious enthusiasm into the rather stagnant channels of the established church. They were determined to enliven the learning, dignity, respectability, and formality of the Church with a subdued and guided form of Wesley's ecstasy. They were not themselves preachers, but a group of business and professional men who carried on a decorous crusade in the midst of family and neighborhood life, a sort of pruned and quieted Methodism within the Church of England.

The group gathered for its conferences at Battlesea Rise, the large and impressive home of Henry Thornton, facing Clapham Common. William Wilberforce, a kinsman, lived with him up to the time of his marriage and afterward lived in a house which Thornton built for him next door. The faces of the two men show a similarity, though no actual likeness. Both have good foreheads, high cheekbones, sensitive mouths, steady, friendly eyes, and the expression of humorous, kindly understanding. There was this difference between them: Wilberforce was a fascinating conversationalist with a flexible, musical voice, while Thornton was a man of few words. Wilberforce could hold his audience in the House of Commons for hours, while Thornton's popularity was enhanced by the brevity of his parliamentary speeches. Thornton, who had great wealth and uncommon generosity, was the financial backbone of the Clapham Sect, while Wilberforce was its inspiration. Wilberforce's widowed sister married a member of the group, James Stephen, also a member of Parliament, and lived close by. Another important member of the colony was Lord Teignmouth who chose to live there after his return from being Governor General of India. Zachary

Macaulay and his brother-in-law Thomas Babington might be designated as members-at-large of the group for, although they did not live near the others, they were closely associated in the activities. John Newton was also especially sympathetic.

It was natural enough that Hannah should become closely associated with these men. The More sisters had known Zachary Macaulay and his wife intimately from the days of the Bristol boarding school. William Wilberforce was a visitor in their Bath home, at Cowslip Green, and at Barley Wood. Hannah made a trip up the Wye River with Miss Wilberforce, his sister, and corresponded with her thereafter. She knew the group also through John Newton. After she became acquainted with the Thornton family there was visiting back and forth between Clapham Common and Cowslip Green. With Lord Teignmouth she had friendly relations and could count on his assistance in her philanthropies. These were the members of the party with whom she became most intimately associated and she had a visiting acquaintance with some of the others. Thackeray, in *The Newcomes*, draws a depressing picture of the spiritual severity contrasted with the physical comforts of wealth in these homes around Clapham Common, but he may have overemphasized their seriousness. Certainly Hannah enjoyed the company of these idealists and she kept her lively social sense in spite of being deeply religious.

It would be difficult to exaggerate Wilberforce's influence on Hannah's life. He liberalized her views and gave her a worthy outlet for her splendid zeal. They were attracted to each other from the day they met in Bath in 1786, in spite of a difference of fifteen years in their ages, and they continued to be friends until their deaths which occurred within a few weeks of each other forty-seven years later. When H. W. Pickersgill painted Hannah's portrait in duplicate for two of her admirers, Lowell Gwatkin and Sir Thomas Acland, he showed a bright-eyed, white-haired old lady, who sat very straight, and had just finished writing a letter. If you look closely at the superscription on the envelope you can decipher a faint "Wilberforce"—although the portrait was paid for by another man! There was a bit of the coquette in our lady even when she was seventy-six and a saint.

A visit by Wilberforce at Cowslip Green was a treat to the entire More family and one of his visits may be said to have been an event of national importance, for the Somerset Sunday Schools resulted from it. Wilberforce was at this time around thirty, with charm, ability, and religious zeal. Mrs. Elizabeth Montagu called him "The Red Cross Knight," after Spenser's Knight of Holiness. If, as is said, Hannah drew Candidus, in her *Christian Morals*, from Wilberforce, she failed miserably, for Candidus was a prig, while Wilberforce's righteousness was an engaging quality and his passion for service was a part of his amiability. He was undersized and always delicate in health but the amount of work he accomplished was more than most persons achieve with health and vigor.

The visit to Cowslip Green with his sister was preliminary to a trip through Monmouthshire and down the river Wye and Hannah was to accompany them. Patty kept urging him to visit the marvelous, wild, and impressive Cheddar cliffs and caverns ten miles to the south of Wrington. Toward the end of his visit he went, alone. Here is Patty's account of the impression made upon him by the country:

> I was in the parlour when he returned [writes Patty in *Mendip Annals*]. With the eagerness of vanity (having recommended the pleasure) I inquired how he liked the cliffs. He replied they were very fine, but the poverty and distress of the people was dreadful. This was all that passed. He retired to his apartment and dismissed even his reader. I said to his sister [Miss Wilberforce] and mine [Hannah] I feared Mr. W. was not well. The cold chicken and wine put into the carriage for his dinner were returned untouched. Mr. W. appeared at supper, seemingly refreshed with a higher feast than we had set before him. The servant, at his request, was dismissed, when immediately he began, "Miss Hannah More, something must be done for Cheddar." He then proceeded to a particular account of his day—of the inquiries he had made respecting the poor. There was no resident minister, no manufactory, nor did there appear any dawn of comfort, either temporal or spiritual. The method or possibility of assisting them was discussed until a late hour. It was at length decided in a few words by Mr. W.'s exclaiming, "If *you* will be at the trouble, *I* will be at the expense."

No immediate plan seems to have been adopted. Mr. Wilberforce, his sister, and Hannah left in a day or two for the trip on the Wye River. No one can doubt that discussions of methods and means were carried on during the delightful tour. The decision was—a Sunday School in Cheddar.

The credit of inaugurating the Sunday School movement belongs to Robert Raikes of Gloucester, for although a few unsuccessful attempts had been made by others, he was the first with sufficient understanding, persistence, and tact to work out a method. Mr. Raikes owned a printing press and the *Glouceester Journal* and was kind, honest, and well-to-do. His portrait shows a man of full habit, with a plump, high-colored face, a generous mouth, and a double chin. He was a man with imagination and directness. Walking down St.

Catherine Street in Gloucester one Sunday morning, he was appalled at the roughness and the filth of the factory children playing in the street. It seemed to him that someone ought to teach them to read and write and clean themselves and he stopped at a nearby house and began making inquiries about schoolrooms and teachers.

When his first school opened, there was no problem about persuading children to attend. They came rushing, stayed long hours, attended services, and some carried their books to the factories to study in odd minutes. They even washed their faces and combed their hair to get in.

These religious reading, writing, and good conduct schools spread like wildfire through England, Scotland, and Wales. In ten years time thousands and thousands who would otherwise have grown up illiterate learned to read their Bibles and from that book passed to other books and to newspapers. These schools raised the general culture of the English people and also affected the politics of the nation, for though the leaders designed the instruction to teach the working class to be obedient to their betters, it is not clear that this was the result. Children who could read the Bible could later read Tom Paine and Wilkes, and many did.

CHAPTER XVII

The Cheddar Sunday School

THE CHEDDAR school was the first one established by the Mores. Here techniques were worked out, innovations tested, and routines established. There was never any serious trouble in connection with this school; it was the most fully successful of all the More Sunday Schools and the dearest to the hearts of its founders. Although the other schools differed among themselves according to environment and circumstances, a description of this school pretty well describes them all.

The village of Cheddar was pleasantly situated under the ridge of the Mendip Hills, along the edge of a large green on which fed the cows belonging to the villagers.[1] Some two hundred houses were scattered along three or four irregular streets, near the church. It had a Market Cross but no market.[2] The inhabitants were engaged in farming, cheese-making, spinning, and knitting. The poverty was extreme and the people were wild and lawless, some of them actually living in caves and selling roots and stalactites to tourists for their living.[3]

The vicarage was in the gift of the Dean of Wells and the incumbent lived at Oxford where he was connected with the university. There had been no resident curate for forty years; instead a galloping curate rode over from Wells on Sundays. Although the farmers had a right to a resident curate, they did not press their claim for fear their tithes would be raised. A large legacy had been left for the relief of the poor in Cheddar, but it had been in Chancery for thirty-seven years.

The state of this parish is an illustration of the abuses too common at that time. Those clergy of the established church who were conscientious preachers and parish workers stand out against a too large number of fox-hunting, hard-drinking divines. Some of the clergymen were scholars who neglected their parishioners to shut themselves up in their studies, while others preferred to live in London and leave their duties to curates. Salaries of clergy were shockingly small, and from this arose the custom of giving one man several parishes, often widely separated. An example of the extent to which this was sometimes carried was the case of Dr. Watson, who when Bishop of Llandaff (in South Wales) held also two livings in Shropshire, two in Leicestershire, and three in Huntingdonshire.

The circumstances under which the Cheddar school was started are recorded at length both in Hannah's letters and in Patty's journal, published long after her death under the title of *Mendip Annals*. When the sisters went to look the ground over, toward the end of September, 1789, their first interview heartened them to endure future discouragements. They stopped at the Market Cross to talk with a Quaker rabbit-catcher, who was shabby and serious; a tear rolling down his cheek convinced the ladies there was grace in his heart. "You will have much difficulty," he told them, "but let not the enemy tempt you to go back; and God will bless the work."[4]

Learning from the rabbit-catcher that they must win the approval of a rich farmer designated as Mr. C., who lived ten miles away, the two ladies made the journey, evidently on horseback, across the ploughed fields and along almost impassable roads. They arrived "at the den of this monster, in a country as savage as himself, near Bridgewater," when he was sitting down to dinner. From him they heard for the first time a point of view which was to grow familiar to them in many neighborhoods.

The idea of schooling for the poor was distasteful to the prosperous farmer. He assured the ladies that religion would be the ruin of agriculture; that it was a dangerous thing and had produced much mischief since it was introduced into Glastonbury. They put the matter in a pleasanter light by mentioning that they were not soliciting subscriptions.

Hannah and Patty made eleven more visits in the neighborhood, realizing that the approval of "these rich savages" must be secured. "Miss Wilberforce would have been shocked," Hannah wrote Wilberforce, "had she seen the petty tyrants whose insolence I stroked and tamed, the ugly children I praised, the pointers and spaniels I caressed, the cider I commended, and the wine I swallowed." She told the farmers that a Sunday School would keep the poor from robbing orchards, poaching, and like misdemeanors, and might even lower the poor rates. This was definite and some of the farmers promised that they would "discharge or favor the poor in proportion as they were attentive or negligent in sending their children."[5]

The sisters spent the first night of their canvassing at an uncomfortable inn at the Market Cross and started out again the next morning. They now visited, not the farmers, but the laborers' families from which they would draw their pupils. They went about their work methodically, learning in advance about the character, employment, wages, and members of each family. As much opposition was shown by the persons whom the school was to benefit as had been displayed by their employers. The rumor spread that the teachers would have the right to sell the children across the seas after seven years' attendance. The mothers thought the children should be paid for attending. They were all willing to send the babies to get them out from under foot, but they wanted the older girls at home to help with the housework.

The Mores persevered. They found a house that after some repairing was suitable for the schoolmistress, and an ox barn which with new flooring, roof, and windows made a schoolroom. They engaged a schoolmistress. They gathered in some pupils and the Cheddar school was formally opened on Sunday, October twenty-fifth, 1789.

Even after children had been induced to come to school, the problem remained how to keep them coming. In addition to exerting pressure on employers to use influence, and themselves cajoling and scolding the mothers, the Mores relied on a system of small rewards. A penny was given to each child who came in time for morning prayer for four successive Sundays. Once in six or eight weeks gingerbread treat was provided. Bibles, prayerbooks, and tracts were distributed according to merit once a year. Clothing was given out once a year, each boy in good standing getting a hat, a shirt, and a pair of shoes and each great girl receiving a calico apron or a cap. A small girl had a cap and a tippet of calico. So exceedingly poor were these people that the prizes were worth striving for.

The Mores made the Sunday School sessions as entertaining as might be in those times. When the children were tired they stood up and sang. The first effort was to teach the children to read and to learn Scripture by heart. A penny a chapter was paid for proficiency in reciting such sections as the ninth chapter of Isaiah, the Beatitudes, and some of the Psalms. The early chapters of Genesis were read again and again to fix in infant minds the fall of man. The parables were in favor as a groundwork in teaching.

Hannah wrote some of her own textbooks. Her *Questions and Answers for the Mendip Schools* was a tiny volume one inch square.[6] Some of her tracts were also used in teaching. Copies of the Church Catechism were framed and hung on the walls. The main reliance was placed on the Bible, the New Testament, the Psalter, the Book of Common Prayer, and spelling books.

The eagerness with which the children learned was notable. Five weeks after the Cheddar school opened, thirty pupils said their catechism correctly and forty could sing three psalms. Several great girls could read a little. The children were taught cleanliness, decency, and honesty as a part of religion, and children who had never known school discipline endured the long sessions and the church services which were a part of the curriculum. All over England it was the same; rowdy, hard-boiled youngsters came week after week to learn to read, although the Bible is a far from easy primer.

The yearly cost of a Sunday School was figured as:

	£
House-rent	7
Repairs, whitewashing, benches	2
Salary, headmistress	30
Under teachers	10
Bibles, prayers and other books	8
Caps and tippets, 100 girls, etc.	15
Shirts, 20 young men	5
Club subscriptions and expenses	6
Incidental charities	6
Total	£89

On Sunday nights a meeting was held for the parents at which a printed sermon was read, a printed prayer read, and a printed psalm sung. Hannah was apologetic at having music, saying that, though she herself did not delight in music, she had observed that singing was a help to devotion in others. Tuesday nights one of the instructors expounded the Scriptures; that is, he or she read a chapter and explained the hard words; and Wednesday night a class of adults met. No extemporaneous sermons or prayers were allowed, for that raised an angry cry of Methodism and meant broken windows and general disorder on the part of the rougher element of the neighborhood.

Securing efficient teachers was difficult. A general impression prevailed among families with problematic relatives that a schoolroom was a good spot to place a reduced gentlewoman or a bad-tempered aunt, but Hannah's pedagogical background gave her strength to refuse unsuitable applicants. She knew that if the instructor was not zealous the work would be neglected, while if she was too energetic, conservative neighbors were made uneasy. The zeal of a reformer, tempered by experience, and applied with tact, was necessary to carry on the work in the face of apathy and suspicion. Hannah always tried to find an intelligent, religious, industrious woman, preferably with a husband having the same qualities. The wife taught the girls and women, while the man taught the boys.

The salary of the Cheddar headmistress, Mrs. Baber, and her twenty-five year old daughter Betsy who assisted her in teaching, was thirty pounds a year, free rent of house and garden—which came to seven guineas a year—coal, and candles. Under-teachers received ten pounds a year. These salaries were fair according to the standards of the time.

The success of the Cheddar school must be attributed partly to Mrs. Baber, who was a woman of fine character and unusual efficiency. She was a widow whose profligate son and drunken husband had, according to Patty, been the means of subduing an originally proud spirit and awakening a sense of seriousness. Both Hannah and Patty admired and loved her. Her death, after six years, was a grief and a misfortune. Her funeral was characterized by the indulgence in loud grief which was good form at that time. The school children were led two by two, after the funeral service in the church, to the graveyard, in black, if they had black, with a black ribbon at least. First went the coffin, next Mr. Boake the curate, then Betsy, the daughter, and other chief mourners, followed by the gentry and two hundred children. A sermon had already been preached in the church in which Mrs. Baber's deathbed was described in detail and her last words dwelt upon. At the grave the children sang a hymn, nosegays were flung upon the coffin and everyone sobbed. "The undertaker from Bristol wept like a child, and confessed, that without emolument, it was worth going a hundred miles to see such a sight," Patty wrote Hannah, who was in London.

Patty took the children into the schoolroom and made a speech. "I said a great deal to them as well as I could, and wrung their little hearts; for I knew but too well that the world and young blood would make an excellent sponge to wipe out, full soon, the awful business of that day. . . . Excellent, laborious Betsy had hitherto all her life been an indefatigable slave. She will now suddenly be called into great power, and Satan, I presume, will be more active about her than ever; and therefore the truest tenderness will be, to keep a tight rein ourselves, and let her out gradually, as we have not that exalted opinion of human nature which some gentlemen and ladies have." [7]

Betsy was now in her early thirties and her thoughts turned to marriage. In spite of Patty's tight rein and against the advice of her friends, she engaged herself to one of the teachers, a serious young man considered not her equal. According to the custom of the time a female teacher, regardless of her efficiency, was discharged when she married or even upon her betrothal. Betsy tried to hold on to her position by concealing her attachment. This gave rise to gossip and even scandal and she was dismissed. Another teacher was found and the school continued successful.

The great event of the school year in the Mores' schools was the Feast, held out-of-doors in one of the lovely spots of the Mendip Hills. Patty was a fine organizer and the success of the Feasts was due to her good management. The distant children were carried from their schools to the meeting place in carts decorated with greenery, forming a procession.

Other wagons contained servants, and food: great roasts of beef, huge plum puddings, bread, hundreds of cakes, and plenty of cider.

Festivities began with a procession. The Boy of Best Character led, waving a flag. Next came Hannah and Patty. Then the teachers. Then the children two by two. The children sat on the grass. A clergyman said grace, and after the meal said grace again. The entertainment was the examination of children in repeating chapters of the Bible. After the excitement was over, all sang "God Save the King" and the children walked off the field, singing, into the distance until they could be heard no more.

The Bath Chronicle for Thursday, August twenty-second, 1793, gives an account of one of these feasts:

> Friday last an entertainment was given on Mendip-Hills by the Miss Mores to near one thousand children, collected from the different Sunday Schools in nine neighbouring parishes. The fineness of the day attracted an immense number of spectators; not less than ten thousand persons being present, consisting of most of the respectable families in the vicinity, and a great number of ladies and gentlemen from this city and other parts of the country. The spot was advantageously selected—the summit of a lofty hill, on which formerly had been erected a castle, and round which might be distinctly traced the limits of an extensive Roman fortification. In the area of this venerable spot it was that the children from the different neighbouring parishes first assembled, when they moved in a regular procession to another part of the hill, prepared for the company and themselves to dine on; and a more captivating sight cannot be conceived than of this infant cavalcade marching from the camp to the place we have been describing. They were preceded by a numerous band of rustick musicians, who played in the most animating manner, the favourite song of "God Save the King," till they arrived at a laurel arch, which formed the grand entrance into the circle, when the children (conducted by their

respective teachers) burst into songs of praise to their Maker, and paraded round the fence, singing hymns with that fervent and artless simplicity which touched the heart and roused the tear of sensibility in the eyes of all present. The children seated themselves in circular divisions on the grass, and were helped by the company present to their bread, and their beef and their pudding, and their cyder. When the repast was over, the children arose, and sang hymns in their respective divisions till they were again summoned to attend the band and company in the loyal song of "God Save the King," when they were joined by the multitude in one grand chorus, marching at the same time from whence they had first proceded; and after a sentiment from a respectable neighbouring clergyman, complimentary to the founders of the institution (which was received with the most enthusiastick applause) they departed in separate divisions to their respective homes, highly gratified at the liberality of their entertainment.

CHAPTER XVIII

Sunday School Extension Work

THE SUNDAY SCHOOL movement included more than religious instruction and training in personal cleanliness and decent behavior. A School of Industry was frequently associated with a Bible School, and in it girls were taught spinning, weaving, knitting, sewing, cooking and other household techniques needed in one's own home or in domestic service.

A Cheddar School of Industry with a spinning mistress was opened the Monday following the launching of the Sunday School. Hannah expected this project to pay its own expenses, for stocking-makers in Uxbridge promised to take the output of yarn, but little learners were not as quick at spinning as at reading and memorizing psalms and the stocking-makers could not use their rough product. Much material was wasted by beginners and the children would not work steadily at their tasks. Hannah fell back on domestic service, where skilled work, though desirable, was not absolutely necessary. The girls were taught housework in the school and sent on certain days to the houses of well-to-do families who had sober servants, to help the housekeeper, the cook, the parlor maid, or the laundress as apprentices, to practice by helping the servants. After a time servants

trained in the Cheddar school were in demand. There is no record of craft training for boys; perhaps the regular apprentice system took care of that.

Writing was taught only in special cases to especially gifted children. When a boy showed unusual ability in figuring, he was sent to a master for instruction.

At Cheddar, at Shipham and Rowberrow, and perhaps in some of the other localities, Hannah and Patty established women's clubs patterned on men's friendly societies, those mutual benefit organizations which were increasing in Somerset. As many as one hundred and fifty women belonged to some of the women's clubs, each paying in three halfpence a week. Those who could not afford this were privately helped with their subscriptions. When a club was successful, the gentry sometimes contributed to the fund. The lady of the manor in Cheddar left a legacy to that club and about ten years after the club was started the treasury had a capital of between two and three hundred pounds.

A sick woman drew three shillings and sixpence a week. Seven shillings was the amount for a lying-in. A guinea was expended for a funeral, after the women of Shipham and Rowberrow had fought fiercely for the concession, against Patty's indignation. Patty declared: "those wretches, half naked, and I believe some of them half starved, had a long contention, with as much fury as they dared exhibit before us, declaring that they would rather relinquish the comforts and blessings of assistance at their lying-ins, to enrich the stock and procure a handsome funeral. . . . 'What did a woman work for, but in hopes she should be put out of the world in a tidy way?'" The lying-in stipend was not as generous as that calculated by the kindly Anglican clergyman in Berks, David Davies, who made weekly visits to his parishioners computing a budget for them. He counted a lying-in as a biennial family expense and his budget ran: "Child's linens 3 or 4 shillings; Midwife, 5 shillings; Midwife's gin or brandy, 2 shillings; Nurse, 5 shillings; Brewed malt and hops to minister for churching, 1 shilling." [1]

The annual club day was to the women what the Mendip Feast was to their youngsters. After divine service and a sermon, the club women, with husbands, parents, and children, adjourned to the decorated schoolroom. The gentry came to sit on the platform, tea and cake were served, and an account of the year's club doings was read. Any girl about to be married was given—provided she produced a written certificate of good character from her minister—a marriage portion consisting of a pair of white worsted stockings of the Mores' own knitting, five shillings, and a Bible.

Last on the program of the meeting was the annual Charge delivered by Patty or Hannah, after the fashion of a bishop exhorting his clergy. The club members endured an extraordinary amount of scolding. Girls were warned that dancing led to dishonor. Children were told that if they came to Sunday School for tarts and clothing instead of from a sense of duty, the One who knows the secrets of all hearts would remember it on their deathbeds. Here are typical extracts from *Mendip Annals:*

> Your ministers and some few friends here can recollect, if *you* have forgot, the melancholy, ragged, impudent, lying set of children who first entered these doors; can recollect how long it was before you had patience to have your children served—before you had patience to have them cleaned and clothed—and above all before you had *any* patience to have them trained for heaven.

There are still too many of you who have not yet discovered that a prating tongue commonly slanders an innocent neighbor. . . . We understand that the intolerable gossip and idle slander at the paper mill and bakehouse, by a few idle women, are sufficient to set a whole village together by the ears. I wish the next time a woman carries a loaf to be baked, she would think what a mercy it is to have a *loaf* in these times. . . .

I now turn to the club. . . . I daresay there is no woman here but will forgive my gently hinting to her, that her own three-halfpence a-week would make but a poor figure in a fit of illness, if it was not for the kind contributions of so many good friends, who condescend to make part of the company with you every year, and to whom, I trust, every member feels very much obliged for *both* favors.[2]

The women had to swallow all of this, along with their tea and cakes, in the presence of their families, their neighbors, and the gentry on the platform, but the women were not always so docile as their benefactors thought they should be, having their own ideas and sometimes compelling the ladies to give in to them.

Hannah believed in the responsibility of the family in the Great House for the welfare of the poor of the parish as firmly as she believed in the duty of the employees to be submissive, and she scolded the gentry for neglect as vigorously as she got after their dependents. The lord of the manor, the squire, or the clergyman was the magistrate, and the orderliness of alehouses, the honesty of storekeepers, and the general tone of the village depended largely upon him. Hannah wrote Mrs. Garrick on December eleventh, 1790, that she had been going to all the justices in the country to obtain redress for the poor in the matter of underweight loaves of bread. In the Mores' country neighborhood, purchasers were receiving two pounds less bread for a shilling than in Bristol, Bath, and other towns. Hannah righted this injustice in forty Somerset parishes.

Landowners came in for a goodly share of Hannah's attention. She begged them to allow their workmen to plant a few greens in odd corners of the fields; she told them that they should sell some of their corn to the laborers at a low price, instead of sending it all to the cities; she made a plan for well-to-do folks to buy rice in large quantities at wholesale price and resell it in small quantities without profit. The gentry were requested to buy the prime pieces of meat since they could afford to pay for them, and to leave the coarse cheap joints and soup bones for those who had little money.

This was a period of gross eating among many of the rich and of food shortage among the poor. A squire's family usually had a late, hearty breakfast, a heartier dinner during the afternoon, and a supper before bedtime. A proper dinner displayed mutton, beef, game, fowl, and fish, all on the table at once. A table "groaned" and wine "flowed." Family portraits show gentlemen bursting with plumpness. Oddly enough, the women were likely to be thin, but that is probably because they were painted in their youthful beauty while their husbands were depicted when they were older and famous or rich. Hannah herself seems to have been slender as a young woman, plumper in middle age and in old age a mere wisp of a woman, although her voluminous dresses may deceive us.

Though Bristol was famous for its good eating, Somerset laborers were as badly off there as anywhere. They lived on bread, potatoes, and a few green vegetables raised where they could tuck them into the ground. A piece of meat for father was hard to come by. To teach the wives to make the most of scanty supplies Hannah wrote a cookbook called *The Cottage Cook*. She may have taken the idea from Dr. Stonehouse's book, *Receipts for Making Cheap and Wholesome Food*, published some fifteen years previous. She explained the advantages of cooperative arrangements, gave advice on buying, and furnished recipes for making coarse food palatable. Diet should be varied, she told the housewives. A laborer got six to eight shillings a week. If he was a careful man he brought it all home. Saturday night after market, he could buy meat to the best advantage. If he laid out a shilling or two on a bit of coarse beef or a hog's head, his wife could throw a couple of pounds of it into the pot with two or three handfuls of dried peas and pepper. She could add a cabbage or a turnip or any garden vegetable that was available and stew it for two or three hours. The man should have the meat, because he needed meat, and the children would have thick soup.

Another recipe was thin, sliced raw potatoes baked with a little water in a deep pot with onion and pepper for seasoning. A bone or a strip of salt pork or a few pickled herring were added and the pot covered closely. This could be cooked slowly over the fire or baked in the oven. The children got the potatoes with dish gravy. Rice pudding was made of a half pound of rice, two quarts of skimmed milk, two ounces of brown sugar, and a bit of allspice. It would not cost above sevenpence and was good cold, too.

The Mores taught the housewives to brew their own beer as a substitute for gin and tea. The brewing would also provide them with yeast for breadmaking. If wheat flour was dear, bread could be made of half wheat and half potato flour. Cutting bread hot from the oven was wasteful; day-old bread was economical.

Hannah taught the villagers how to run community schemes, like building a village oven for baking bread and puddings. The saving of fuel was important, now that heaths were being enclosed and turned into farm land, making turfs and faggots hard to come by. Such an oven was fired three times a week and a halfpenny was the fee for baking a great loaf or a rice and milk pudding. She dinned it into the villagers' ears that a store which sold on credit against next season's wages must needs charge more than one which sold for cash and the goods were likely to be inferior. If the big dairy farm would not bother to sell milk by the pennyworth, some person must be persuaded to buy a cow and make a business of small sales, for babies must have milk and babies' fathers must have rice and milk puddings. If a man had only a small garden, she pointed out, it was better to plant six pennyworth of parsnip seed instead of potatoes. This crop would furnish more food than potatoes and parsnips are good the second day warmed up with a little rasher of bacon to flavor them.

Neglected old folks in almshouses came in for a share of attention. Morning and evening prayers were instituted in poorhouses at Wrington, Rowberrow, Churchill, and Winscombe. Shipham could not have such services because not one of the inmates could read. Those inmates who attended regularly received a Christmas treat of beef, peas, and a shilling. One feels sure the Mores did not limit their attention to spiritual needs, but concerned themselves also with food, clothing, and beds.

It is true that Hannah inquired into very personal matters,

but she gave advice based on experience which her beneficiaries lacked, and she incited them to efforts they would not by themselves have undertaken. She frequently lamented that she spent more time working for God than in meditating upon Him, but at no time does she show herself in a more pleasing light than when she thus helps the poor in their distress, placing her talents, her knowledge, her hands, and her pocketbook at their disposal.

CHAPTER XIX

Mining Village Schools

During the winter season many of the Somerset roads were impassable. The schools had to proceed on their own momentum without More supervision, while Hannah spent months with Mrs. Garrick and Patty sometimes joined her for a round of visits among their friends. During the summer the sisters were accustomed to visit as many as three schools a Sunday, making a circuit of from ten to thirty miles. They often traveled on horseback for the roads were terrible; some of them being only lanes, narrow, stony, deep with ruts, or soupy in mire. When a chaise met a van it was sometimes necessary to lift the lighter vehicle over a hedge to make room for the van to pass. The country was picturesque but difficult. Hannah and Patty, riding sidesaddle with sweeping skirts, doubtless attended by a servant, pushed ahead through rain and heat, up and down steep hills in one neighborhood, in another through swampy fens or over ploughed fields where there was no road at all. Once they had to abandon a chaise and proceed on pillions behind men on horseback.

They promoted, started and administered schools at Axbridge, Barnwell, Barley Wood, Belmont, Blagdon, Cheddar, Congresbury, Cowslip Green, Flax Bourton, Nailsea, Rowberrow, and Shipham, Wedmore, Weston, Winscombe, and Yatton. All this in ten years. Concerning some of the schools we know nothing save that they existed. The schools were all formed on the Cheddar model, but differed among themselves according to their environments and the amount of interest shown by the gentry and the clergy of the locality.

The mining villages of Shipham, Rowberrow, and Nailsea were a variation from the farming districts. The union school which the Mores started to serve both Shipman and Rowberrow was preliminary to the adventure of Nailsea. The rector of Shipham had claimed tithes for fifty years, for forty of which he had not preached a sermon nor catechised a child, but his curate, Mr. James Jones, was a different type, and on the rector's death Hannah was able to have him appointed rector. When Mr. Jones died at the age of eighty-six, he had a record of having missed service only four times in sixty-one years. The school could hardly help going well under the influence of a man like that. The first teachers were especially satisfactory. They were half-sisters, two dairymaids with deeply religious natures, one of whom had already started a Sunday School on her own initiative in another part of the county. They were glad enough to leave dairy work for teaching and the school was progressing well under them when they engaged themselves to marry two young men of the hamlet. The Mores regretfully but promptly discharged them.

Encouraged by the success of the Cheddar and Shipham-Rowberrow schools, the Mores explored the Nailsea situation. Nailsea was singularly placed on the skirts of a large moor. A part of it was in the midst of a thicket and had the appearance of a neglected forest of timber trees, holly and briar.

Four coal pits in the parish produced excellent fuel which burned into a fine white ash.[1]

The school at this village when first started drew only children of the poorer farmers and the colliers. When the classes were in good running order the Mores advanced upon the glassmakers' families, their object from the beginning. Let Martha tell the story of that first visit:

> We now made our appearance, for the first time, among the glass-house people, and entered nineteen houses in a row (little hovels), containing in all near two hundred people. Whatever we had seen before was of a different nature, and, though we had encountered savages, hard-hearted farmers, little cold country gentry, a supercilious and ignorant corporation, yet this was still new, and unlike all other things—not only differing from all we had seen, but greatly transcending all we had imagined. Both sexes and all ages herding together; voluptuous beyond belief. The work of a glass-house is an irregular thing, uncertain whether by day or by night; not only infringing on man's rest, but constantly intruding upon the privileges of the Sabbath. The wages high, the eating and drinking luxurious—the body scarcely covered, but fed with dainties of a shameful description. The high buildings of the glass-houses ranged before the doors of these cottages—the great furnaces roaring—the sweating, eating, drinking of these half-dressed, black-looking beings, gave it a most infernal and horrible appearance. One, if not two joints of the finest meat were roasting in these little hot kitchens, pots of ale standing about, and plenty of early, delicate vegetables. We had a gentleman with us who, being rather personally fearful, left us to pursue our own devices, which we did by entering and haranguing every separate family. We were in our usual luck respecting personal civility, which we received even from the worst of these creatures, some welcoming us to "Botany Bay" others to "Little Hell," as they themselves lovingly called it.[2]

With their usual tact—which explains much of their success—the Mores did not mention religion but talked about training for domestic service, getting top places and going out into the world. "Religion here," comments Martha, "would have been a very indiscreet, and, I fear, unsuccessful beginning." They left with the promise of twenty-seven children for their school.

These wild and independent people took to the idea of a school from the first. Martha describes a second visit:

> From the cottages, which exhibited the usual scene of filth, feasting and great ignorance, we proceeded to enter the very glass-houses, amidst black Cyclopean figures, and flaming, horrible fires. However, we were again agreeably surprised as well as affected, for every one of these dismal looking beings laid down their tools, and immediately surrounded us, speaking in the civilest terms, calling all the great boys out of their black holes, and using really persuasive language to them to induce them to listen to us and do what we wished.[3]

The glassmakers, the men who worked in the coal pits, and probably some of the farmers were called "Nailsea Headsmen," or, less respectfully, "Nailsea Savages." Rough they might be, but lawless they were not. They ran the affairs of the parish and they had the welfare of the people at heart. They took to the idea of a school from the first, welcomed our ladies, and cooperated in running the school. In fact, they took on more responsibility than the ladies wished. The Headsmen agreed among themselves to attend classes two by two, each to forfeit a shilling for absence. When they had accumulated fourteen shillings they spent the money on a gooseberry-tart treat for the children. After a while the Headsmen fell out with the teacher and demanded his removal.

Mr. Younge, the teacher, and his wife came from Bath, well recommended for zeal and industry. Younge must have had good qualities and ability for both Hannah and Patty stood by him through all the trouble he made them in Nailsea and later in Cheddar, admitting only that pride and a consciousness of really tolerable parts were his besetting sins. He began disorganizing Nailsea plans when one of the Headsmen insulted him at a school feast and a serious quarrel ensued. Younge repented his own impetuousness, but the Headsmen insisted on his removal. There were charges and countercharges and angry meetings and threats of closing the school, before the Mores were obliged to give in and shift the Younges to another village.

The Headsmen chose their next teacher themselves, a young collier who had been too severely injured in the pit to return to mining. Each Headsman subscribed a sixpence a week to pay for his training as a teacher during his convalescence that he might be able to carry on a weekday as well as a Sunday School. He made an excellent teacher until his death. Two other young colliers then took over the work and were successful in managing the proud rough parish where the better educated Younge had lamentably failed.

If one admits that the Mores brought many of their difficulties upon themselves by their dictatorial attitude, one must also realize that that was the accepted method of carrying on humanitarian projects. The idea of community direction of community ventures had not yet dawned on philanthropists. Probably most parishes had not reached the point where they were capable of taking such responsibility. Nailsea stands out as a very early example of local collective action.

CHAPTER XX

The Blagdon Controversy

THE PHRASE "Blagdon Controversy" was on many lips and was printed in many newspapers, magazines, and books in the years between 1800 and 1804.[1] Hannah's friends called it the "Blagdon Persecution." The struggle was between the evangelical branch of the Church, which favored Sunday Schools, and the conservative faction, which considered them dangerous Methodist propaganda. As the Methodists became organized and grew in strength, reactionary members of the Church of England took alarm and felt that the Evangelical Party in the established church was too friendly with the new denomination. Hannah More's Sunday Schools became the focus of a malignant attack.

The trouble began at Wedmore, a large hamlet some fifteen miles from Cowslip Green, stretching along a ridge of hills, over moors and around marshes. The name was derived from the swampy character of much of the land. One of the industries was cutting turf from pits six to eight feet deep. There were in all three hundred and twenty-nine houses and some eighteen hundred inhabitants. The section in which farmhouses clustered around a large Gothic church was called "The Borough."[2]

The school was started at the request of William Eyre,

curate at Wedmore from 1793 to 1803. Even greater opposition than usual immediately developed from the nervousness of the prosperous farmers and the superstitions of the laborers. A well-to-do farmer summed up his fear in the words: "Then it is all over with property; if property is not to rule, what is to become of us?" The first session of the school was unfortunately held in a Wedmore orchard high with weeds and grass, the schoolhouse not being ready. One of the farmers remembered that Methodists had once held a meeting in his mother's orchard with the result that the apple tree under which they stood withered and bore no more fruit.[3]

Undeterred by the outcry, to which they were now becoming accustomed, the Mores added to the children's classes evening meetings for their parents. These sessions were always a delicate problem. They could not be held in the church because they were not church services, but held in a schoolhouse they suggested religious nonconformity and tempted enemies to attack them under the excuse of the Conventicle Act, an act passed in 1664 decreeing punishment by fine, imprisonment, and transportation for all meetings of more than five persons for worship other than the established forms of the Church of England. The Act was no longer enforced but it was still used as a threat.

The abusive opposition, added to overwork in the damp unfinished Wedmore schoolhouse, broke Hannah down. Spasms in her head, probably neuralgia, came on one Saturday night, making it impossible for her to accompany Patty to Wedmore on Sunday. On Monday, being left alone, she fell from her chair in a fainting fit, bruising her face against a stone wall. Her sisters found her bleeding and unconscious.

She wrote to Wilberforce; "It was a good while before I had any clear idea, but a sort of stupid serenity, no emotion but a general feeling that I had not done enough for God, and what would poor Patty do by herself . . . you will be very glad to hear that my mind has been very clear and that I felt this visitation was in mercy."[4] She frequently mentions that her severe illnesses were accompanied by great peace of mind, as if her emotional suffering passed into physical pain.

Sometime during the Wedmore struggle Mr. Eyre joined the opposition. He had not foreseen the upheaval. He may in addition have been angry because the school, instead of being under his supervision, was directed by Mr. Harvon, a teacher whom the Mores brought over from their Axbridge school where he had got himself into trouble by his rashness and indiscretion. Mr. Eyre was having difficulty in bringing up on his small salary his six children to whom he was devoted, and he may have resented that Mr. Harvon in addition to his stipend received a house and garden and free coal and candles. Moreover, Mr. Eyre had an excitable personality, if one may judge from two letters which turned up a hundred years later in a curious way. When workmen razed a low stone wall separating the old Wedmore Vicarage garden from the garden next door, they uncovered a bottle containing the following letters, written while the controversy was still raging. Although it has no direct bearing on the quarrel, it does throw light on Mr. Eyre's ineffective way of meeting difficulties:

April 15 1801
My dear fellow mortal,

If any of my family, I mean my children, shoul'd settle here. Be good—Be good—My children—In goodness is happiness—

how often has my heart bled for your little wants and misfortunes. I pray God grant you grace and gratitude to think of me—and how I have toil'd for you—I am dead and rotten—Tho' now only 38 years—My children are registered in this p'sh—

.... Wm. Eyre

April 15th 1801

This wall was built at the expense of the Revd. William Eyre by the Tilly's (masons of Allerton)—The great scarcity of bread is likely to bring on troubles—the quartern loaf sells for one shilling and ten pence—pease at 6/6 per peck and everything in proportion—Potatoes even exceed this ration—they have sold at from one guinea to thirty shillings per sack—I write this in full strength of body and perhaps it may fall into hands yet unborn.—O think!—think!!—think!!! of eternity.

Adieu, adieu, adieu

Wm. Eyre [5]

A clergyman who could write so hysterical a letter for posterity was likely to have various troubles. Moreover, the parish lacked adequate oversight from higher church officials. Wedmore parish was a "particular" under the Dean of Wells, who came to Wedmore only when he kept his residence at Wells some distance away. The bishop, Dr. Charles Moss, was so aged that his son concealed all trouble from him. Wedmore had no rector in residence. Given a failing bishop, an absentee dean, and an absentee rector, an hysterical curate, a trouble-making teacher, alienated parishioners, and the unconciliatory Mores, the bitter struggle which followed was a logical outcome. This preliminary outbreak of the controversy was quieted by the dismissal of Mr. Harvon on the ground that he had no teaching license, and the appointment of Mrs. Carol who had made a good record at Axbridge where Mr. Harvon had his first failure.

The center of the storm shifted to the parish of Blagdon where the curate was Thomas Bere, a friend of William Eyre. The Blagdon school had been opened in 1795, three years before the Wedmore school, and had been running harmoniously for some four years when its trouble broke out.

Mr. Bere had asked the Mores to open the Sunday School. The immediate occasion of his request was his horror at the fate of a woman living at Charterhouse, a hamlet high up in the Mendip Hills. She was condemned to death "for attempting to begin a riot and purloining some butter from a man who offered it for sale at a price they thought unreasonable." The school started with one hundred and seventy pupils, not one of whom knew the answer to "Who made you?" The opening session was an affecting sight. Several of the older boys had been tried at the last assizes, three of the children of the woman condemned to death were present, and several known thieves were there. When Mr. Bere saw this vicious crew on their knees in his church he burst into tears.

As Hannah came out of the church surrounded by her "ragged regiment," some "musical gentlemen" drawn by curiosity struck up the hymn, "Inasmuch as ye did it to the least of them." In the afternoon Hannah and Patty led the children again into the beautiful Gothic church, the procession being headed this time by a club of men carrying ornamental sticks and the "musical gentlemen." [6]

The course of events at Blagdon was similar to that in Wedmore. Here also was a disgruntled curate, a defiant teacher with a record of trouble behind him, the same aged bishop and absentee dean, an absentee rector, and the stiff-necked Mores. The disagreement broke out over Monday-night meetings for adults, the sort of prayer meetings that had caused difficulty in other localities. Hannah was probably less able to deal with the situation because of an emotional attitude toward Blagdon. John Langhorne had been vicar there and Hannah had been his honored guest and might have been the lady of the manse. With her tenacious memory and her loyalty to the past, the founding of the school must have been an offering to a hallowed memory. It was natural that she should be impatient with Thomas Bere, so greatly Dr. Langhorne's inferior.

Mr. Bere had a strong personality, an important position in the community, and probably a feeling of insecurity, for he had made his way up from humble beginnings. His father had kept a tavern in Wales and Mr. Bere was said to have eloped with the daughter of an apothecary. He was now not only Curate of Blagdon, but also Rector of Butcombe, near Bristol, and a magistrate. He was a sensitive, emotional man, irritable, quickly offended, with a tendency to think himself persecuted. Mrs. Bere started the quarrel by criticising the Monday-night prayer meeting at which the men gave personal testimony as to their spiritual state. She made the criticisms to the teacher, Mr. Younge from Nailsea. For four years after being put in charge of the Blagdon school he had lived peaceably with the Beres, but he now flared up and intimated that the prayer-meeting testifiers were in a higher spiritual state than was Mrs. Bere who criticised them. Mrs. Bere told Mr. Bere and Mr. Bere wrote Hannah that Younge was Methodistic. Patty directed Younge to cease holding prayer meetings, but trouble continued.

The Mores ignored the affair as long as they could, but the Beres insisted on Younge's dismissal, making various charges against him. Hannah refused to remove him because the demand seemed to her an attack on herself. She felt that her antagonists were striking at the principle of all her schools, which was probably true. By the time Hannah gave in and sent Younge to a position in Ireland as private secretary to the Peter LaTouche family of Bellevue, County Wicklow—a philanthropic, religious family—the damage was done. Many people had been drawn into the controversy and the argument had shifted to whether or not Hannah was Methodistic. As the Methodists became organized into a formal church, the members of the established church became, in general, less tolerant of their activities and the Evangelistic Party in the established church was looked upon with disfavor for trying to maintain friendly relations. Hannah, being a close friend of the leaders of this group, was regarded with suspicion.

Hannah was passionately defended by lords and ladies and bishops. Mr. Bere was backed by many conservative church folk. Magazines took up the cause on either side. A tremendous amount of letter-writing took place. Mr. Bere published a pamphlet, *The Controversy between Mrs. Hannah More and the Curate of Blagdon; Relative to the Conduct of her Teacher of the Sunday School in that Parish; with the Original Letters and Explanatory Notes. By Thomas Bere, M.A. Rector of Butcombe, near Bristol, MDCCCI Price 3 shillings.* Sir Abram Elton, a gentleman of the neighborhood to whom Hannah applied for justice, replied with an unsigned pamphlet entitled *A Letter to the Rev. Thomas Bere, Rector of Butcombe, Occasioned by his unwarrantable attack on Mrs. Hannah More. Price 1 shilling 6 pence.*

Twenty-three pamphlets were put forth, some of them

extraordinarily malign. Edward Spencer wrote one of the best-known, entitled *Truths respecting Mrs. Hannah More's Meeting Houses and the Conduct of her Followers*, in which he represented Hannah as "the founder of a Sect, by every artifice, every insidious plausibility, drawing within the vortex of her petticoat, numerous bodies of the regular Clergy of the land," accused the teachers of having "small base children," and said he refrained from mentioning "small fornications between the grown-up Ladies and Gentlemen" who attended prayer meetings."

A scurrilous bill was posted at the turnpike in Blagdon advertising a circus at the Green Cowslip in Wrington with five female savages, etc. The type of humor suggests that Mr. Spencer wrote the poster as well as the pamphlet.

The ridiculousness of these accusations made pamphlets like Spencer's less hurtful than one written by Rev. William Shaw, rector of Chelvey, Somerset, entitled *The Life of Hannah More with Critical Review of her Writings.* His *nom de plume*, "Archibald MacSarcasm," was derived from Sir Archy M'Sarcasm, a character in Charles Macklin's *Love à la Mode*, produced in 1759. The pamphlet is chiefly a clever distortion of facts; misrepresentation of events that actually occurred. A tiny bit of truth is dexterously woven with lies. Mr. Shaw begins by stating that Jacob More was a servant in the employ of Norborne Berkeley, Esq., at Stoke House, Gloucester; that he married a fellow servant and became the teacher of twenty poor boys and ten poor girls at a salary of twenty-five pounds a year. The name of the patron and the fact of a teaching position is all that can be relied on. A statement that Hannah wanted to be a singer is a slur at her complete deafness to music. Her suitors are listed as: a gentleman on the stage, an army officer, a sea captain, and a gentleman of good fortune. "It was at this time, too, that she met with an advantageous bargain, by purchasing an annuity of 200 pounds a year, at a very easy rate." In this vicious jumble one may recognize the actor as Garrick, the sailor as Rev. John Newton, and the benefactor as Mr. Turner. The army officer is more difficult; maybe he was put in to make the riddle harder.

Hannah was prostrated by this attack. Dr. Thomas Sedgewick Whalley, friend and neighbor, wrote a return pamphlet when Patty applied to him, saying: "The emissaries of Satan are spreading strange things in London. . . . My sister Hannah is ill again, we are alarmed about her. This affair will I fear destroy her." [7]

Dr. Whalley's pamphlet was called *Animadversions on the Curate of Blagdon's THREE PUBLICATIONS entitled The Controversy between Mrs. Hannah More and the Curate of Blagdon, etc. An Appeal to the Public and an Address to Mrs. Hannah More; with some Allusions to his Cambrian Descent from 'Gwyr Ap Glendour, Ap Cadwaller, Ap Styfnig' as affirmed and set forth by Himself in the Twenty-eighth page of his Appeal to the Public.* The pamphlet was anonymous and was written in a scoffing tone, sneering at Bere for boasting of his Welsh forebears, for having a father who kept a tavern called The Three Pigeons, and for having made a discreditable marriage. While not as vulgar as the pamphlets on the other side, it reflects no credit on Dr. Whalley who wrote it, Patty who incited the writing, nor Hannah who allowed it to be printed.

When Dr. Moss, the very old bishop, died, Dr. Richard Beadon who succeeded him tried to bring the scandalous controversy to an end by appointing a board of five magistrates, three clergymen, and three private men to meet at Blagdon. The matter had grown extremely complicated, involving side issues; whether or not Mr. Bere's sermon at Axbridge had attacked the doctrine of the Trinity; whether one witness against the Mores had been in a lunatic asylum and another had illegitimate children; and whether laymen at the prayer meetings had preached sermons or only commented on the Scriptures as they read.

Much of the controversy centered on the exact degree to which Hannah was tainted with "enthusiasm." She had several times attended the chapel of the popular preacher Rev. William Jay of Argyle Chapel in Bath. She was herself a member of the Church of England and regularly attended Dr. Randolph's congregation when in Bath, but she found it hard to explain away the fact that she had once received communion in Dr. Jay's chapel. Patty defended her with a curious argument: "I know many high church people, and one gentleman and lady with 10,000 pounds a year, who have always the church prayers performed morning and evening in their family, did the same. . . ." [8] In the early days of the school Hannah had even hired teachers on Dr. Jay's recommendation.[9] In brief, Hannah found it impossible to prove that she was as prejudiced against religious sects other than her own, as her critics felt she should be.

Dr. Beadon did his best, but his activity was no more effective than Dr. Moss' inaction had been. The board of magistrates, clergy, and gentlemen recommended that the school be closed. Hannah closed it. Bishop Beadon reversed the decision of the board and Hannah allowed herself to be persuaded to reopen the school. The Bishop dismissed Mr.

Bere but later found that Mr. Bere could not legally be removed. Mr. Bere came back; Hannah again closed her school and he opened one. The curate was final victor.

When the matter was finally settled and after the cruel attacks had ceased, Hannah collapsed completely. From 1803 to 1805 she had what she always referred to as "my great illness." The memory of that prostration remained long with her. Ten years later she recalled in writing to Mr. Wilberforce: ". . . in that long affliction, though at one time I very seldom closed my eyes in sleep for forty days and nights, I never had one hour's great discomposure of mind, or one moment's failure of reason, though in health very liable to agitation." Those who nursed her were wont to exclaim in admiration: "Would that her enemies and traducers could be in her sickroom." [10]

CHAPTER XXI

Ill Health

Hannah's attention to her health increased with her years until she became a hypochondriac. Her letters are full of complaints of ailments: headaches, coughs, colds, bowel complaint, rheumatism in the face, dreadful spasms, fainting fits, fevers, shiverings and sweats, paralyzed legs, pains that lacerated like knives, dizziness, nausea, and like ills. In writing to Mrs. Garrick she would apologize for not writing before because she had been ill and she knew how Mrs. Garrick disliked complaints and would then go on to details of her seizure. Next she would inquire about Mrs. Garrick's health, after which the real letter would begin.

She had an odd difficulty in getting started on her yearly journey to visit Mrs. Garrick. If she set a definite date, she was very likely to take a severe cold, and her colds were terrible. She gave herself up completely to her disorders, while Sally and Patty wrote postponing her departure, perhaps several times. Sally's letters on these occasions, while not unsympathetic, were calm; but Patty's were disturbed and anxious. After the bout of illness, Hannah would get into the coach and travel to London. It seems as if she must have had some unconscious conflict about leaving her sisters to go to

Mrs. Garrick's, for while she never missed the trip she almost always found difficulty in beginning it.

Hannah's early life was punctuated with blinding headaches which, being especially troublesome in the morning, prevented her from conforming to the early rising habits of her family. When she was visiting the Cotton cousins in Bungay she read while the others slept at night and had her morning headaches and late rising as usual. Headaches were common among the *Bas Bleu* ladies and were generally attributed to overtaxing the female brain.

Certain headaches are famous in history. Elizabeth Carter, who studied Latin, Greek, Hebrew, French, Italian, Spanish, German, Portuguese, and Arabic, visited the various spas and drank the waters for such an affliction, though Lord Bath told her harshly to stop drinking green tea and taking snuff to keep herself awake to study at night. The Duchess of Portland recommended a piece of stale bread the size of a walnut eaten upon awakening. Hannah put blisters on her own temples. Sophia Peabody had a headache for twenty years before she married Nathaniel Hawthorne. Maria Edgeworth and Harriet Martineau were other well-known sufferers. While the cause lay largely in fine print, flickering candlelight, and faulty eye-glasses, one wonders if there was not an emotional component. The women must have felt that such wonderful headaches were a distinction; they talked so much about them.

Hannah expected a siege of illness every winter and she was not disappointed. She shut herself up in her room for long periods, never venturing out except in a chair and only to church. When the Mores lived in Bath the sisters attended Laura Chapel in Henrietta Street, Rev. Dr. Randolph's private property, with fireplaces in recesses, carpeted floors and like comforts. But Hannah gave up churchgoing for weeks at a time, because even when she sat next to one of the hot fires in church she took cold. Patty was frantic over Hannah's frailness and it seemed to many as if her weak body could not survive the repeated racking illnesses. Nevertheless she lived into her eighty-ninth year.

Illnesses were Hannah's rest periods. She went into retreat from the world. She laid aside for a time her lifelong struggle to be more meritorious than she was and to make others more meritorious than they wished to be, and on her sickbed recuperated from physical and spiritual fatigue and gathered strength for her next onslaught. One notes that she complained about her maladies but did not complain about her troubles; when life bore hardest on her she wailed loudest about her illnesses.

Hannah believed that God sent her poor health to turn her thoughts toward Him. When she was depressed, she thought about God, while cheerfulness attended her practical activities. She served the Lord with joy; she worshipped Him in gloom. Once she wrote regretfully in her journal: "I had rather *work* for God than *meditate* upon him. . . ."

Hannah wrote in her journal on Sundays as a religious exercise. She made entries about her infirmities, the deaths of her friends, and the unsatisfactory state of her soul. She had a pretty regular Sunday headache.

1798 Sunday, April 29th. Had a bad headache all day—nothing done for God—in pain my religion vacillates. . . .

. . . .

Teston [home of Mrs. Bouverie and the Middletons] Mar. 1. Arrived here Monday—seriously ill all the way. . . . Several bad nights—violent cough—not comforted by religious but tormented by worldly thoughts. . . . While attending on the dying bed of Mrs.——I did not feel my heart properly afflicted.

. . . .

Saturday, Sept. 22. Head seldom free from pain—Pain does not yet purify my heart, though my Gracious Father purposes it for that end.

. . . .

Sunday, December 23. Ill for above a week with a violent cough—blistered, etc.—by the Grace of God I am resigned to pain; but my thoughts, which at such times ought to be devoted to heavenly things, are not always in my own power. . . . An awful dispensation! The curate of—visited with a sudden blindness for three days—It seems to have been a supernatural awakening. . . .[1]

She was never sure that she had won what she passionately desired—God's complete approval. Her attention was focused on the details of religion rather than its sweep and inspiration; she kept as it were an account book of petty sins and was absorbed in the minutiæ of righteousness. "How many ways there are of doing wrong," cries a character in one of her books. She fled from the profundities of religious experience, for emotional excess of any kind was abhorrent to her and the ardors of the saints must have seemed to her not quite nice.

Hannah's appreciation of pious deathbeds increased to morbidity during her later years. The suspense of a deathwatch fascinated her, the sufferer's agonies, in those days of inadequate narcotics, were a part of the grim drama, and the religious exaltation of the departing soul confirmed her belief in her own salvation. In an undated letter from Barley Wood to a clerical friend congratulating him on his wife's recovery, she relates, for the edification of his "nine fine young creatures," the conduct of a dying child whom she and Patty had just visited:

In the school consisting of over three hundred I missed a little favorite who used to hail our approach. She is daughter of two of our teachers, eminently pious young people, to whom we taught their alphabet about twenty years ago. They were then grown up. The child is more than ten years old, but so little that she does not appear to be eight. We went to their cottage and found her lying on a little couch in a scarlet fever, with all the marks of approaching death, burning head and obstructive respiration. She had been fervently praying she might see my sister and me once more. When she spied us she said, "I thought I should not see you till we met in heaven, for I am sure I shall go there." She then expressed a strong sense of her own corruptness and of her firm reliance on the Saviour. "He has forgiven me," added she, "I know it, I feel it. I have been a great sinner, but he has told me tho my sins are as scarlet they are become as wool," and went on through the whole passage. I asked what sins they were, beside heart sins, which layd so heavy on her. She wept and said that she had twice gone to bed without saying her prayers but had solemnly vowed never to do it again. . . .[2]

And so it goes on, covering in all more than two closely written pages, ending: "I have not heard she is dead, but I feel sorry she should return to such a world as this. Forgive this story, but my mind is full of this little saint, I might add, full of envy at her superiority."

During these periods of suffering and morbidity the sisters protected Hannah from even her dearest friends. The watchfulness was so extreme as to suggest that she may have had mental as well as nervous breakdowns which the family kept secret from outsiders. That would explain Patty's excessive anxiety at such times. Miss Mary Butt, later Mrs. Sherwood, author of *The Fairchild Family*, gives an account of a call at the Bath Pulteney Street house in 1799.

A mutual friend took Miss Butt and her brother to meet Hannah More. A footman opened the door of the handsome house and ushered them into a large dining room, to which the four sisters came down, excusing Hannah on the plea of ill health. The friend persisted in begging that Miss Butt and her clergyman brother be allowed to meet Hannah.

"The four old ladies looked unutterable things, but never once uttered their sister's name. It was always 'she' and the voice fell to the lowest key when 'she' was uttered." The visitors finally won their point and "were then ushered upstairs to the drawing-room which was next to the presence chamber. After a little further delay they were led into a dressing room where sat the lady, looking very much like the picture which was commonly known then, though considerably older, and wearing a cap.

"She sat in an armchair in true invalid style, and though a strong featured woman of a dark complexion, she had a magnificent pair of dark eyes. She was very gracious to her visitors, and spoke well, those about her gathering up her words carefully, though in rather a Boswellian-like manner."

After the adoring, dominating sisters gave up their Bristol school, they were free to devote more attention to Hannah than was good for her. Hannah was the victim of family affection; the prisoner of her sisters' love. Although every spring for more than twenty years she escaped their devotion to visit her friends in London and vicinity, yet from each respite she returned to her sisters' influence. She found it pleasanter to be pampered and ruled than to be independent. From the time of Garrick's death the struggle grew weaker between her desire for adventure and her need to be safe in familiar scenes, until she ceased her London visits and settled down with her sisters. Although she was up and about, engaged in humanitarian activities, a good part of her later life, yet between periods of activity she retreated into the sanctuary of her sickroom.

CHAPTER XXII

Early Tract Writing

In order fully to appreciate the brilliancy of Hannah More's tract writing the reader must accept from the outset the fact that she acquiesced in the prevailing middle- and upper-class view that rigid social distinction was God's own benevolent plan and that it was therefore wrong for the poor to try to raise themselves to higher economic or social levels by means of workers' unions or by efforts to change laws which bore harshly upon them. Ambition to leave a lowly station was reprehensible, discontent was sinful, and rioting was atrocious. Her writings reflect the general—but not universal—uneasiness at the possibility of laborers getting out of hand. Her plan for avoiding this was to make the poor physically comfortable by showing them how to utilize what they had, and submissive by teaching them that joy in heaven was the recompense for deprivation on earth.

The poverty of Somersetshire laborers was terrible. A man's usual wage for a day's work was a shilling. A skilled woman could make a shilling and a half spinning linen and near three shillings a week spinning wool. A child could pick up a shilling a week scaring off crows, picking out stones from the field, or keeping birds from cherry trees. A dilapidated two-room cottage rented for fifty shillings a year; four rooms in good repair for eighty.

The agricultural workers got no benefit from the prosperity which had come to their employers from the improvement in agricultural methods. Farmers were learning how to make the soil produce better grain and root crops. This improved feed encouraged the breeding of finer herds, and cattle improved in weight and quality; sheep were heavier and their wool thicker. Tools and implements were better designed. Great landowners began to take a personal interest in the way their land was farmed and many of them reserved home farms for personal supervision, while professional men took up farming on the side.

The result of this widespread interest was a marked increase in profits for owners and tenant farmers, but not for their wage laborers. Landowners could charge very high rent to tenant farmers, who in spite of rent rise could make good profit, especially in the years of poor harvests when prices soared. All this was fine for the country at large but hard on farm laborers and their families, many of whom, although working their hardest, were on relief all or a part of the time. Areas of common land on which the poor had been accustomed to dig fuel turf or to pasture a pig and ducks and geese were now being enclosed to be a part of the owner's farm or park. Intensive cultivation utilized even the odd corners of land which laborers had been allowed to use as gardens. The dairy and wheat farms selling their produce to the cities would not bother with selling by the shilling's worth. A further cut in workers' income came during the last quarter of the century when the invention of improved machinery took spinning and weaving and knitting out of the cottages into city factories along river banks, so that the women and children at home could no longer contribute to the family income.

A condition so advantageous to the upper and middle classes seemed to them the decree of God. Wages at subsistence level, it was held, kept the laboring class from either increasing or decreasing unduly. It was thought that if the laborer had a bit of extra money he would stop work, and the idea of the lower class having liberty to be idle was most upsetting to the idle of the upper class. The reformers who held opposing views were thought infected by French radicalism.

The French Revolution had been putting ideas into the heads of some factory and farm workers, and men who learned in Sunday School to read the Bible later used this accomplishment to read Tom Paine and Wilkes and Godwin. The dangerous idea was advanced that the English government was not perfect, and the comfortable middle class was alarmed lest revolution spread from France. The Bishop of London, Beilby Porteus, meeting Hannah in Bath in 1792, begged her to write something in simple words to open the eyes of uneducated people dazed by the words "liberty" and "equality." Mrs. More at first refused on the plea that it was not in her line, but the idea stuck in her mind and one day when she was sick she occupied herself in writing her first tract, *Village Politics, by Will Chip, a Country Carpenter.*

She was ashamed of the little piece because it was written in such un-Johnsonian language, but she must have had pride in it too, for she sent it to the publishers, F. and C. Rivington, choosing a new firm lest she be suspected of being the author. An excerpt from this tract will illustrate the usual theme and treatment of the majority of the tracts which followed:

A dialogue between Jack Anvil, the blacksmith, and Tom Hod, the mason.

Jack. What's the matter, Tom? Why dost thou look so dismal?

Tom. Dismal, indeed! Well enough I may.

Jack. What, is the old mare dead? or work scarce?

Tom. No, no, work's plenty enough, if a man had but the heart to go to it.

Jack. What book art reading? Why dost look so like a hang dog?

Tom. (Looking on his book) Cause enough. I find here that I am very unhappy, and very miserable; which I should never have known if I had not had the good luck to meet with this book. Oh, 'tis a precious book!

Jack. A good sign though; that you can't find out that you are unhappy without looking into a book for it? What is the matter?

Tom. Matter? Why I want liberty.

Jack. Liberty? That's bad indeed! What, has anyone fetched a warrant for thee? Come, man, cheer up, I'll be bound for thee. Thou art an honest fellow in the main, though thou dost tipple and prate a little too much at the Rose and Crown.

Tom. No, no, I want a new constitution.

Jack. Indeed! Why I thought thou hadst been a desperately healthy fellow. Send for the doctor directly.

Tom. I'm not sick; I want liberty and equality, and the rights of man.

Jack. Oh, now I understand thee. What! thou art a leveller and a republican, I warrant!

Tom. I'm a friend to the people. I want a reform.

Jack. Then the shortest way is to mend thyself.

Tom. But I want a general reform.

Jack. Then let everyone mend one.

Jack points out that the English already have the blessing for which the French are striving, that jails are necessary for the protection of the honest, that if everybody had an acre of land each would be busy tilling it and there would be no tailors, shoemakers, doctors (for the doctors would be busy tilling too), that without the present superiors, the strongest would take all, and that there is no such thing as perfection in government, "though Sir John says we come nearer to it than any country in the world ever did."

Jack does not hold the gentry perfect either, but useful in spite of occasional follies.

Jack. Now in this village, what should we do without the castle? Though my lady is too rentipolish, and flies about all summer to hot water and cold water, and fresh water and salt water, when she ought to stay at home with Sir John; yet when she does come down, she brings such a deal of gentry that I have more horses than I can shoe, and my wife more linen than she can wash. Then all our grown children are servants in the family and rare wages they have got. Our little boys get something every day by weeding their garden and the girls learn to sew and knit at Sir John's expense, who sends them all to school of a Sunday besides.

Tom. Ay, but there's not Sir Johns in every village.

Jack. The more's the pity. . . . No poor rates in France, Tom . . . But when this levelling comes about, there will be no infirmaries, no hospitals, no charity schools, no Sunday Schools. . . . For who is to pay for them? Equality can't afford it. . . . Those poor French fellows used to be the merriest dogs in the world; but since equality came in, I don't believe a Frenchman has ever laughed.

Tom. What then dost thou take French *liberty* to be?

Jack. To murder more men in one night than ever their poor king did in his whole life.

Tom. And what dost thou take a *democrat* to be?

Jack. One who lives to be governed by a thousand tyrants, and yet can't bear a king.

Tom. What is *equality?*

Jack. For every man to pull down every one that is above him; while, instead of raising those below him to his own level, he only makes use of them as steps to raise himself to the place of those he has tumbled down.

In like manner Jack (who as Tom bears witness never told a lie in his life) shows Tom the meaning of all the political terms which have seduced his imagination, like *new Rights of Man,* etc.

Tom. And art thou very sure we are not ruined?

Jack. I'll tell thee how we are ruined. We have a king, so loving that he would not hurt the people if he could: and so kept in that he could not hurt the people if he would. We have as much liberty as can make us happy, and more trade and riches than allows us to be good. We have the best laws in the world, if they were more strictly enforced; and the best religion in the world if it was but better followed. While old England is safe, I'll glory in her, and pray for her, and when she is in danger, I'll fight for her and die for her.

Tom. And so will I too, Jack, that's what I will. (Sings) "Oh, the roast beef of old England!"

Four arguments used to lecture the laborer into contentment were: the gentry look after the worthy poor; no relation exists between government and want; government is no concern of the common man; God knows what is best for his people.

Gentle, kindly Dr. Porteus and his friends were so confident that the malcontents would be influenced by Will Chip's reasoning that they paid for the printing and distribution of Will Chip's argument. Whether or not Chip quieted the restive folk, he certainly gave comfort to the upper classes. Hester Thrale Piozzi at her home in Wales paid twelve guineas to have *Village Politics* translated into

Welsh and distributed, but Mr. Piozzi made his contribution toward the good of the nation by giving his cottagers a feast of roast beef and dumpling and leading them in "God Save the King." Chip's dialogue was translated also into French and Italian.

The next political writing from Hannah's quill was an indignant reply to the atheistic speech of Jacob Dupont in the National Convention at Paris, December fourteenth, 1792, in favor of establishing anti-religious public schools. The two hundred pounds brought in by the sale of Hannah's printed reply were devoted to the benefit of the destitute refugee French clergy. The sisters opened their home in Bath to these unfortunate Frenchmen even as their father had shown hospitality to the paroled French officers in Fishponds many years before, and this despite Hannah's intense antipathy to French thought, customs, and actions.

Only four pieces of Hannah's vast output deal primarily with government; the two already mentioned, a second tract, and a ballad. The tract is entitled *The History of Mr. Fantom, the New Fashioned Philosopher and his Man William,* and records the harm done by a vain, selfish, hypercritical atheist who spouts a misinterpretation of Tom Paine's doctrines. The piece is dull and without distinction.

The political ballad is a different matter. Hannah had a pretty talent for turning a rhyme and one of her best story-poems is *The Riot: or Half a Loaf is Better than No Bread, in a Dialogue between Jack Anvil and Tom Hod. To the tune of—"A Cobbler there was." Written in Ninety-five, a Year of Scarcity and Alarm.* Impetuous Tom Hod tried to incite cautious Jack Anvil to rioting. Jack explains to him that famine conditions are from the weather and not from misgovernment and that the less one has, the harder one should work.

But though poor, I can work, my brave boy, with the best,
Let the king and the parliament manage the rest;
I lament both the war and the taxes together,
Though I verily think they don't alter the weather.
The king as I take it, with very good reason,
May prevent a bad law, but can't help a bad season.
Derry down.

. . . .

And though I've no money, and though I've no lands;
I've a head on my shoulders, and a pair of good hands;
So I'll work the whole day, and on Sundays I'll seek
At church how to bear all the wants of the weak.
The gentlefolks too will afford us supplies,
They'll subscribe—and they'll give up their pudding and pies.
Derry down.

Then before I'm induced to take part in a riot,
I'll ask this short question—What shall I get by it?
So I'll e'en wait a little, till cheaper the bread,
For a mittimus hangs o'er each rioter's head;
And when of two evils I'm ask'd which is best
I'd rather be hungry than hang'd I protest.
Derry down.

Quoth Tom, thou art right; if I rise, I'm a Turk;
So he threw down his pitchfork, and went to his work.

This ballad was reported to have stopped a riot near Bath.

CHAPTER XXIII

Cheap Repository Tracts

THE WIDE circulation of *Village Politics* encouraged the Clapham group of religious laymen to underwrite the *Cheap Repository Tracts*, a series of readable moral tales, jolly, edifying ballads, and special Sunday readings of sermons, prayers, and Bible stories, aimed at offsetting the influence of vicious broadsides and chapbooks hawked about the countryside by peddlers and popular with uneducated folk who had recently learned to read. As in the matter of Sunday Schools, the same men promised to raise the money if Hannah would do the work. Henry Thornton was treasurer, and subscriptions to defray the initial cost poured in. Since the tracts were sold at a little under cost to encourage circulation, there was a deficit to make good.

The first publishers were Samuel Hazard, Bath, and John Marshal, London. Later the printing was transferred to Evans and Hatchard, London. The first publication date was March, 1795, and, with two reorganizations, the tracts came out monthly for three years. The last year the Mores severed their connection with the undertaking and inferior work was produced. Some twenty years later, in 1817, the scheme was revived under a London committee, the first issue being a reprint of *Village Politics*, under the title *The Vil-*

lage Disputants. Hannah furnished some new or revised songs. The second venture was not as successful as the first had been.

The tracts sold by the thousands; in one year over two million were bought by the well-to-do and distributed among the poor, some through hawkers, others in prisons, in the army and navy, and in schools. To what extent they were read by the malcontents for whom they were designed we have no means of knowing. The Archbishop of Canterbury was active in the distribution and the Bishop of London saw to it that the Royal Family at Windsor had a good supply. "Shiploads" went to the West Indies and the natives of Sierra Leone were reported to read with avidity these essays on English workers' vices and virtues.

To the amusement of Hannah's friends, that well-bred lady made a startling collection of chapbooks; anti-governmental and anti-church tirades, histories of notorious murderers dying on the scaffold, careers of thieves, vulgar ballads, bawdy songs, and obscene jests. She studied these seriously to learn the secret of their popularity, and borrowed their form for her own works. Her tracts were printed on coarse brown paper, adorned with lively woodcuts, and titled to attract attention. For example: *The History of Idle Jack Brown: Containing the Merry Story of the Mountebank, with some Account of the Bay Mare Smiler, being the Third Part of THE TWO SHOE MAKERS.* The title-page cut shows a merry andrew in a huge cocked hat, long-skirted coat, and knee breeches, standing on a table, attended by a fantastic assistant. In front of the table are three bemused dupes; under the table a ruffian menaces a terror-stricken victim; beside the table a scoundrel is mugging his prey; the background is a gin house. The story was written by Hannah. A similar woeful tale of derring-do, unsigned, may have been written by spritely Sally for it is entitled *The Story of Sinful Sally: Told by herself: Showing how from being Sally of the Green she was first led to Become Sinful Sally, and afterwards Drunken Sal; and how at Last she came to a Melancholy, and almost Hopeless End; being therein a Warning to all Young Women both in Town and Country.*

Hannah wrote forty-nine of the first one hundred and fourteen of the pamphlets, signing them "Z." Sally contributed several, full of gaiety and zip, signing them "S." The initials "S.S." on others stood for Sappho Search, the pen name of Rev. John Black of Bentley, Suffolk.[1] Other contributors were William Mason, Hester Mulso Chapone, William Gilpin, and others. Henry Thornton contributed some prayers; excerpts from John Newton's sermons were included; Selina Mills helped editorially, and probably Sarah Trimmer gave some aid. Hannah scrutinized offerings sharply and refused many. She rejected one of Mason's because it had too much love in it.[2]

The tracts written by the Mores are far more readable than the others, because they were drawn from life. An eighteenth-century village is spread before us, with its trades, its sports, its problems and its habits. We meet Sir John, the great man of the place, rich, thoughtless, lavish, and indolent, subscribing to a ball match or a charity school, indulging his tenants in bell-ringing, bonfires, and drunkenness at Christmas, but considering it folly to teach them and madness to try to reform them. We regret that Sir John's lady is giddy and extravagant, but realize that she provides work for villagers in the great house laundry, kitchen, and stable. The young ladies do not always assume their rightful obligation of teaching village girls cooking and sewing. The squire, in contrast, though close with money, is a conscientious magistrate, willing if sufficiently pressed to close a disorderly house or fine a Sabbath-breaker. Mr. Bragwell, the foolish farmer, bred up his daughters to be fine ladies, vain and showy; while Tom White, his opposite number, was kind and honest without detriment to his model farm. We are acquainted with the shopkeepers, the baker, the blacksmith, the thatcher, the rat-catcher, little boys turning an honest penny harrying the crows, little girls collecting sheep's wool from pasture brambles, great girls working in dairies, and the housewives at home, all of whom—or almost all of whom—are real human beings with a generous supply of faults and excellencies. The general atmosphere is, perhaps, a little on the sad side. One unsigned tract is entitled *The Troubles of Life, being a Familiar Description of the Troubles of the Poor Labour; the Little Shop Keeper; the Great Tradesman; the Disappointed Lover; the Unhappy Husband; the Widower; and, lastly, the Child of Sorrow. To which is Added the Story of the Guinea and the Shilling. Being a Cure for Trouble in General.*

Many passages are obviously drawn from life, as, for example, Hannah's exasperation with a ne'er-do-well family:

Poaching Giles lives on the borders of those great moors in Somersetshire. . . . He lives at that mud cottage with the broken windows, stuffed with dirty rags, just beyond the gate which divides the upper from the lower moor. . . .

The common on which Giles's hovel stands is quite a deep marsh in a wet winter: but in summer it looks green and pretty enough. To be sure it would be rather convenient when one passes that way in a carriage, if one of the children would run out and open the gate; but instead of any one of them running out as soon as they heard the wheels, which would be quite time enough, what does Giles do but set all his ragged brats, with dirty faces, matted hair, and naked feet and legs, to lie all day upon a sand bank hard by the gate, waiting for the slender chance of what may be picked up from travelers. At the sound of a carriage, a whole covey of these little scare-crows start up, rush to the gate, and all at once thrust out their hats and aprons; and for fear this, together with the noise of their clamorous begging, should not sufficiently frighten the horses, they are very likely to let the gate slap full against you before you are half way through, in their eager scuffle to snatch from each other the halfpence which you have thrown out to them. I know two ladies who were one day very near being killed by these abominable tricks.

Black Giles, the father of these little wretches, was by profession a rat-catcher. Whenever he was sent to a farm-house to clear out the vermin, it was his custom to leave a few to breed and to transfer some to nearby granaries to increase his business. When he was hired to plant beans, he put most of the seed in his pocket and blamed the sparse crop on mice and rooks. Tawney Rachel, his wife, was a slut. She used her red coat as a blanket by night and an ironing sheet on Sunday. She tramped the roads with a basket on her arm, pretending to sell laces, cabbage nets, and chapbooks, and to buy rags and rabbit skins, but her true profession was telling fortunes and thieving. She preyed upon the country girls through their superstitions and the story, *Tawney Rachel, or the Fortune Teller*, gives a fine lot of information about the credulity of the folk and their belief in signs and omens.

One group of stories, centering on the social service activities of Mrs. Jones, a widow in reduced circumstances, is a fictionized account of the village welfare work of Hannah and Martha. *The Sunday School* and *The History of Hester Wilmot* narrate their trials and successes in setting up Sunday Schools, and the improving influence of the institution on family life. Mrs. Wilmot, Hester's mother, fed her vanity on compliments to her housekeeping; she was poison neat and made her family unhappy, although she drew flowers on the whitewash with a charcoal stick and taught Hester to draw patterns on the sanded floor. Hester was lazy and impudent. The father fled to the tavern. The Sunday School opened a new world to Hester as it did to many smart, frustrated children, and thanks to the instruction she received she changed into an ambitious, eager child and was helpful at home. Gradually the whole family felt the influence of the school. Not only was this probably a true story of one family, it was the story of hundreds of families all over England.

The almshouse furnished copy for two tracts. Hannah's is a mild affair entitled *'Tis All for the Best*, but Sally's galloping quill ran away with her in *The Hubbub, or the History of Farmer Brown, Hard-Hearted Overseer:*

> The oldest man living at Compton-Ashby cannot call to mind such another Hubbub as that which happened there some months ago on the common, just before the poorhouse door. . . . Never was such a hissing and hooting and hallooing heard. . . . Betty Jobbins beat the frying pan with the key of the door, Sally Gore pounded the pestle and mortar, Nellie Shepson rung the warming pan, Dick Devonshire blew the ram's-horn, whilst Nick Stafford and other gingled the sheep's bells. . . .

Here is the description of the instigator of the mutiny:

> Amy Talbot seemed to be about sixty years of age, but time had not cured Amy of gossiping, nor taught her to mend her

clothes. . . . Wherever there was a gossiping in the parish, thither ran Amy with her rags flying about her, like a scarecrow in a cherry tree. Her skin which was quite tawny was never washed; her hair had worked itself through the borders of her mob; half the border of which was lost; the pigs had one day eaten a hole through her hat as it lay on the ground, and a piece of it now hung over her eye like a black patch; her petticoats were all in tatters, and her gown reached but a little below her knees; it had worn away bit by bit, till it was ravelled out to the above dimensions; her stockings had no feet, and her feet were slipped into a miserable pair of shoes which she had not taken the trouble to draw up at the heel, even when they were new; in one hand she clutched her rags together, whilst with the other she held a short pipe in her mouth, resting her elbow on her knee, as she sat cross-legged.

It is unnecessary ever to relate the plot of any of these tracts, for the good are always rewarded or taken to heaven, while the rascals repent or go to jail or are hanged. Yet one feels that the Mores had more actual enjoyment in writing about their rowdies than their paragons.

The principal figure in Hannah More's best-known tract, *The Shepherd of Salisbury Plain*, was an actual Somersetshire character, David Saunders by name, who lived on Littleton Downs, at the top of Saunders Lane. He worked for the same farm for thirty years although the property changed masters several times in that period. He was at one time summoned before a magistrate on the charge of "preaching in his own house," but convinced that official that though he read the Bible to shepherd boys and shepherdesses on Littleton Downs, and though he rose an hour earlier on Sunday mornings to have time for a hymn and a prayer and perhaps a bit of Bible reading, yet he was never guilty of preaching. The magistrate, a clergyman, severely reprimanded the accuser, advising him to go and do likewise. Saunders could read and write and toward the end of his life he opened an evening school.

The shepherd had sixteen children and his wife was badly crippled with rheumatism. He earned six shillings, threepence a week. The younger children helped out by cow-tending and by plucking knobs of wool from the bushes in the sheep run.[3] The crippled mother in the chimney corner cleaned and carded this and the children spun it into yarn which they knit into stockings or sent to Potterne or Cheverill where a few weavers lived who wove it into blankets or flannel for petticoats. When pitied for his poverty, the father was accustomed to say: "Cut your last loaf as cheerfully as your first; they (the children) are growing and want plenty of victuals; if God sends children he will send bread."

This estimable old man died in his sleep in his eightieth year, in the middle of September, 1796, while visiting friends in Wyke. He was buried with unusual solemnity in the north-east corner of West Lavington Church. He left a fortune of about six guineas, part of which was the remainder of a legacy from Sir James Stonehouse, who was his vicar, and part from the sale of two or three sheep which he had been allowed to keep from his master's flock when he was too old to work any longer.[4]

The Mores seem never to have met Saunders personally, but knew him through their lifelong friend Sir James Stonehouse, the vicar of Cheverill, and his curate. Hannah used a writer's privilege by slightly altering some details of Saunders' circumstances and making his living conditions and income toward the end a little easier than they actually were.

The description of the family and their cottage, given in the tract by Mr. Johnson the vicar (Sir James Stonehouse to us) might apply to many a Somersetshire cot of that period. Mr. Johnson, looking in at the door on a Sunday, saw:

. . . the shepherd (who looked so respectable in his Sunday coat that he should hardly have known him) his wife and their numerous young family, drawing round their little table, which was covered with a clean but very coarse cloth. There stood upon it a large dish of potatoes, a brown pitcher, and a piece of a coarse loaf. The wife and children stood in silent attention, while the shepherd with uplifted hands and eyes, devoutly begged the blessing of heaven on their humble fare. . . .

The shepherd and his wife sat down with great seeming cheerfulness, but the children stood; and while the mother was helping them, little fresh-coloured Molly, who had picked the wool from the bushes with so much delight, cried out, "Father, I wish I was big enough to say grace, I am sure I should say it very heartily today, for I was thinking what must *poor* people do who have no salt to their potatoes; and do but look, our dish is quite full.". . .

The trenchers on which they were eating were almost as white as their linen, and notwithstanding the number and smallness of the children, there was not the least appearance of dirt or litter. The furniture was very simple and poor, hardly amounting to bare necessities. It consisted of four brown wooden chairs, which by constant rubbing were become as bright as looking glass; an iron pot and kettle; a poor old grate, which scarcely held a handful of coal, and out of which the little fire that had been in it appeared to have been taken, as soon as it had answered the end for which it had been lighted—that of boiling their potatoes. Over the mantle stood an old-fashioned broad bright candlestick, and a still brighter spit; it was pretty clear that this last was kept rather for ornament than for use. An old carved elbow chair, and a chest of the same date, which stood in a corner, were considered the most valuable part of the shepherd's goods, having been in his family for three generations.

The English Sunday School plan in which the Mores played so early and important a part attained an importance unforeseen by its originators, whose primary object was to discipline wild children through Bible study. No sooner were the children enticed into classes than the instructors realized that they must be taught also to wash their faces and mend their manners. As they grew older it was necessary to train them in crafts to earn a decent wage to support decent living. All this brought the parents into the picture and the scheme had to be enlarged to include adults in religious, moral, and technical instruction. It is no exaggeration to say that the More sisters helped raise the standards of living, of techniques, of ethics, and of grace, in generations then unborn.

CHAPTER XXIV

Didactic Books

THE BOOKS which Hannah herself considered her most important contribution to ethics and to literature are today her least interesting work. At the time of publication the demand for them was truly extraordinary. They sold by the thousands, edition after edition, in England; were tremendously popular in the United States; and were translated into French, German, and other languages.

Thoughts on the Importance of the Manners of the Great to General Society, published in 1788, went through seven editions in a few months, the third edition selling out in four hours. *An Estimate of the Religion of the Fashionable World*, 1790, was equally popular. Both books were published anonymously and Hannah did not acknowledge them until so many had guessed the authorship that the secret was no longer a secret. She expected her fashionable acquaintances to turn on her for her criticism of their frivolity and was braced for anger, not realizing the tendency to apply general criticism to one's neighbors' faults instead of one's own. She expected to find every door shut against her but thought that would not be important, for, she confided to a sister, it would only send her to her "darling retirement," that illusive solitude which she so seldom attained and so quickly abandoned. All her friends recognized the style and content of the books and played the guessing game only to please Hannah. When she dined with the Bishop of Salisbury, her two dear friends Dr. Porteus and Mrs. Montagu talked the book over with the greatest warmth and commended it. When she visited Horace Walpole he scolded her with pretended severity for being so serious and Hannah knew he was referring to "the little sly book." He explained to her with mock earnestness that the Sabbath was made to afford a rest period for the hard laboring poor and the beasts of burden, and was not intended to be kept by persons of fashion who never did anything on weekdays but rest. Hannah was a trifle nervous when Mr. Walpole got after her in his amusing sacrilegious way, but she loved it just the same. Kind Mrs. Chapone wrote to Hannah as if the *Estimate* had been by "the same good gentleman who sometime ago gave his excellent Thoughts to the Great."

The didactic books are from a literary viewpoint the least admirable of Hannah's writings. Her mind was not clear cut. Against a blurred background, certain opinions stood out boldly, so protected from inquiry that they should be called prejudices rather than principles. Any questioning of church, government, social distinctions, distribution of wealth, legal discrimination, and like matters shocked her. Criticism of the Church was to her sacrilegious and theories looking toward governmental changes were treasonable. Avoiding all speculation, she enjoyed that conviction of being right which is the reward of wholehearted acceptance of authority.

In spite of her practice in verse writing and her training as a dramatist, Hannah threw aside all rules of literary structure in these books. She wrote with dreadful ease and was not in the habit of revising. She felt it necessary to make few corrections. Ink flowed from her quill like tepid water from a tap.

The Manners of the Great, etc. sets forth the importance of reformation in high society that it may seep downward to the lower classes which draw their beliefs from the gentry's and model their conduct on that of their betters. Therefore the example afforded them must be good. Hannah was roused by individual domestic failings rather than by the general social evils which characterized the fashionable world. In a period of heavy gambling, repudiation of debts, a dissolute attitude toward women, drunkenness, gluttony, and irresponsibility among some of the great, she chose to speak severely of the custom of calling in the hairdresser on Sunday, of allowing servants to get "card money" by selling the packs of cards to the guests in a private home, of the deception of saying "Not at home" instead of "Not receiving," the evils of Sunday concerts, and loose conversation.

Hannah was a critic of her times, but a mild one. Her words did not bite like Swift's nor lash like Pope's. No one writhed under her scorn. She was satisfied with mild reforms and was pleased to learn that, after reading her books, the Queen stopped summoning an outside hairdresser on the Sabbath and had her tresses arranged by an attendant already on duty.

The *Estimate* takes up the decline of Christianity, the neglect of religious education, the negligent conduct of Christians, and the inadequacy of morals without religion. A sample will show the rather loose style in which she expressed shrewd insight:

Even allowing the boasted superiority of modern benevolence, still it would not be inconsistent with the object of the present design to inquire whether the diffusion of this branch of charity, though the most lovely offspring of religion, be yet any positive proof of the prevalence of religious principle.

Three books on education were enthusiastically received: *Strictures on the Modern System of Female Education*, 1799, went through thirteen editions and sold nineteen thousand copies; *Hints for Forming the Character of a Princess*, 1805, had but a limited appeal; while *Coelebs in Search of a Wife*, 1809, her only novel, went through twelve editions in a year, clearing that year two thousand pounds. Thirty thousand copies were sold in America before the author's death and this appreciation went far toward reconciling Hannah to the wicked rebellion of that country.

The *Strictures* is an inclusive, somewhat rambling arraignment of women and their ways. It commences with an address to women of rank about their influence and takes up such varied subjects as children's balls, the religious employment of time, a routine of prayer, conversation, false sensibility, and the doctrines of Christianity. This book roused abundant praise but also more antagonism than had the preceding ones. Hannah's friend and admirer, Beilby Porteus, extolled the work in a charge to his clergy:

Mrs. Hannah More, whose extraordinary and versatile talents can accommodate themselves equally to the Cottage and the Palace, who, while she is diffusing among the lower orders of people an infinity of little Religious Tracts, calculated to reform and comfort in this world, and to save them in the next, is at the same time applying all the powers of a vigorous and highly-cultivated mind to the instruction, improvement, and delight of the most exalted of her own sex. I allude more particularly to her last work on Female Education, which presents to the Reader such a fund of good sense, of wholesome counsel, of sagacious observation, a knowledge of the world and of the female heart, of high-tone morality and genuine Christian piety; and all this enlivened with such brilliancy of wit, such richness of imagery, such varied and felicity of allusion, such neatness and elegance of diction, as are not, I conceive, easily to be found combined and blended together in any other work in the English language. . . .

This panegyric was too much for John Wolcot, the Peter Pindar who had satirized Hannah in her early days. Her rigid views and Bishop Porteus' admiration furnished him with a subject for six fulminations, four of which were addressed to the bishop, one to Hannah, and one to the *Bas Bleu.* The theme was the same in all six, that Hannah had borrowed the bishop's ideas, a theme which the satirist wore out long before he ceased worrying it.

A selection from one set of verses will illustrate Peter Pindar's brand of vituperation:

NIL ADMIRARI

Miss Hannah More a Rhyme and Prose Gentlewoman born at Bristol

. . . .

MISS HANNAH'S graces dazzle not the view—

. . . .

No bonfire she—no SUN's meridian blaze—
A rush-light *'midst the illumin'd FEW:*
A farthing rush-light, *with it's winking rays.*

. . . .

MISS HANNAH has no eagle wings to flee,
Whom thus your adulation can befool;
Alas! a poor ephemeron is SHE!
A humming *native of a Bristol Pool.*
Indeed, MISS HANNAH has a so-so lyre;
So out of tune it murders all the NINE:
She really playeth not with taste or fire:
No, DR. PORTEUS, no thou GREAT DIVINE!

. . . .

With smiles her eulogy Miss Hannah hears
Laughs in her sleeve at all thy pompous praise:
In silence wrapp'd, perceives the ass's ears,
And sits complacent while her STENTOR brays.[1]

The same Richard Polewhele who as a lad had been very critical of Hannah and her writing, now himself a writer and Rector of Mannacan in Cornwall, rose up in her defense and slaughtered Pindar in *A Sketch of the Private and Literary Character of John Wolcot, M. D. commonly called Peter Pindar.*[2]

Bishop Porteus was distressed at Pindar's attack on Hannah but it made no difference in their friendship. Shortly before his death some years later, Hannah received from him a strange letter requesting her fervent and frequent prayers because he was in great difficulties and distresses. A note followed three days later saying that prayer had its usual effect and all was perfectly right. Hannah learned that the bishop's sick mind had been upset by a rumor that the Prince of Wales had started a social club which met Sundays. A devout Sabbath-keeper, the bishop secured an audience and was half carried into the presence of the

Prince to implore him to desist. The Prince, who was usually charming and tactful in his dealings with the clergy, assured the dying man that it was not a club but a charitable association, and that the day of meeting should be changed. After the bishop's death his writing-table drawer was found full of pious jottings and brief prayers written on scrap paper. Bishop Porteus left Hannah two hundred pounds in memory of their long friendship, and she on her part erected a cenotaph to him in the grounds of Barley Wood.

Hints for Forming the Character of a Young Princess, 1805, was designed for the education of the Princess Charlotte, the only child of the Prince of Wales, later George the Fourth. The development of the Princess Royal was a matter for anxiety on the part of thoughtful and religious subjects, although this concern could not be openly spoken, lest royalty be admitted imperfect. Her father could hardly be considered a guide for youth, since he quarreled with his royal father, separated from his wife, piled up debts, and conducted himself in a rowdy fashion. The mother was a woman of dubious conduct, probably half mad. The Princess, high-spirited and immature, was England's future queen and England's problem child. Rev. Dr. Grey, then prebendary of Durham, later Bishop of Bristol, suggested that Mrs. More write of the education suitable to a future ruler, for the assistance of the ladies who had charge of Princess Charlotte's training, and Alexander Knox added his entreaties. While the work was in the press, Dr. Fisher, Bishop of Exeter, was appointed preceptor to the Princess of Wales, putting Hannah in a quandary; should she suppress the book or take the chance of offending the bishop? She decided to publish it anonymously, with an apologetic dedication to the eminent divine. A copy was sent him through the publisher and Hannah was pleased that the Bishop's reply was addressed to "Sir." When it was clear that the Bishop was not offended, when the Queen had expressed approbation, and the Princess was said to have praised the book, the authorship was announced at a public breakfast given to the author by her friend the Duchess of Gloucester, Horace Walpole's niece.

The book is a sort of college course in one volume. It contains remarks on forming the mind; on the acquisition of knowledge; something of ancient history and historians; a good deal about English history; the necessity of religion; the true arts of popularity; the importance of the royal example; conversation; manners; moral calculation; observations on flattery, books, writers, the Holy Scriptures, the Church, and like subjects; not forgetting warnings against esteeming Louis XIV, accepting Voltaire's opinions, or being in any way influenced by the French; the whole written in generalities which could offend no one. It was reported to Hannah More that this volume was the last which Princess Charlotte read before her marriage to Prince Leopold and the last also which she read before her early death.

The full title of *Coelebs* is *Coelebs in Search of a Wife: Comprehending Observations on Domestic Habits and Manners, Religion and Morals.* Coelebs (the name indicating a bachelor) is a very prudent young man who inspects a series of young women, object matrimony. Mr. Stanley, the model father of the model Lucilla whom the model Coelebs finally selects, was commonly supposed to be drawn from the character of Hannah's beloved father. Maria Edgeworth stated that Coelebs was drawn from young Mr. Harford, of

Blaize Castle, Bristol, who was a young friend of the Mores and one of the gentlemen who later assisted Hannah in moving from Barley Wood to Clifton, a few years before her death; but a similarity exists between Coelebs' courting technique and actions of that strange man Thomas Day, the author of *Sanford and Merton*. Day first courted Edgeworth's sister and put her on an unsuccessful probation of one year. He courted in turn the sisters Honoria and Elizabeth Sneyd, losing them both in turn to Maria's much-married, much-widowed, fascinating father. Hopefully he adopted two girls to train, discarding one early and the other later as unworthy of his hand. Thomas Day finally married Elizabeth Milnes, a paragon of beauty, sense, submission, and devotion. This unusual inspection of possible wives must have been known to Hannah even if she never met Day himself, for they had acquaintances in common, among them Fanny Burney and Anna Seward, the Swan of Lichfield. The Mores may have been acquainted with some of the Edgeworths too, for that family visited Hotwells at Bristol while the Mores lived in Barley Wood. Since Thomas Day, strange as his personality seems to us, was deeply loved by his friends, surely *Coelebs* was not obnoxious to the sensibilities of that day. The book is less a story than a series of essays modeled on those of *The Spectator* and *The Rambler*, over which Hannah had pored in her youth.

Hannah More's views on women's education were in advance of those of most people in her time. Her moderate demands carried more weight than radical demands would have done. She made many excellent observations on the subject, pointing out that it was unjust to keep women ignorant and scorn them for it, holding that education should be a preparation for life rather than adornment; she advocated only for exceptional girls the classical education which she and her sisters had received. She would have the average girl trained in whatever "inculcates principles, polishes taste, regulates temper, subdues passion, directs the feelings, habituates to reflection, trains to self-denial, and more especially, that which refers all actions, feelings, tastes, and passions to the love and fear of God." She would have history taught to show the wickedness of mankind and the guiding hand of God, and geography to indicate how Providence has graciously consulted man's comfort in suiting vegetation and climate to his needs. She had extreme faith in the disciplinary value of study. Mr. Stanley, in *Coelebs*, quelled the superabundant vivacity of one daughter by a course of arithmetic with "a tincture of mathematics," while he rewarded another with lessons in Latin. Cooking and sewing were considered desirable not only for use, but for an indirect moral effect. Physical training was ignored. No school at that time offered any other exercise than walking out two by two.

As Hannah's absorption in religion grew stronger and stronger, her interest in literature lessened, until she came to fear that most literature was an evil influence on The Young Person. *Coelebs* contains the melancholy story of a girl who was ruined by reading poetry to excess. By the time Hannah brought out the collected edition of her own works, she had turned against the stage, but with very human inconsistency she republished her own plays with a preface condemning drama. She stated that she had felt that "the stage under certain regulations might be converted into a school of virtue," but had finally decided that it could not be purged of its improprieties until human nature itself changed; no plays were consistent with Christian principles because, in place of peaceableness, long suffering, gentleness and forgiveness, the stage upheld a code of honor involving love, jealousy, hatred, pride, and revenge; young men were led by these false standards into dueling and suicide and the representation of love scenes impaired the sober-mindedness of young females. She advised "the discriminated, the guarded, the qualified perusal" of Shakespeare by young people in company with a judicious friend, in order to satisfy the curiosity about so famous a writer and prevent the young reader from disastrous investigation by himself. This, from one who in her youth had made up a game with her friends in which no phrase could be used that was not a quotation from Shakespeare.

Three books on Christian Duties and *An Essay on the Character of Saint Paul*, 1815, rounded out Hannah's writing career. *The Spirit of Prayer*, published in 1825, when she was eighty years old, was made up of extracts from previous work, rather than fresh matter. The books on Christian Duties were *Practical Piety, or the Influence of the Religion of the Heart on the Conduct of Life*, 1811; *Christian Morals*, 1812; and *Moral Sketches of Prevailing Opinions and Manners, Foreign and Domestic, with Reflections on Prayer*, 1819. A pleasing quality of eighteenth-century titles is that they tell definitely what books are about.

The first edition of *Practical Piety* was sold out before publication and quickly ran into ten editions. It was translated into Icelandic. Two Persian gentlemen, waiting on the author, received a copy from her hands, and declared it should be the first book printed on the printing press they were carrying back to their native land. *Moral Sketches* sold its first edition on the day of its appearance. In this book, written at seventy-five, the old lady talked about the disobedience of children, the impudence of servants, the rebellion of laborers, the levity of society, the extravagance of the poor, and the depravity of foreign lands. Though she held that not all in England was good, she was convinced that all that was foreign was bad. Hannah was forever England. She wrote to Walpole, January seventh, 1793, during an illness: "They have been worrying me to go abroad, as if it were not better a thousand times to be sick, and even die, in this country, than to be alive and well in almost any other."

It is a noticeable fact that Hannah More is remembered today as a hymn writer. Actually, she wrote only a very few hymns, the dates of which are not given. Their first verses are:

True Heroes: or The Noble Army of Martyrs.

You who love a tale of glory,
Listen to the song I sing;
Heroes of the Christian story,
Are the heroes I shall bring.

A Christmas Hymn

O How wondrous is the story
Of our blest Redeemer's birth!
See the mighty Lord of Glory
Leaves his Heaven to visit earth!

A Hymn of Praise, for the Abundant Harvest of 1796.
After a Year of Scarcity.

Great God! When famine threaten'd late
To scourge our guilty land,
O Did we learn from that dark fate
To dread thy mighty hand?

CHAPTER XXV

Mrs. Garrick's Old Age

IT WAS inevitable that Mrs. Garrick and Mrs. Hannah More should grow apart during the later years of their lives. The journey to London seemed longer to Hannah as her strength grew less, and the two women had fewer interests in common and more to occupy them apart. Hannah's closest London friends were dead: Mrs. Montagu, Mrs. Boscawen, Lady Middleton and her friend Mrs. Bouverie, Frances Reynolds, and Mrs. Carter. Still the four sisters who had sucked Hannah back into family life were as good company as could be found in England. Barley Wood became a social center, with Hannah as the shining focus. Visitors came from far and wide; lords and ladies from drinking the waters in Bath, young poets visiting Joseph Cottle, the publisher, in Bristol, Americans, clergy, foreign missionaries, admirals, occasionally a royal duchess or even a prince, and humble folk by the score, drawn as to a shrine.

The shift in Hannah's social interests from London to Wrington was one factor which loosened the bond between her and Mrs. Garrick. Another was her absorption in religion and religious work. Although Mrs. Garrick's Catholicism had never come between the two women in the slightest degree, yet Hannah's increasing zeal in church work was not something that she could share with Mrs. Garrick. Her letters to Mrs. Garrick contain few references to her three main interests: didactic books, tracts for farm and factory workers, and Sunday Schools. In the end the sisters gathered Hannah completely into the Sisterhood and she went no more to visit her old friend.

Mrs. Garrick turned to relatives for close companionship and her German and Austrian kinfolk came over in numbers after her husband's death. Horace Walpole, writing to Miss Mary Berry, August twenty-fifth, 1795, describes a call on Mrs. Garrick at Hampton: "She met me at the door and told me she had a hundred head of nieces with her and in truth so I found; there were six gentlewomen, a husband of one of them and two boys. An elderly fat dame affected at every word to call her Aunt." This hundred head, more or less, may well have been one of the factors that discouraged Hannah's visits.

When she was over ninety Mrs. Garrick gave to these relatives twelve thousand pounds which she had saved from her income in the twenty-six years since her husband's death, a generosity which was the result of the extreme thrift with which she lived. She was accused of letting both her houses run down. When a portion of her late husband's property was divided among the "next of kin" in 1807, she petitioned to be included as one of the recipients. She was represented in court by the second son of Hannah's friend Sir William Pepys, Charles, who later became Lord Chancellor and was created Earl of Cottenham. Sir William wrote Hannah that Mrs. Garrick's claim failed because the whole tenor of the will was against it, but that it had afforded his son an opportunity of distinguishing himself by the speech he made on his client's behalf.

Mrs. Garrick was intimate with all her husband's nephews and nieces, especially George's daughter Catherine who had lived with them as a girl, later marrying John G. Payne; and with Emma Hart Garrick, widow of nephew David, later wife of Evan Jones, a Welsh minister. Mrs. Garrick dearly loved "Little Emma," a child of Emma Hart by her Garrick marriage, and grieved at her early death. A child by the second marriage was given the same name and this second Little Emma was able to speak English, French, and Welsh at the age of eight. The Joneses lived near Bristol for several years and Hannah met them frequently.[1]

As Mrs. Garrick grew older she developed a peppery temper and once quarreled with Little Emma's mother, refusing for a year to be reconciled in spite of letters and a gift of two geese. She had continuous trouble with Wallis over the estate and her diary for 1819 (brief entries in the trembling hand of a very old lady) contains petulant references to various persons.[2]

A definite estrangement between Hannah and Mrs. Garrick took place in the spring of 1801. Hannah's letters of the previous year are as cordial as ever although her visit was curtailed at the start by a heavy cold which delayed her setting off for London and then by Mrs. Garrick's illness. Hannah and Patty made a rather long stay at Barham Court, Teston, the Middletons' home, and stopped only for a call on Mrs. Garrick on their return journey. The first letter written on January fourth of this year has the usual friendly, intimate tone, but on April eleventh Hannah wrote, refusing Mrs. Garrick's hospitality rather tartly, saying they would not want a bed, that they must take their chance of finding her when they called as the date had not been fixed.[3]

The correspondence fell off from then on, yet the few letters which we have express deep affection and regret at hearing so seldom. In 1813 Hannah and Patty, although they spent a night with Lady Waldegrave at Strawberry Hill, merely called at Mrs. Garrick's the next day and, not finding her at home, went on without even stopping to rest.

They were returning from a visit to Lady Olivia Sparrow, at Brampton Park, Huntingdonshire.[4] They were going on to stay with Lord Barham (formerly Sir Charles Middleton) at Barham Court where they had so often visited in the lifetime of Mrs. Middleton and Mrs. Bouverie, and had almost reached there when they received word of Lord Barham's sudden death. Hannah was stricken by the news. Each new bereavement recalled to her the long succession of deaths; the loss of her father, Dr. Langhorne, Dr. Johnson, the *Bas Bleu* ladies, Bishop Porteus, and above all—David Garrick. Each death was Garrick's death all over. Hannah sank into one of her states of lassitude, pain, and depression, and Patty was probably anxious to get her home quickly. Knowing Patty's dominating ways, one suspects it was her decision to break the journey at Strawberry Hill rather than at the Garrick villa.

Mrs. Garrick wrote a letter of loving reproach to "My beloved Friend," saying that if she had only known that her most dearest friends were in Hampton she would have walked on foot from London if she could have found no conveyance. Mrs. Garrick was then in her ninetieth year, her handwriting was cramped, many words struck out, and some sentences unfinished, but it is a long letter full of love and regret.[5]

Old Mrs. Garrick lived a full life despite the infirmities of age. In summer she had her garden at Hampton. She was passionately fond of fruit, raising oranges in her hothouse and sending presents of fruit to her friends. She was ninety-four years old when, visiting a friend and finding him absent, she demanded a ladder from a reluctant servant and herself climbed a tree to pluck coveted fruit.

In winter she had her easy chair, her snuffbox, a blazing fire, and her histories and volumes of philosophy to read and reread. No newspapers nor novels, she wrote Hannah, perhaps remembering how Hannah felt about novels—except the one Hannah wrote.[6]

Then, too, she had the theatre. A box at Drury Lane was reserved for her till her death. Her diary of 1819 records that she sometimes attended as often as three times a week. She was in fact dressing for the theatre when she suddenly expired.

Lady Louisa Stuart wrote to Elizabeth, Duchess of Buccleuch, in an undated note after she had, as Mrs. Garrick's guest, been to see Kean acting Richard III:

> The old lady was as great a treat in her way as Mr. Kean. I never saw such vivacity and sense as her own, with a sort of captivating good breeding, that sends one back fifty years, without being in the least stiff or old-fashioned. The most modern girl of fifteen would not think her either, but be pleased and yet kept in order, yet not knowing why. She calls herself ninety-one, but my friend who knew her in Garrick's time, doubted her being so much. She has now a box on the ground floor, and the first time she came into it after the opening of the Theatre, the audience gave a loud clap. She told this to my friend and said it overset

her entirely, "but I knew not what to do; I was not to come forward and curtsey like the Queen; who was I? Besides they did not clap me, you know; they did better—I could do nothing: I went back and I cried."

Kean's acting reminded Mrs. Garrick of her husband's. She showed her favor by giving him Garrick's stage jewelry, having him sit in Garrick's own chair when he came to see her, visiting him at his own home, and criticising his acting when his interpretation differed from that of David.[7]

The old lady was on terms of informal intimacy with royalty. King George III, Queen Charlotte, and the Royal Dukes used to drop in to see her at Hampton. The story goes that when Queen Charlotte found her peeling onions, the Queen demanded another knife and helped. This shrivelled, bent old lady who had all her wits and a good bit of life left in her was almost as great a celebrity in her old age as she had been in her youth when she was the toast of the town.

Mrs. Garrick, who was born February twenty-ninth, 1724, died October sixteenth, 1822. She came fairly near to rounding out a century. Her funeral was a very quiet one, only a few close friends being admitted to Westminster Abbey where she was buried in her husband's grave.

Mrs. Garrick remembered Hannah and Martha More in her will, drawn January twenty-eighth, 1817. This would seem to indicate that the coldness which had once existed between them had been entirely wiped out.

> To my friend Mrs. Hannah More the sum of one hundred Pounds which I request she will kindly accept as a small token of my sincere esteem.
>
> To my friend Mrs. Martha More the sum of one hundred Pounds as a small memorial of my sincere regard.

Patty had died between the time the will was drawn and Mrs. Garrick's death. Mrs. Garrick left legacies to her relatives, servants, friends, and charitable institutions, bequeathing the residue for life, with remainder to grandchildren, to Madame Elizabeth de Saar, who was Betty Fürst, the niece who was living with the Garricks at the time of David's death more than forty years before.

Recording her quiet burial beside her husband in Westminster Abbey, James Boaden says: "His widow after an hourly regret of forty-three years, sleeps with him in the same sanctuary." [8] A truer phrase than "hourly regret" would be "constant memory," for though she was "Davie's widow" to the end, she had full and happy years after she outlived the initial heartbreak.

CHAPTER XXVI

Hannah's Last Years

THE MORE sisters lived together at Barley Wood until the death of Mary; that blunt, inflexible woman, who had created and run the best girls' school in Great Britain, died in 1813 on Easter Sunday. The five had grown up together, been educated together, worked together, retired together. This devoted sisterhood was now broken by death. The four remaining went courageously on with their common interests, but it was not the same. Three other sisters died within what was a brief period compared to the years they had been together. Elizabeth, the gentle homebody, died in 1816; spritely Sarah, the following year; Patty, two years later.

So long as Patty was left her, Hannah was able to rally from the loss of the other sisters, although they had all been bound together in more than usual interdependence. She and Patty occupied themselves with their schools and their friends. They did not make many trips out into the world, but their particular world came to them. They started a Wrington branch of the British and Foreign Bible Society. For several years annual meetings were held in a "waggon-yard," there being no hall large enough, and once over a hundred were entertained at Barley Wood for dinner, the overflow from the house being fed at tables in the garden, and some two hundred came to tea. They had given up the great school feasts, but some other school activities went on under their supervision and the very year she died the indefatigable Patty distributed rewards to more than thirteen hundred children and parents.

Wilberforce was visiting Barley Wood at the time of Patty's death. "Patty sat up with me," he wrote in his diary, "till near twelve, talking over Hannah's first introduction to a London life, and I, not she, broke off the conference. I never saw her more animated. About eight in the morning when I came out of my bedroom I found Hannah at the door—'Have you not heard Patty is dying? They called me to her in great alarm.' " She had been taken ill two or three hours after she had said good-night, and died in about a week. Wilberforce says of her: "Never was there a more generous, benevolent creature, more self-denying to herself, or kind to others." [1]

Patty, dying in 1819, left an estate of approximately ten thousand pounds to be distributed after Hannah's death, naming as executors and residuary legatees John Lintorn Simmons and the two Miss Roberts, Mary and Margaret. She left money to three hospitals, several missionary societies, and some relatives, remembering her godchildren, six of the schoolmasters, and other friends with small sums.

Patty's death broke Hannah's heart, for this youngest sister had been like a mother, a servant, and an adorer. Although Hannah wrote Selina Mills Macaulay that not one rebellious thought had risen in her heart for Patty's death, she was in truth a desolate, broken woman, with fourteen years of loneliness ahead of her. The family invalid was to live the longest of them all. After Patty's death she did not often leave her chamber, for in her own room where she had long been accustomed to be much alone she could sometimes forget her fourfold bereavement, while the downstairs rooms were too filled with associations to be endurable.

Hannah's letters from now on are one long wail, not about the loss of four beloved sisters, but about her bad health. She relieved her spirit of its violent grief through incessant complaints of pain. She would remark, holding her medicine in her hand, that it was a token of God's mercy that she had lost her sense of taste and smell long ago, since she had to take such nauseous draughts, or she would piously remind her attendant that the gall and vinegar was more bitter than what she had to swallow. By absorption in her sufferings, she tried to crowd out the thought of her exceeding loneliness. "I write to you on the anniversary of my seizure," she begins a letter; and another the same day, "I continue to this day which is the anniversary of my last seizure." In other letters she would calculate the exact number of nights she had slept during this bad period or that one. Her friends told her and each other that she was wonderful and their sympathetic admiration was balm to her wounded heart.

The year after Patty's death, the poor woman enacted, during a serious breakdown, the first of a series of edifying deathbeds. She had a second deathbed two years later and a third one in another two years. Weariness and grief struggled with natural love of life; she wanted to die and she wanted to live. When the actual end came, a decade later, she slipped quietly and not unhappily, first out of her mind and then out of her body, without farewell scenes or affecting utterances. Her devoted friends must have understood that this constant dwelling on her infirmities was really expression of loneliness, for they rallied round with letters and love and the praise on which she fed.

After she was eighty, a strange thing happened to Hannah; her health improved. It seemed as if she reconciled herself to life as death approached. Perhaps the struggle had ended between her natural nature, somewhat faulty, and the high standard of saintliness she imposed upon it. Her days were not unhappy. She kept pinned to her bed curtain a little bag from which she sent by the hand of her physician daily doles to poor homes where there was sickness or some other calamity. She sat in her bow window planning improvements for the garden and the grounds which had been Patty's special care. Small unexpected pleasures came her way. A dignitary of the cathedral of Lincoln, of whom she had never heard, left her a twenty guinea legacy with a heartening eulogy, and she spent the money redeeming two little slaves in the Burman Empire, where she had heard the people were "not so much idolaters as atheists, an ingenuous, acute people, very argumentative." She knit "garters and muffatees a little decorated" and the money from their sale went to the Barley Wood school maintained by the American Board of Missions in Ceylon. "Halfpenny papers" written by her sold for a shilling each in charity bazaars at Bristol, Clifton, and Bath. Through her devoted companion, Mary Frowd, she kept in touch with her schools and her mothers' clubs.

Hours of her time were taken up with her huge correspondence from all over the world, especially from America. She discovered "cultivated minds" among the Americans who came to see her and was glad to have her prejudices against that vast republic softened. She reported that they were imitating all the English religious and charitable institutions and were fast acquiring taste, the last quality, she felt, that republics acquire.

Friends resented her squandering her failing strength on letters to strangers. They worried, too, over her seeing visitors by the hundreds—literally hundreds—not realizing that the old lady received a tremendous lift from meeting new people. She could still charm, and her natural gaiety flared out in the joy of greeting these pilgrims to her home, although she was afterward overwhelmed with fatigue. She explained: "If my visitors are young, I hope I may perhaps be enabled to do them some good; if old, I hope to receive some good from them. If they come from far, I cannot refuse to see them after they have incurred (though so little worth it) so much trouble and possibly expense to visit me; and if they live near, I could not be so ungracious and so unkind as to shut out my neighbors."[2] The truth of the matter was, she wouldn't have missed a single visitor for all the headaches and fatigue in the world. Although Heaven was her destination and she was in haste to get there, still she found much to enjoy by the way.

The devotion which Hannah More had given her older friends when she was young was now returned to her by younger people. She had long outlived the Johnson circle, *Bas Bleu* was only a name, and all the dear, dear elderly divines were gone. But she had never ceased replacing lost friends by living ones. She could follow the long roll call of her dead with an impressive list of the younger generation who loved her for her kindness, affection, lively interest, and social spirit.

Her moods varied, as they had all her life, from periods

of lonely depression to intense enjoyment of company. A visit to this Saint of Barley Wood is recorded by Mrs. S. C. Hall, a magazine writer well known at that time. With her husband she journeyed to Wrington over roads crackling with January snow and turned into the frozen driveway. She noted the bare rose vines twined about the veranda pillars, the swallows sheltered in the thatch, and the bird food set out for them. The visitors were received in the upstairs sitting room. Three ladies were already calling and with them was a little boy whose plate Mrs. More delighted in piling with cake. When this group had departed, Mr. and Mrs. Hall were asked to take a walk through the grounds while their hostess had a short nap.

Upon their return indoors they found her refreshed by her rest and able to enjoy their company. Although she was small and shrunken and aged, she conveyed no suggestion of feebleness. She was light on her feet and vivacious, laughing and chatting in a voice as strong and clear as that of a girl. Mrs. Hall describes her as a sparkling, light, bright, summery old lady. Her white hair was frizzed in a bygone fashion under a white cap with a full double ruffle of rich lace, and she wore a silk pea-green dress and a white China crepe shawl.

Tripping from console to console, the old lady showed her treasures, mementos of her life: South Sea curiosities collected during her later absorption in foreign missionary work, Patty's memo book for which Hannah had collected contributions during her London years, and "some gift that bore a name immortal, some cherished reminder of other days—almost of another world, certainly of another age; for they were memories of those whose deaths were registered before the present century had birth." Among her treasures were cards of admission to *Percy* and a playbill of the tragedy, and an inkstand made from Shakespeare's mulberry tree and given her by David Garrick. Her eyes were what most impressed Mrs. Hall. "Those bright, immortal eyes of hers, not marred by looking at the world for more than eighty years, but clear and far-seeing." When she spoke of Garrick the expression of her countenance became more earnest, more affectionate than it had been at the mention of any other name. Certainly her eyes in youth must have been glorious, says Mrs. Hall; when she spoke of the great master of his art, they expressed the utmost tenderness. She recalled his ability, his energy, his kindliness, and his expressive face. "I should have liked to have looked upon his face once more, but they only showed me his coffin," she said. "Ah, if he had been alive, it would have been a trial to have retired from the world." [3]

The memory of David Garrick was with Hannah all the days of her life. Not that he was her last love, for she flirted with devoted bishops, young members of Parliament, and elderly generals and visiting noblemen, as long as her bright eyes could flash and quick tongue snap out repartee, but Garrick was her great love.

The old lady had to move from Barley Wood a few years before her death. She had always spent her money generously and as she grew old it slipped too easily through her fingers; people took advantage of her. Her staff of servants had increased to eight, although she never left her room, and was constitutionally afraid of giving trouble. Matters were brought to a crisis by the extraordinary behavior of servants who cheated her outrageously, as if a contagious disease had broken out among them. They gave personal orders to tradesmen in their employer's name, they diverted money which she supposed was being expended in charities, they ate the game sent by her friends, and they kept hidden in the house a servant she had discharged. Some nights they gave parties in the coach-house, with music and brandy and a table set with More silver. The ringleader had lived with the More family twenty-six years and the coachman for eighteen, and all were to have received bequests.

The poor old lady refused to hear of their misdeeds and refused to believe what she could not help knowing. To avoid taking any steps—for she was now too old to grapple with domestic trouble—she held as long as possible that it was God's will she should be thus mistreated.

Hannah, now so old that she was Mrs. More to even her nearest and dearest, was finally persuaded to move to a house belonging to her friend Rev. Dr. Whalley in Windsor Terrace, Clifton, where she would be near friends who could watch over her in comfort and well-being.

The dishonest servants were not notified until the day of their employer's departure, three months' wages being given in lieu of notice. John Harford sent his carriage, since her own coachman was one of the treacherous domestics. Among the bodyguard who gathered about her on this occasion to protect her from unpleasant demonstrations were sons and daughters of her early friends; the daughter of Mrs. Simmons, schoolmate and a cousin of Mr. Turner; and John Lintorn Simmons, Esq., who was one of her executors. Richard Lovell Gwatkin came, too; he for whom Hannah had written an Epilogue to speak after the performance of Dr. Young's tragedy, *The Brothers*, acted by the young gentlemen of the Bristol grammar school when he was twelve years old, more than fifty years before. Friendship with Hannah More was handed down in such families as the Simmons' and the Pepys' and the Macaulays', and the Bathursts', along with ancestral silver and portraits.

Mrs. More had been downstairs only once before in seven years. "She descended the stairs with a placid countenance," reported one of the party, and walked silently around the lower room, the walls of which were covered with the portraits of all her old and dear friends, who had successively gone before her; and as she was helped into the carriage, she cast one pensive parting look upon her bowers, saying, 'I am driven like Eve out of Paradise; but not like Eve, by angels.' "

Barley Wood was disposed of to one of the Harford family, and her expenses being materially reduced by satisfactory arrangements, she was able to give in charity every year as much as ever. Some of her American friends, hearing of the way she had been defrauded, thought she was in financial straits and wrote offering to collect a fund for her maintenance. Of greater gratification to her than this thoughtful but unnecessary offer was the information that *Hints for the Education of a Princess*, hitherto excluded from publication in republican America, was now adopted as "a generally useful work." "I have conquered America," she exclaimed.

Clifton was close to Bristol though not then a part of the city where she had lived so many years. It was a return to an earlier home rather than a change to a new place. Here she lived her last five years, in the serenity which had descended so late on her uneasy, striving nature, leaving the world little by little, never quite realizing that she was at last actually approaching that death on which her troubled thoughts had dwelt so long and earnestly.

She must have been indeed a lovable old lady to call forth so much devotion from so many friends for so many years. Her resident companion was Mary Frowd, of whom we know only that she had a mother, five sisters, and a brother John who was a clergyman, to all of whom Hannah left small bequests. The Misses Roberts made long, greatly appreciated visits. Several years before, when Hannah's clothing caught on fire from the fireplace, Mary Roberts had saved her life at the cost of severe burns on her hands. Margaret Roberts was her literary executor and the William Roberts who edited the four-volume edition of Hannah's letters immediately after her death was their brother.

Lady Olivia Sparrow was, next to the Misses Roberts, Hannah's greatest comfort in her lonely years. Hannah met her through mutual friends in the religious Clapham group. Her portrait shows a tall woman swathed in voluminous black relieved with white lace. Her lovely face is framed by a lace hood and her blond or white hair brought forward in a coil on each temple. She has a beautiful forehead, serene eyes, and a determined chin. It is the picture of a great lady. She was Hannah's constant correspondent and occasional visitor. Hart Davis, Mr. Harford's brother-in-law, was one of Hannah's friends who wrote her frequently. Wilberforce died within a few weeks of Hannah and his obituary in *The Christian Observer*, January, 1834, contains a long letter about the friendship existing between the two.

One occupation which filled Hannah's hours while her strength ebbed slowly away was deciding how to distribute her property among her many philanthropic interests and her multitude of friends. She drew her last will in 1830 and the following year began writing codicils. The failure of her mind seems to have begun early in 1832, for in the first nine months of that year she added fourteen codicils, mostly very trivial, after which there were no more entries although she lived a year longer.

Her fortune of some thirty thousand pounds was distributed among some seventy religious societies and charitable projects, only three of the donations being as large as one thousand pounds and many of them fifty pounds or less. Well over a hundred friends were remembered. To her relative Mrs. Harriet Mills she left a thousand pounds, and to Miss Mary Frowd one thousand one hundred and twenty. Several received five hundred pounds, but most of the bequests were small. Nineteen guineas was a favorite sum as there was no legacy duty on bequests under twenty pounds. The residue went to the endowment of the new church of St. Philip and St. Paul in an out-parish of Bristol.

She made no arrangements for continuing her schools, but wrote:

> Deeply regretting the necessity of dissolving my schools at Nailsea, Shipham and Cheddar I direct that the rents, teachers and all outgoings be paid off and discharged six months after my decease.

Her concern for the welfare of her schools, with which she had had no personal contact since Patty's death, had been superseded by her desire for the emancipation of slaves, for which Wilberforce ardently worked, and her absorption in foreign missions. The Negroes of Africa and the Red Indians of

Ohio delighted her imagination. Primitive man stood in a romantic glow of innocent nobility.

Hannah's treasures were carefully distributed among her close friends. One feels she spent many hours deciding that "to Miss Mary Roberts should go my tall mahogany scrutoire with a glass at the top and the little carriage," and Mary Roberts should receive "the pair of worked fire-screens glazed, the small wooden Barley Wood candle screen and small silver inkstand," while a list of books was bestowed on them in common. She selected the books which were to go to various friends and distributed her table silver, bedding, and some furniture among more intimate associates. It is evident that a great deal of thought went into the document, although the bequests are unclassified either by the nature of the gift or the relationship of the beneficiaries, and names are so repeated that the distribution of the estate must have been a piece of work. Eight of the codicils are additional bequests to Mary Frowd, as if the invalid felt her obligation to her companion to an exaggerated degree.

One codicil records a pathetic situation—the old lady's alienation from her beloved Tom Macaulay. In the body of the will she had left her library to this young man whom she herself had trained in the selection of books, for the friendship between the man just becoming famous and the woman who was leaving fame behind was a pleasure to both of them. Unfortunately, he called on her when she was living in Clifton, soon after he was elected to Parliament. He was full of spirit and vivacity and argued about politics with her, not making sufficient allowance for an old lady's old-fashioned views.[4] He evidently realized this afterward for, when his mother asked him for franks to send to Hannah a copy of his speech advocating the Reform Bill, he replied: "Oh, no, don't send her it. If you do she will cut me off with a prayer book." [5] As it turned out, he got not even a prayerbook, for on August eleventh, 1832, the old lady revoked her legacy to Thomas Babington Macaulay, leaving her books to her relative, Charles Mills. The alteration in her will was made only a few weeks before the dear old lady's wits wandered out of her control, and one regrets that the approaching shadow should have darkened a unique friendship.

The aged Mrs. More died September seventh, 1833, and was buried on the thirteenth beside her four sisters in the Wrington churchyard. A funeral procession in deep mourning came to Barley Wood from Bristol, where the shops were closed and the church bells tolled. These carriages were joined by those of the neighborhood gentry, clergy, and farmers, and at the church the children of Wrington schools lined the pathway to the door. The Rev. Thomas Tregenna Biddulph, Rector of St. James's, Bristol—the Mores' church for many, many years—conducted the services. The sisters' common grave is covered with a flat stone on which is cut an inscription in which the ages given, according to the custom of the time, are of the coming and not the past birthdays:

Here Lie the Mortal Remains of Five Sisters

Mary More	Died 18th of April	1813	Aged 75 Years
Elizabeth More	Died 16th of June	1816	Aged 76 Years
Sarah More	Died 17th of May	1817	Aged 74 Years
Martha More	Died 16th of Sept	1819	Aged 72 Years
Hannah More	Died 7th of Sept	1833	Aged 89 Years

All these died in the Faith
Accepted in the Beloved

Hebrews 11:13 Ephesians 1:6

Author's Notes and References

ANY LIFE of Hannah More must be based on William Roberts' *Memoirs of the Life and Correspondence of Mrs. Hannah More* in four volumes, the first edition of which was published by R. B. Seeley and Sons, London, in 1834, the year after Mrs. More's death. Many editions have followed since that first one, but the text has not been altered. The book is compiled from hundreds of letters to which Mr. Roberts had access through his sister Margaret Roberts, Mrs. More's literary executor. Mr. Roberts was himself but slightly acquainted with the subject of his biography, but he knew much about her through fellow members of the Clapham Sect, Zachary Macaulay, William Wilberforce, the Thornton family, and through the long close friendship of his two sisters, Mary and Margaret Roberts, with Hannah. Being himself an intensely religious man, his interest centered on her work and personality in the latter part of her life, leading him to neglect her early, gayer years, and to present her later years in a somewhat dreary light. Reviewers criticised him severely at the time, and it is difficult even now to be patient with his biased viewpoint. Nevertheless one must draw lavishly from his rich storehouse of information and I acknowledge my indebtedness, even while I regret his preoccupation with only one side of her nature. Mr. Roberts edited with abandon, eliminating and altering sections of the letters, and even changing dates to achieve unity of subject and time. This one discovers in comparing his work with the original manuscripts of such letters as have come to light.

Rev. Henry Thompson, who published a shorter biography, *Life of Hannah More with Notices of her Sisters* (Cadell, London, 1838), was a curate who came to Wrington three years after Hannah's death. The book contains information drawn from Wrington sources; but, like Roberts' book, it was written of a very old, deeply religious lady. Other biographies which deserve mention are: *A New Memoir of Hannah More or Life in Hall and Cottage,* by Mrs. Helen Cross Knight (American Tract Society, New York, 1851); *Pilgrimage to English Shrines,* by Mrs. S. C. Hall (Virtue, London, 1853). From these have been drawn a number of shorter biographies, written with care but containing no additional information. The best of these are by Annette Meakin, Charlotte M. Yonge, Mrs. C. L. Balfour, Marion Harland, and Margaret Tabor.

Other important sources of information are *Mendip Annals,* a journalistic record of the organization and carrying on of the More Sunday Schools, by Martha More (Carter, New York, 1859), edited by Arthur Roberts, and *Letters of Hannah More to Zachary Macaulay, Esq.* (Carter, New York, 1860) edited by the same hand. Letters by Hannah More are to be found in volumes of correspondence exchanged by her contemporaries; especially Horace Walpole, David Garrick, Rev. William Jay, Thomas Sedgewick Whalley, D.D., Boswell, Elizabeth Montagu, Elizabeth Carter, Frances Burney, Mary Hamilton, Frances Boscawen, Joseph Cottle, Thomas De Quincey, and William Wilberforce. Collections of unpublished letters are listed in the Acknowledgments.

CHAPTER I

1. Some pleasing information about this school came to me in response to my queries in the Bristol newspapers. Miss Ball of that city wrote:

My father, a tradesman of Fishponds, was born in 1832. His name was John Henry Ball and he attended the school in the house where Hannah More was born, on Fishponds Common, Fishponds, near Bristol, and he was at school when Her Majesty Queen Victoria was crowned in 1837. The scholars were each given a new penny and a mug and all shouted, "Hulloa, boys, let the bells ring! Hulloa, boys, hulloa, boys, God save the Queen!" This birthplace of Hannah More is now used, I believe, for church work as it adjoins Fishponds Church.

2. M. G. Jones, *The Charity School Movement* (Cambridge University Press, 1938), tables pp. 355, 366. The Stapleton school is not included in the 1724 list of Gloucestershire free schools, but is in a much later list.

3. Somerset House, London, PCC 484 Ellenbro; PCC 646 Farquhar.

Martha, who predeceased Hannah, in a will drawn 1819, made bequests to William Grace the younger, Martha Grace, and Susan Grace, four hundred pounds each; forty pounds to William Grace the elder and twenty to his sister Mary Jacobs. The Baskervilles and the Williams likewise living at Stoke Gifford were beneficiaries. These and additional legacies were not to be distributed until after Hannah's death. Hannah, in a will drawn 1830, left four hundred pounds apiece, kitchen utensils, wearing apparel, and all the silver spoons but six to Martha Grace and Susan Baskerville. Charles Mills [later the Rev. Charles Popham Mills, Principal of the Malta Protestant College] is mentioned as a relative in connection with his legacy and Mrs. Harriet Mills is also a beneficiary, but nothing indicates to which side of the family they were kin.

CHAPTER II

1. John Latimer, *The Annals of Bristol in the 18th Century* (printed for the Author, 1893), pp. 190, 241.

2. Joseph Cottle, *Early Recollections* (Longman, Rees & Co., London, 2 V, 1837), I, p. 80 n.

CHAPTER III

1. Latimer, *op. cit.*, p. 331.

2. Daniel DeFoe, *A Tour through the Islands of Great Britain* (London, 1778, 4 V.), II, p. 236.

3. When I climbed Park Street hill in 1938, the boarding school had been converted into a shop on the ground floor and offices above. It was a flat-faced building, close to the sidewalk. The house had spacious rooms and a good stairway, but one marvelled that it could have held sixty pupils and their teachers. A meeting house filled what must formerly have been a garden in the rear. All the houses up and down the hill had been converted into shops and offices, but one could still picture demure school girls, dressed like little women in long skirts, walking two by two in those dreary promenades which were their only form of exercise. As I stood at College Green, at the foot of the steep hill, looking across Park Street, after the evening lights were lit, I could see through upper windows large,

lofty rooms with lovely carved ceilings, former drawing-rooms converted into workshops and salesrooms.

Bristol must have been a beautiful city in the Mores' day although it had not the fame of Bath. From biographies and letters one gets an impression of comfortable living combined with intellectual liveliness, like a prosperous university town. It was a pleasant city when I visited it, the charm of ancient buildings and canals still lingering amid commercial activity. Now Park Street hill lies a mass of stone and brick and mortar, old buildings gone forever. Some of the Bristol rubble was sent overseas as ballast in ships hurrying to America for munitions and when discarded was used in constructing the East River Drive in New York City. A part of old Bristol is now a part of New York.

4. This bill, faded ink on worn, stained rag paper, came to me by a delightful route. My advertisement in *The Times Literary Supplement,* London, for unpublished More letters, was answered by Charles L. Simmons, Esq., descendant of John Lintorn Simmons, Esq., Parish of Keynsham, Somerset, the executor of Hannah More's will in 1833. Mr. Simmons put me in touch with a relative, Mrs. Lintorn Orman, who was so pleased to find someone who would appreciate what she had treasured that she gave me faded letters written to Martha Lintorn by Hannah and Martha and this itemized school bill.

5. Rev. Richard Polewhele, *Reminiscences in Prose and Verse* (London, 1836), II, p. 167. Also, *Traditions and Recollections* (London, 1826), I, p. 87.

While on a second visit to Bristol, the young jackanapes, now an Oxford student, but still an admirer of his former teacher, had the bright idea of showing Hannah Peter Pindar's recent verses, *A Supplicating Epistle to the Reviewers,* in which the satirist touched up Hannah. Young Polewhele slipped the poem into his pocket and hot-footed it to 43 Park Street, where Hannah received him surrounded by a group of "parlour-boarders." One sees the circle of young ladies busy with their embroidery frames and knitting needles, young ladies in voluminous skirts spreading from slender well-stayed waists, sitting very straight in wooden chairs, hands busy, ears open to culture, thoughts free to roam, very conscious of the young dandy, while Hannah read aloud.

The strutting young blade made his bow and produced the satire, begging Hannah to read it aloud to them. Imagine the excitement of the young ladies when they heard Peter Pindar citing "the volumes of Miss Hannah More" as an example of overpraised work! Those little high-set eyes of the impudent young sprig must have twinkled when Hannah read:

> *The Search for Happiness,* that beauteous song,
> Which all of us would give our ears to own;
> *The Captive Percy,* that like mustard strong,
> Makes our eyes weep, and understandings groan.

Hannah paused. Polewhele waited hopefully. The young ladies probably gasped; perhaps some stifled giggles. Hannah inquired what the writer meant by *The Captive Percy,*—for Pindar had telescoped the names of two plays, *The Inflexible Captive* and *Percy* into one title. Polewhele was disappointed that there was no indignant explosion and considered Hannah affected in pretending not to understand.

6. Henry Thompson, *The Life of Hannah More* (Cadell, London, 1838), p. 166 n.

CHAPTER IV

1. Reginald Blount, ed., Mrs. Montagu, *Queen of the Blues* (London, n.d., 2 V.), II, p. 213.

2. The thought of the Bronte sisters comes to one in this connection. The social position of the two families was similar and their incomes probably about the same. The sisters in both families were brilliant, ambitious, and passionately attached to each other. In each case they saw a girls' boarding school as the solution of their financial troubles. Charlotte and Emily courageously went to Brussels to learn French. The Mores learned it from each other and from prisoners on parole. The Brontes were like the Mores in sex, lack of money, and ambition, but very different in personality. The Brontes failed to get one pupil. The imaginative, hapless Brontes could only write immortal books and die young. The practical, determined Mores could run a successful school and live to a wealthy old age.

3. Robert Isaac and Samuel Wilberforce, *Life of William Wilberforce* (Philadelphia, 2 V., 1839), I, p. 248.

4. Thompson, *op. cit.*, p. 25.

5. *Ibid.*, p. 27.

This was not the end of the verse-making, for Burke, offering himself as a messenger, carried back to Hannah's friend Frances Reynolds in London a letter which, opened and read in the presence of Dr. Johnson, turned out to be a poetic address to Burke. The Doctor exclaimed, "Human language can soar no higher." Hannah laid on her poetic compliments rather thick, but it was the fashion of the day. Anyone who could write eulogistic verse, did so; and many recorded in ephemeral lines friendships, enmities and other emotional upsets. Light verse fluttered round Hannah like doves around their cote.

6. Viscountess Knutsford, *Life and Letters of Zachary Macaulay* (London, 1900), p. 141.

CHAPTER V

1. Rev. John Collinson, *The History and Antiquities of the County of Somerset* (Bath, 1791, 3 V) III, p. 155.

2. William Roberts, *Memoirs of the Life and Correspondence of Mrs. Hannah More* (Seeley, London, 1834, 4 V), I pp. 31–3.

3. Clementina Black, *The Linleys of Bath* (Secker, London, 1926), p. 28.

4. Collinson, *op. cit.*, III, p. 156.

5. *Ibid.*

CHAPTER VI

1. The Theatre Royal, Bristol, the oldest theatre in Great Britain, was sold, January 28, 1942, for £10,500, at a dramatic auction which lasted seven minutes. It was announced later that this perfect miniature eighteenth-century theatre was to be England's first nationally owned theatre.

2. Guy Tracy Watts, *Theatrical Bristol* (Bristol, 1915).

3. These sentiments, which long outlasted Hannah's time, remind one of Kingsley's "Be good, sweet maid, and let who can be clever."

4. Thompson, *op. cit.*, p. 25.

5. Richard Brinsley Peake, *Memoirs of the Colman Family* (London, 1841).

CHAPTER VII

1. Roberts, *op. cit.*, I, p. 54.
2. *Ibid.*, I, p. 66.
3. Daniel Wilson, *Chatterton* (London, 1869).
4. Roberts, *op. cit.*, I, p. 261.
5. *Ibid.*, I, p. 251.

CHAPTER VIII

1. Roberts, *op. cit.*, 68–9.
2. Pigot papers.
3. James Boaden, ed., *The Private Correspondence of David Garrick* (London, 1831, 2 V), II, p. 148.
4. Folger Shakespeare Library, *Garrick Correspondence*. Dated, Adelphi, Decr. 17. 76. The last page of the letter is missing. This same letter is published by Roberts, I, 119, mutilated, misdated, and combined with another letter.
5. *The Clerical Guide or Ecclesiastical Directory* (London, 1822).

In Hannah's correspondence only one later reference to the Cotton family is found. Writing home while visiting Lady Spencer at Holywell House, St. Albans, in 1784, she wrote: "I had intended to call on Dr. Cotton, but he is grown very old and I was afraid he would not recollect me." This must have been Dr. Nathaniel Cotton, poet and philosopher, who died at St. Albans three years later, aged eighty-three, and one is justified in supposing that it was during the visit to the Cotton family in Bungay that Hannah had previously met him. We have no information why the well-connected Cotton relatives dropped out of Hannah's life when one of her outstanding traits was passionate loyalty to old friendships. Neither the name of Cotton nor of Hayle occurs in the will of either sister.

6. Roberts, *op. cit.*, I, 201.
7. Boaden, *op. cit.*, II, 278. (Roberts erroneously states that this review was published in *The Gentleman's Magazine*.)

CHAPTER IX

1. Boaden, *op. cit.*, II, p. 241.
2. Roberts, *op. cit.*, I, p. 123.
3. *Ibid.*, I, 132.
4. *Bath Chronicle*, Feb. 21, 1793, p. 3. Reviewed in: *The Monthly Review*, V, LVII (1778), p. 23; *The Gentleman's Magazine*, V, 48 (1778), p. 33. Also, Clementina Black, ed., *The Cumberland Letters* (Secker, London, 1912), p. 175.
5. Rev. John Genest, *Some Account of the English Stage* (Carrington, Bath, 1832), XI, pp. 115, 117, 162, 211, 237, 384.
6. William Heard, *A Sentimental Journey to Bath, Bristol, and their Environs* (Sewell, London, 1778).
7. Pigot Papers.
8. John S. Harford, *Recollections of William Wilberforce, Esq.* (Longman, Green, Longman, Roberts, & Green, London, 1865), p. 277. Elizabeth and Florence Anson, eds., *Mary Hamilton* (Murray. London, 1925), p. 137. Rev. Montagu Pennington, *Memoirs of the Life of Mrs. Elizabeth Carter* (Greenleaf, Boston, 1809), pp. 358–9, 359 n.
9. Roberts, *op. cit.*, I, p. 113.
10. *Accounts of Chippendale, Hairg & Co. for the Furnishing of David Garrick's House in the Adelphi* (Victoria and Albert Museum, 1920).
11. Roberts, *op. cit.*, I, p. 146.

CHAPTER X

1. Folger, Gar. Cor., *op. cit.*
2. Roberts, *op. cit.*, I, p. 147.
3. *The Life and Death of David Garrick, Esq.* Anon. (London, 1779).
4. *The Life of the Rev. Sir James Stonehouse, Bart., M.D.* (Oxford, 1844).
5. Roberts, *op. cit.*, I, p. 149.
6. *Ibid.*, I, p. 192.
7. *Ibid.*, I, p. 172.

CHAPTER XI

1. Countess of Ilchester and Lord Stavordale, *Life and Letters of Lady Sarah Lennox* (London, 1902), II, p. 293.
2. Pigot Papers.
3. Roberts, *op. cit.*, I, p. 167.
4. *The Gentleman's Magazine,* V. 49 (1779), p. 462.
5. Roberts, *op. cit.*, I, p. 72.
6. *Ibid.*, I, p. 212.
7. *The Gentleman's Magazine,* V. 70 (Sept. 1800), p. 908.
8. Roberts, *op. cit.*, I, p. 319–20.

CHAPTER XII

1. Collinson, *op. cit.*, I, p. 206.
2. Folger, Gar. Cor., *op. cit.*
3. Anson, *op. cit.*, p. 291.
4. Folger, Gar. Cor., *op. cit.*
5. Although Barley Wood has been a good deal altered since Hannah's time, the general effect of the outside is much like the old pictures. The present owner has more than doubled the width of the building in front, added a great organ room in the back, added another story, and put on a modern roof, yet the old charm of the place has not been lost.
6. *The Christian Observer* (1833), p. 632, prints a letter from "an American Clergyman" in which he makes special mention of this garden house.
7. Harford, *op. cit.*, pp. 268–73.
8. *Tait's Edinburgh Magazine* (Dec., 1833; Aug., 1840).
9. Arthur Roberts, *Letters of Hannah More to Zachary Macaulay* (Carter, New York, 1860), p. 138.

CHAPTER XIII

1. Henry E. Huntington Library and Art Gallery, *Montagu Collection*. Hannah More to Mrs. Montagu, Aug. 27, 1784 and *circa*.

2. John Wesley, *Works* (Printed at the Conference Office, London, 1810), V, p. 355.
3. *Ibid.,* VI, p. 42.
4. *Bath Chronicle* (1791, Mar. 31, Apr. 7, Apr. 14, Apr. 21, Apr. 28, May 12, June 16, June 23, Aug. 11; 1792, Apr. 5; 1793, Mar. 28, May 15). *Sarah Farley's Bristol Journal* (1791, Mar. 28, Apr. 2). *Felix Farley's Bristol Journal* (1791, Apr. 19). Roberts, *op. cit.,* II, p. 335. Folger, Gar. Cor., *op. cit.*
4. Latimer, *op. cit.,* p. 493.

CHAPTER XIV

No author's notes.

CHAPTER XV

1. Roberts, *op. cit.,* I, p. 206.
2. *Ibid.,* I, p. 270.
3. Elizabeth Bouverie inherited Barham Court from Sir Philip Boteler. The Barham Barony is among the Gainsborough titles. For Mrs. Bouverie's descent and inheritance see Folkstone Peerage. Also, *Ireland's History of Kent* (1829), IV, pp. 476, 279.

CHAPTER XVI

No author's notes.

CHAPTER XVII

1. Daniel De Foe, *A Tour through the Island of Great Britain* (London, 1778), II, 28.
2. Collinson, *op. cit.*
3. Helen Cross Knight, *A New Memoir of Hannah More* (American Tract Society, 1851), p. 129.
4. M. More, *op. cit.,* p. 14.
5. *Ibid.,* p. 17.
6. Emanuel Green, *Bibliotheca Somersetensis* (Taunton, 1902).
7. M. More, *op. cit.,* pp. 120–2. Roberts, *op. cit.,* III, pp. 439–43.

CHAPTER XVIII

1. Witt Bowden, *Industrial Society in England* (Macmillan, 1925), p. 219 ff.
2. M. More, *op. cit.*, pp. 147, 152, 163.

CHAPTER XIX

1. Collinson, *op. cit.*, II, 162.
2. M. More, *op. cit.*, pp. 61–2.
3. *Ibid.*, p. 90.

CHAPTER XX

1. *The British Critic,* Vol. 17, p. 444; Vol. 18, p. 216; Vol. 19, p. 90. *Anti-Jacobin,* Vol. 5, pp. 80, 314, 340, 459; Vol. 9, pp. 277–296; Vol. 11, pp. 13, 87–99, 195, 199–201, 201–7, 326, 530.
2. Collinson, *op. cit.*, II, p. 187.
3. M. More, *op. cit.*, p. 212.
4. Roberts, *op. cit.*, III, p. 40–1.
5. *Notes and Queries of Somerset and Dorset,* Vol. XVI (1918), p. 255.
6. M. More, *op. cit.*, pp. 167 ff.
7. Ed. Rev. Hill Wickham, *Journal and Correspondence of Thomas Sedgewick Whalley, D.D.* (Bentley, 1863).
8. *Ibid.*
9. Ed. George Redford and John Angell James, *Autobiography and Reminiscences of the Rev. William Jay* (Hamilton, 1854).
10. Roberts, *op. cit.*, III, p. 243.

CHAPTER XXI

1. Roberts, *op. cit.*, III, p. 58 ff.
2. Hopkins papers; *Hannah More to Rev. W. Cooper* (undated).

CHAPTER XXII

No author's notes.

CHAPTER XXIII

1. Emanuel Green, *op. cit.*

2. G. H. Spinney, *Cheap Repository Tracts* (Biographical Society, London, 1940).

3. At a "Do and Mend" exhibition held in 1942 at the Northumberland Rooms, Northumberland Avenue, London, garments were exhibited made from the fleece plucked from the hedges in Kent and carded, spun, and woven on homemade hand instruments, after the old-fashioned methods.

4. *David Saunders, The Shepherd of Salisbury Plain* (The Religious Tract Society, London, n.d.). Rev. H. Atley, *Reminiscences . . . Also . . . Authentic History of David Saunders, the Pious Shepherd of Salisbury Plain* (Salisbury, 1855).

CHAPTER XXIV

1. Peter Pindar, Esquire (Dr. John Wolcot), *Works* (Wood, London, 1805), I, p. 3.

2. Richard Polewhele lost much of the prancing complacency that made him so annoying in his youth although his later praise of Hannah seemed as important to him as his earlier criticism. Hannah answered his letters but never included him among her friends. His admiration for Hannah increased year by year and in *The Unsex'd Females,* a diatribe directed at Mary Wollstonecraft, he did not mention Mrs. Macaulay in his list of approved female writers although he included Barbauld, Montagu, Carter, Chapone, Seward, Piozzi, Burney, with others of lesser note, and above all, beyond all—More. The footnote attached to Hannah's name contains a long quotation from the introduction to her early *Essays on Various Subjects, Principally designed for Young Ladies* in which, intent on showing that women's minds are different from men's, she succeeds in showing them inferior. Hannah's lifelong belief that women were inferior to men inclined the gentlemen to consider *her* an exception to the rule.

CHAPTER XXV

1. Folger, Gar. Cor., *op. cit.*
2. *Ibid.*
3. *Ibid.*
4. Lady Olivia Sparrow, eldest daughter of Arthur, first Earl of Gosford, married (1797) Brigadier-General Robert Sparrow of Brampton Park, Hunts. He died 1805. Lady Olivia died 1863. Mrs. Warrenne Blake, *An Irish Beauty of the Regency,* compiled from the unpublished Journals of Hon. Mrs. Calvert (John Lane, London, 1911), p. 162 n.
5. Folger, Gar. Cor., *op. cit.*
6. *Ibid.*
7. F. W. Hawkins, *Life of Edmund Kean* (London, 1869), pp. 205–9.
8. Boaden, *op. cit.,* preface.

CHAPTER XXVI

1. Wilberforce, *op. cit.,* I, p. 220.
2. Roberts, *op. cit.,* IV, p. 253.
3. Mrs. S. C. Hall, *Pilgrimages to English Shrines* (Virtue, London, 1853). Mrs. Hall speaks especially of this green silk dress, saying that it was odd but in keeping with Mrs. More's personality. Two miniatures, duplicates, neither signed, show her in this gown. One is in the Bristol Museum and Art Gallery and the other in the possession of Cuthbert Becher Pigot, Esq.
4. A. Roberts, *op. cit.,* pp. 207–8.
5. George Otto Trevelyan, *Life and Letters of Lord Macaulay* (Detroit, 1878), I, p. 118.

Index